THE DECLINE AND FALL
OF THE ROMAN EMPIRE

THE DECLINE AND FALL
OF THE ROMAN EMPIRE

James W. Ermatinger

Greenwood Guides to Historic Events of the Ancient World
Bella Vivante, Series Editor

GREENWOOD PRESS
Westport, Connecticut • London

Library of Congress Cataloging-in-Publication Data

Ermatinger, James William, 1959–
  The decline and fall of the Roman Empire / by James W. Ermatinger.
    p. cm.—(Greenwood guides to historic events of the ancient world)
  Includes bibliographical references and index.
  ISBN 0–313–32692–4 (alk. paper)
    1. Rome—History—Empire, 284–476. 2. Rome—History—Germanic Invasions,
3rd–6th centuries. I. Title. II. Series.
  DG311.E75   2004
  937'.09–dc22   2004014674

British Library Cataloguing in Publication Data is available.

Library of Congress Catalog Card Number: 2004014674
ISBN: 0–313–32692–4

First published in 2004

Greenwood Press, 88 Post Road West, Westport, CT 06881
An imprint of Greenwood Publishing Group, Inc.
www.greenwood.com

Printed in the United States of America

The paper used in this book complies with the
Permanent Paper Standard issued by the National
Information Standards Organization (Z39.48–1984).

10 9 8 7 6 5 4 3 2 1

Copyright Acknowledgment

The author and publisher gratefully acknowledge permission for use of the following
material:

From Roman to Merovingian Gaul: A Reader, edited and translated by Alexander
Callander Murray (Peterborough, ON: Broadview Press, 2000). Copyright © 2000 by
Alexander Callander Murray. Reprinted by permission of Broadview Press.

To Angela, Michelle, and Ian

CONTENTS

Illustrations follow Chapter 6.

Series Foreword

As a professor and scholar of the ancient Greek world, I am often asked by students and scholars of other disciplines, why study antiquity? What possible relevance could human events from two, three, or more thousand years ago have to our lives today? This questioning of the continued validity of our historical past may be the offshoot of the forces shaping the history of the American people. Proud of forging a new nation out of immigrants wrenched willingly or not from their home soils, Americans have experienced a liberating headiness of separation from traditional historical demands on their social and cultural identity. The result has been a skepticism about the very validity of that historical past. Some of that skepticism is healthy and serves constructive purposes of scholarly inquiry. Questions of how, by whom, and in whose interest "history" is written are valid questions pursued by contemporary historians striving to uncover the multiple forces shaping any historical event and the multilayered social consequences that result. But the current academic focus on "presentism"—the concern with only recent events and a deliberate ignoring of premodern eras—betrays an extreme distortion of legitimate intellectual inquiry. This stress on the present seems to have deepened in the early years of the twenty-first century. The cybertechnological explosions of the preceding decades seem to have propelled us into a new cultural age requiring new rules that make the past appear all the more obsolete.

So again I ask, why study ancient cultures? In the past year, after it ousted that nation's heinous regime, the United States' occupation of Iraq has kept that nation in the forefront of the news. The land base of Iraq is ancient Mesopotamia, "the land between the rivers" of the Tigris and Euphrates, two of the four rivers in the biblical Garden of Eden (Gen. 2). Called the cradle of civilization, this area witnessed the early development of a centrally organized, hierarchical social system that utilized the new technology of writing to administer an increasingly complex state.

Is there a connection between the ancient events, literature, and art coming out of this land and contemporary events? Michael Wood, in his educational video *Iraq: The Cradle of Civilization*, produced shortly after the 1991 Gulf War, thinks so and makes this connection explicit—between the people, their way of interacting with their environment, and even the cosmological stories they create to explain and define their world.

Study of the ancient world, like study of contemporary cultures other than one's own, has more than academic or exotic value. First, study of the past seeks meaning beyond solely acquiring factual knowledge. It strives to understand the human and social dynamics that underlie any historical event and what these underlying dynamics teach us about ourselves as human beings in interaction with one another. Study of the past also encourages deeper inquiry than what appears to some as the "quaint" observation that this region of current and recent conflict could have served as a biblical ideal or as a critical marker in the development of world civilizations. In fact, these apparently quaint dimensions can serve as the hook that piques our interest into examining the past and discovering what it may have to say to us today. Not an end in itself, the knowledge forms the bedrock for exploring deeper meanings.

Consider, for example, the following questions. What does it mean that three major world religions—Judaism, Christianity, and Islam—developed out of the ancient Mesopotamian worldview? In this view, the world, and hence its gods, were seen as being in perpetual conflict with one another and with the environment, and death was perceived as a matter of despair and desolation. What does it mean that Western forms of thinking derive from the particular intellectual revolution of archaic Greece that developed into what is called rational discourse, ultimately systematized by Aristotle in the fourth century B.C.E.? How does this thinking, now fundamental to Western discourse, shape how we see the world and ourselves, and how we interact with one another? And how does it affect our ability, or lack thereof, to communicate intelligibly with people with differently framed cultural perceptions? What, ultimately, do we gain from being aware of the origin and development of these fundamental features of our thinking and beliefs?

In short, knowing the past is essential for knowing ourselves in the present. Without an understanding of where we came from, and the journey we took to get where we are today, we cannot understand why we think or act the way we do. Nor, without an understanding of historical development, are we in a position to make the kinds of constructive changes necessary to advance as a society. Awareness of the past gives us the resources necessary to make comparisons between our contemporary world and past times. It is from those comparisons that we can assess both the advances we have made as human societies and those aspects that can still benefit from change. Hence, knowledge of the past is crucial for shaping our individual and social identities, providing us with the resources to make intelligent, aware, and informed decisions for the future.

All ancient societies, whether significant for the evolution of Western ideas and values, or whether they developed largely separate from the cultures that more directly influenced Western civilization, such as China, have important lessons to teach us. For fundamentally they all address questions that have faced every human individual and every human society that has existed. Because ancient civilizations erected great monuments of themselves in stone, writings, and the visual arts—all enduring material evidence—we can view how these ancient cultures dealt with many of the same questions we face today. And we learn the consequences of the actions taken by people in other societies and times that, ideally, should help us as we seek solutions to contemporary issues. Thus it was that President John F. Kennedy wrote of his reliance upon Thucydides' treatment of the devastating war between the ancient Greek city-states of Athens and Sparta (see the volume on the Peloponnesian War) in his study of exemplary figures, *Profiles in Courage*.

This series seeks to fulfill this goal both collectively and in the individual volumes. The individual volumes examine key events, trends, and developments in world history in ancient times that are central to the secondary school and lower-level undergraduate history curriculum and that form standard topics for student research. From a vast field of potential subjects, these selected topics emerged after consultations with scholars, educators, and librarians. Each book in the series can be described as a "library in a book." Each one presents a chronological timeline and an initial factual overview of its subject, three to five topical essays that examine the subject from diverse perspectives and for its various consequences, a concluding essay providing current perspectives on the event, biographies of key players, a selection of primary documents, illustrations, a glossary, and an index. The concept of the series is to provide ready-reference materials that include a quick, in-depth examination of the topic and insightful guidelines for interpretive analysis, suitable for student research and designed to stimulate critical thinking. The authors are all scholars of the topic in their fields, selected both on the basis of their expertise and for their ability to bring their scholarly knowledge to a wider audience in an engaging and clear way. In these regards, this series follows the concept and format of the Greenwood Guides to Historic Events of the Twentieth Century, the Fifteenth to Nineteenth Centuries, and the Medieval World.

All the works in this series deal with historical developments in early ancient civilizations, almost invariably postdating the emergence of writing and of hierarchical dynastic social structures. Perhaps only incidentally do they deal with what historians call the Paleolithic ("Old Stone Age") periods, from about 25,000 B.C.E. onward, eras characterized by nomadic, hunting-gathering societies, or the Neolithic ("New Stone Age"), the period of the earliest development of agriculture and hence settled societies, one of the earliest dating to about 7000 B.C.E. at Çatal Höyük in south-central Turkey.

The earliest dates covered by the books in this series are the fourth to second millennia B.C.E. for the building of the Pyramids in Egypt, and the examination of the Trojan War and the Bronze Age civilizations of the eastern Mediterranean. Most volumes deal with events in the first millennium B.C.E. to the early centuries of the first millennium C.E. Some treat the development of civilizations, such as the rise of the Han Empire in China, or the separate volumes on the rise and on the decline and fall of the Roman Empire. Some highlight major personalities and their empires, such as the volumes on Cleopatra VII of Ptolemaic Egypt or Justinian and the beginnings of the Byzantine Empire in eastern Greece and Constantinople (Istanbul). Three volumes examine the emergence in antiquity of religious movements that form major contemporary world systems of belief—Judaism, Buddhism, and Christianity. (Islam is being treated in the parallel Medieval World series.) And two volumes examine technological developments, one on the building of the Pyramids and one on other ancient technologies.

Each book examines the complexities of the forces shaping the development of its subject and the historical consequences. Thus, for example, the volume on the fifth-century B.C.E. Greek Peloponnesian War explores the historical causes of the war, the nature of the combatants' actions, and how these reflect the thinking of the period. A particular issue, which may seem strange to some or timely to others, is how a city like Athens, with its proto-democratic political organization and its outstanding achievements in architecture, sculpture, painting, drama, and philosophy, could engage in openly imperialist policies of land conquest and of vicious revenge against any who countered them. Rather than trying to gloss over the contradictions that emerge, these books conscientiously explore whatever tensions arise in the ancient material, both to portray more completely the ancient event and to highlight the fact that no historical occurrence is simply determined. Sometimes societies that we admire in some ways—such as the artistic achievements and democratic political experiments of ancient Athens—may prove deeply troublesome in other ways—such as what we see as their reprehensible conduct in war and brutal subjection of other Greek communities. Consequently, the reader is empowered to make informed, well-rounded judgments on the events and actions of the major players.

We offer this series as an invitation to explore the past in various ways. We anticipate that from its volumes the reader will gain a better appreciation of the historical events and forces that shaped the lives of our ancient forebears and that continue to shape our thinking, values, and actions today. However remote in time and culture these ancient civilizations may at times appear, ultimately they show us that the questions confronting human beings of any age are timeless and that the examples of the past can provide valuable insights into our understanding of the present and the future.

Bella Vivante
University of Arizona

PREFACE

The Decline and Fall of Rome marked the transition between the classical and medieval world. This period from 250–500 C.E. witnessed the upheaval of the Roman Empire in the third century, its restoration in the fourth, and its ultimate collapse in the fifth century. During this time Rome moved from a global empire to a collection of Germanic kingdoms. Although these kingdoms claimed to be Roman, or the descendents of Romans, the cultural, economic, social, and political map of Western Europe had changed dramatically by 500 C.E.

Crucial to understanding the causes and results of Rome's collapse is an examination of the various forces within the empire. This period has often been seen as culturally, socially, and economically inferior to earlier ages. The religious issues of the age likewise show the varied beliefs and responses among both Christians and non-Christians. Finally, the role and influence of the Germanic invaders, along with the imperial household, clearly dictated most of the political actions, with often disastrous results. These forces led to a distinct separation between the Germanic West and the Byzantine East.

The end of the Roman Empire did not mean an end to the ideals of Rome. Although the West ceased to exist as part of the Roman Empire, the East continued to proclaim its right to call itself the Roman Empire. Furthermore, in the West attempts to recreate the Roman Empire occurred, most notably with Charlemagne in 800 C.E. As we shall see, Rome and its collapse continues to fascinate historians and the public, all of whom try to understand why Rome fell, and what its fall can tell us about the fates of other empires, including our own.

This book begins with a brief historical overview for the period

250–500 C.E. This is then followed by a series of studies examining various components to the Late Roman world. The conclusion places the collapse of Rome in a modern perspective. The book includes a chronology of events, biographies of significant individuals, a selection of primary documents illustrating the various forces in Roman society, and a glossary. An annotated bibliography, divided into primary and secondary works, guides the reader to explore more aspects of Rome's end.

I would like to thank my wife Angela who read, commented, questioned, and discussed this manuscript. I also received valuable input from Bella Vivante of the University of Arizona, the series editor, who helped guide the project and constantly kept me on schedule. Frank Romer of the University of Arizona suggested this project, and I am thankful to him for keeping me in mind. Kate Lau from the Walters Art Gallery, Baltimore, Maryland, and Patricia Woods, from the St. Louis Art Museum, helped in the acquisition of photographs for this work. Larry Easley of the Department of History at Southeast Missouri State University executed the maps under the vaguest of my suggestions. Michael Hermann and Kevin Ohe of Greenwood Publishing Group patiently answered all my questions. I would like to thank Martin Jones, Dean of the College of Liberal Arts at Southeast Missouri State University, for providing assistance. My daughter Michelle and son Ian helped me conduct my work by retrieving materials when asked without too much grumbling. Although all of these individuals helped, I assume full responsibility for the material in this book.

CHRONOLOGY OF EVENTS

Note: Recognized emperors appear in **bold** type.

230s	Rise of the Sassanidae or New Persian Empire.
235	**Severus Alexander** is assassinated; beginning of fifty years of chaos.
244–249	**Philip the Arab** makes peace with Persia.
248	1,000-year celebration of Rome's foundation begins.
249–251	**Decius** defeats **Philip** at Verona and becomes emperor.
250	General persecution of the Christians.
251	**Decius** defeats in battle the Goths who had killed Thrace, who died after crossing the Danube to continue his attack.
253–260	**Valerian** fights the Franks in Gaul, Alamanni in Italy, and Goths on the Danube. He is defeated and captured by the Persians at Edessa.
260–268	**Gallienus** faces general disruption of the empire. Gaul and Spain under Tetricus break away; Palmyra is nominally under imperial control. Goths plunder the Mediterranean.
268–270	**Claudius II** defeats the Alamanni and Goths.

270–275	**Aurelian** makes peace with the Goths by giving up Dacia (modern-day Romania), making the Danube the boundary. He defeats the Alamanni and Macromanni in Italy, defeats Zenobia and Tetricus, and erects the new wall around Rome.
275	**Tacitus** defeats Alani in Asia Minor.
276–282	**Probus** strengthens the Rhine and Danube and drives back the Franks, Burgundians, Alamanni, and Vandals from Gaul.
282–283	**Carus** conquers the Sarmatians and leads an invasion of Persia.
284–305	**Diocletian** restores the empire and enacts a series of reforms. Diocletian and his colleagues secure the empire from invaders and rebels.
285	**Diocletian** appoints **Maximian** as Augustus (co-emperor). Diocletian campaigns in the East, Maximian in the West.
293	**Diocletian** appoints **Galerius** and **Constantius** Caesars (junior emperors) in the East and West, respectively.
303	General persecution of the Christians.
305	**Diocletian** and **Maximian** (reluctantly) retire.
306–313	Civil war between **Constantine**, **Galerius**, Maxentius, Maximian, **Severus**, **Maximin Daia**, and **Licinius**.
312	**Constantine** defeats Maxentius by invoking the Christian God. **Galerius** issues the Edict of Toleration, recognizing Christianity as a valid religion.
313–323	**Constantine** and **Licinius** rule West and East, respectively. Constantine wrestles with the Donatists in Africa.
323–337	**Constantine the Great** rules alone; recognizes and favors Christianity. Arius and his ideas are rejected at Council of Nicaea.

330	Dedication of Constantinople as new capital.
337–361	Sons of **Constantine** rule, with **Constantius II** as sole ruler after 350.
361–363	**Julian** attempts to reestablish paganism, fails.
364–375	**Valentinian I** rules the West while his brother Valens (364–378) rules the East.
378	**Valens** is defeated and killed by the Goths at Adrianople.
379–395	**Theodosius** fights but is forced to make peace with the Goths; promotes Stilicho to supremacy. He divides the empire between his sons **Arcadius** in the East and **Honorius** in the West.
394	**Theodosius** outlaws Paganism.
395–423	**Honorius** rules the West from Ravenna. Stilicho is murdered in 408 by orders of Honorius.
410	Alaric sacks Rome.
425–455	**Valentinian III, Honorius'** nephew, rules ineffectively.
451–453	Attila and the Huns attack the Roman Empire; the city of Rome is saved by Pope Leo I.
455	Gaiseric and Vandals sack Rome for 14 days.
456–472	General Ricimer, who makes and unmakes emperors, rules the West in their names.
476	Odoacer deposes **Romulus Augustus(ulus)** and sends the imperial standards to Constantinople.
481–511	Clovis establishes the Frankish kingdom in Gaul, and is baptized Catholic.
493–526	Theodoric the Great defeats Odoacer and nominally rules in Eastern Emperor's name.

Introduction: Historical Overview

THE SETTING

Rome: Mistress of the world. The Eternal City. The center of an empire. All of these epitaphs suggest that Rome is as much a concept as a location. Indeed, in the first scene of the film *Gladiator* (2000), when the central character, Maximus, and the ailing emperor, Marcus Aurelius talk, the emperor asks:

> *Marcus*: And what would you believe? [of fallen soldiers in a recent battle]
>
> *Maximus*: They fought for YOU and for Rome.
>
> *Marcus*: And what is Rome, Maximus?
>
> *Maximus*: I have seen much of the rest of the world. It is brutal and cruel and dark. Rome is the light.
>
> *Marcus*: Yet you have never been there.[1]

Rome is an ideal, not just a city, or even an empire. Adherence to an ideal explains why Roman legions expanded the empire and conquered the world. To Maximus, Rome is a savior, a light to a cruel world.

The image of light sums up Roman imperial ideology during the republic and the early empire,[2] but what is this ideology in the late empire? Has it changed? And how does the Decline and Fall of Rome touch modern society? In many ways the Roman Empire is like a corpse: Although the person was born, lived, and died, understanding its life leads to an explanation of its death.

An elderly patient, age seventy-five, has died. The coroner determines the cause of death, a stroke, recording it on a death certificate, considering the matter closed. However, by asking why the patient had that fatal stroke, a person's complete life history can be learned. And, if an investigation reveals that the patient smoked cigarettes and drank far too much alcohol, then the assumptions about the cause of death would change.

The Decline and Fall of Rome can be approached in a similar fashion. Traditionally, the date of Rome's fall is given as 476 when the last emperor was removed from the throne. Like the hypothetical patient, the death certificate for Rome might give a date and cause of death. Examining the factors leading to the removal of the last emperor in 476 (Rome's "death") would give a different, more complete, view of the Decline and Fall of Rome.

WHEN DID ROME FALL?

What does the Fall of Rome mean? In popular history the Fall of Rome arrived with the dismissal of Romulus Augustus(ulus) in 476, when the German chieftain Odoacer declared that the West had no need of an emperor dictated by the East. But this removal is only a perceived fall or end of Rome, for Rome had in many ways already ceased to exist. Still, with the perception of Rome's fall occurring in 476, nations have attempted to "recapture" its glory, as in the case of Charlemagne and his Holy Roman Empire (800).

Does the loss of power mean the end of Rome? If it does, a number of dates in which such power was "lost" exist. Honorius (395–424) and Valentinian III (425–455) were weak emperors who allowed their German advisors to wrest power from them. Clearly, these emperors were powerless to stop continual depredations of the Roman state. On the other hand, they may not have cared about their actual loss of power as long as they retained their status. Indeed, Rome's real political and military power may have ended still earlier with Emperor Theodosius the Great (396). He died after his brief union and domination of the empire. Before his death he ensured that his sons received training by his German advisors and generals rather than by Roman advisors, senators, or generals. These new advisors had little Roman heritage, history, or beliefs to impart to his sons. An argument can therefore be made that Theodosius, in his death as well as his life choices, brought about a cessation of imperial Roman power.

This idea of loss of power, however, again assumes that such loss was sudden. If, instead, the Fall of Rome is defined not as a cessation of power but as a decline in Roman influence, then different ways to date this loss and various people to blame exist. Is the loss of influence defined in any special way? Security is crucial to influence, and if the state cannot maintain its security, it cannot keep its influence. In the case of Rome, security appears to have failed at various times. During the 260s it looked as if Rome would collapse, but it did not. In the 350s the Romans contended with invasions from the East, attacks on the Rhine, and internal civil war, but the state recovered. Even after 378, with the disaster at Adrianople (in modern Bulgaria), Roman security held. Many Romans may have assumed that during the 450s Rome would once again rise up and push back the invaders, but it could not. After 476 the Visigoth chieftain Theodoric ousted Odoacer and nominally reasserted Roman rule. Thus security and its maintenance were fluid.

Influence, however, can also be seen as a means of maintaining control. Did the Roman state continue to control its subjects as before? In areas of taxes, law, religion, society, and art Rome continued its dominance. How Rome maintained and carried out this control, however, changed. Taxes were no longer collected only in money, but also in produce or kind. Laws became more absolute, religion shifted from paganism to Christianity, and society and art, along with the economy, became regional. In each area the maintenance of control shifted as well. Once again perception is crucial. But can the Fall of Rome be dated?

What is crucial to understand is that half of the Roman Empire, the East—the Balkans (modern Croatia, Serbia, and Bulgaria), Greece, Asia Minor (modern Turkey), Syria, Palestine (modern Israel, Lebanon, and Jordan), and Egypt—did not fall. In fact, Constantinople (present-day Istanbul, Turkey) controlled the empire for centuries. Constantinople, standing at the bridge between Europe and Asia, joined East and West. The city, well chosen for its strategic, economic, and military position, protected both the East and the West. Invaders moving east through Europe would have to get past the city to cross over to Asia, and any westward-moving invader faced the same hurdle. As such, the city, an isolated triangular landmass with its series of walls and two harbors, guaranteed the protection of both the East and the West. Constantinople, then, would continue its Roman legacy, calling itself the new Rome. The city had its own Roman senate, Roman officials, Roman laws, and of course its own Roman emperor. This continuity helps explain why Rome did not fall in 476 but, in fact, held out for another 1,000 years.

At the same time, the city of Rome did change. No longer the seat of empire, not since 324 or even earlier, Rome nevertheless viewed itself as the traditional ancient capital. The Roman senate still debated topics, not only for the city but the empire as a whole. The city was controlled by a new emperor, the pope. The pope, more than a religious figure, became Rome's protector, administrator, and leader. He saved the city, or at least its inhabitants, when Gaiseric sacked it in 455. The pope administered Rome's political life, ensuring that both menial and important tasks were completed; above all, the pope led the city in times of prosperity and in periods of turmoil. The city of Rome still held an important position in Europe, despite the collapse of the Roman Empire.

Rome and the new Rome, Constantinople, continued the philosophy and history of the Roman Empire. The ideas upon which Rome was founded: law, government, and an ordered society, have constantly been evoked to further the cause of the West. And in the twelfth century, when Constantinople was threatened, it pleaded with the pope and Rome for help. The idea of Rome as a powerful city endured.

HISTORICAL OVERVIEW

The Roman Empire's decline occurred gradually, from 235 to 500. During this time the empire struggled, occasionally regained vitality, and then succumbed to a death in the West and a transition in the East. By 500 the empire in the East was a non-Latin Greek Empire, and in the West it was a series of Germanic Kingdoms (Map 1). The sixth century differed completely from the third century in terms of politics, economics, the military, and social life.

ECONOMY

Political and military upheavals were only part of the problem: Economic turmoil weakened the empire's core. The Roman imperial economy based itself on a system regulated by precious metals. While modern coins have very little intrinsic value, their extrinsic, or stated, value is crucial. In Rome, however, the intrinsic value of a coin was usually tied to its extrinsic value. If the weight of the gold coin decreased, its value relative to silver coins decreased. When the silver content was diluted or debased, its value relative to bronze or gold coins also changed. This relationship influenced the market and the empire. During the first two centuries of the Roman Empire the coinage was relatively stable, but by the early third century the state had troubles meeting its obligations and needed to increase its money supply. One way to do this was to find new sources of gold and silver; the other, more expedient but economically dangerous possibility was to dilute the purity of the silver coin, the *denarius*. Emperors chose the latter course, where the silver percentage in the *denarius* declined to 5 percent. After Caracalla (215 C.E.), the unchanged gold *aureus* equaled 50 *denarii* instead of 25, beginning a process of monetary destabilization and inflation, and causing economic turmoil. Local coinage, struck in bronze, was now used for only small-change purchases, and ultimately disappeared.

Other economic problems arose. First, the government placed an increased burden on cities and wealthy individuals in the form of compulsory labor duty, called liturgies. Rome did not traditionally have an extensive bureaucracy collecting taxes and duties throughout all of the provinces; instead, it relied upon local communities to send in assessed amounts. To accomplish this task Rome required the local cities, through local councilors, who were wealthy individuals, to pay the government. A more serious problem occurred when taxpayers could not pay their taxes. The imperial government then compelled the councilors to make up the difference. During a time of prosperity, this burden was probably light, but during a calamity—natural or otherwise—these payments were heavy.

In addition to liturgies, forced exactions became an even greater burden than regular taxes. These duties, originally imposed only during times of great military hardship, became constant. Exacerbated by numerous usurpers and by foreign wars, the forced exactions became a regular tax during the third century.

EARLY SIGNS OF DECLINE

The third century, 235 to 313, saw first the denigration of traditional Roman society, the collapse of the military frontier, and the restoration of the empire under Diocletian who literally "reformed" it. Severus Alexander's assassination in 235 ushered in 50 years of military anarchy, reaching its climax under Valerian and his son Gallienus in the 250s.

Civil war and disease weakened the frontiers during the mid-third century, and forced Emperor Valerian to face the full rush of the barbarian invasions in 253, when the Goths and Alamanni devastated the Danube region, while the newly formed Franks struck across the lower Rhine in 256 into northern Gaul. Saxons from the Jutish and Frisian coasts began raiding Roman territories on both sides of the English Channel, and the years of civil war left the eastern provinces open to new attacks, allowing the Persian king Shapur to cross the Euphrates and ravage Syria. The former second-century defenses, now understaffed, became underprotected. In addition, a plague reached the empire and by 251–253, caused extensive hardship.

Valerian made his son Gallienus co-ruler, and they attempted to restore order. Valerian attacked Shapur, the Persian king, in 256 only to be defeated, captured, humiliated, and ultimately killed. His son Gallienus, unable to help because of his own troubles in Europe, saw sections of the empire break away, particularly Gaul and the East. Gallienus retook secessionist Gaul and defeated the barbarians in Greece, but was assassinated by his generals Claudius and Aurelian. In 270, Claudius defeated the Goths (earning him the title Gothicus or conqueror of the Goths) and made their remnants _coloni_ or serfs in Roman territory in the Danube Basin. Claudius died of the plague, leaving his lieutenant Aurelian to deal with rebellions in Palmyra (modern Syria) under Queen Zenobia and in Gaul under Tetricus. Aurelian captured Palmyra in 272 but left Zenobia in power. She rebelled again and Aurelian besieged the city, captured Zenobia, destroyed the city's economic importance, and moved quickly to suppress Tetricus and his Gallic Empire. In 273, both Zenobia and Tetricus were made to march in Aurelian's triumph. Afterward, they were given a generous pension and finished their lives in Rome.

Coins celebrating Aurelian's achievements have the legend Restitutor Orbis (Restorer of the World). His restoration, however, had serious flaws, the most important of which was the fear (unrealized at this time) that even the capital could be attacked. To deal with this, in 274 Aurelian began work on Rome's new wall, which ran nearly 12 miles farther than the earlier wall of 390 B.C.E. This fortification and the numerous other forts and walled towns erected during this time, especially in Gaul, Britain, and Germania, indicate Rome's fear of probable barbarian invasion. Aurelian was preparing to meet the Persian monarchy when he was assassinated in 275. Probus, his successor, continued the restoration, as did his successor Carus, who even attacked the Persian Empire in 283. Carus' murder and the political struggles immediately afterwards allowed Diocletian (Document 1.A) to seize power.

The changes, which had occurred over seventy-five years, were tremendous. Taxes, supplemented by forced and often illegal exactions, had devastated cities and their surrounding regions. With the restoration of central control, cities were more and more liable for taxes; this meant city elites were responsible for the tax payments. The economy also changed with the accumulation of land and labor as assets. Capital fled from cities to the rural regions with a growth in villas, and inflation caused by continual debasement in coinage occurred. During the third century, silver coinage became nothing more than bronze coins with a silvery coating. Wealthy individuals attempted to beat inflation by putting their wealth into land and labor.

REBIRTH

Diocletian tried to create an ordered society based on the military camp. He carried out a comprehensive government reform, and saw himself as an almost godlike figure whose job was to watch over society by restoring the economy, simplifying taxes, enhancing the military, and strengthening cities. All of these acts resulted in a renewed empire, but one relying on the emperor as absolute authority and recognized to be in supreme control of all things. This is different from 235, when the emperor actually had this power, but desired to conceal it, to avoid alienating the old elite, the senators, and the rising new elite, the provincials. First, Diocletian instituted a new form of succession, the Tetrarchy, where two senior figures—the Augusti, Diocletian and Maximian—were assisted by two junior colleagues—the Caesars, Galerius and Constantius. Junior figures were tied to the senior members through marriage. When the senior members retired, Diocletian planned for the junior members to take over and appoint two new junior members.

Diocletian also strengthened the military by increasing the number of soldiers. Perhaps realizing their historical role in revolutions, he broke up the great cavalry armies created by Gallienus and Aurelian. Diocletian placed cavalry units on the frontiers, among the traditional legions. His intent was to secure the frontiers and to keep the interior at peace. In addition, Diocletian carried out economic reforms: overhauling the coinage, producing a pure silver coin and a stable bronze coin, standardizing the tax system, and creating a national budget and an anti-inflationary price edict. Thus, Diocletian produced a revival in the cities, witnessed by an increase in building and civic expenditures. He also attempted to reassert the traditional religion by persecuting Christianity and Manichaeanism, which were, in his view, foreign cults. He wished to bring the Christians back into the world of paganism. This process was doomed, but in 303, Diocletian launched his persecution, and, for the next few years the two opposing forces engaged, with Christianity ultimately winning. Finally, Diocletian retired, the first emperor to do so, and in fact, he refused a call to return to power a few years later.

Diocletian and Maximian retired in 305, putting into effect the Tetrarchic plan for succession where Constantius and Galerius became senior members and two new individuals, Maximin Daia (Galerius' nephew) and Severus, became junior members. In 306, Constantius died and civil war resulted between Constantine (his son); Maximian, who returned to power; Galerius; Maxentius (Maximian's son); Licinius (appointed after Severus' death); and Maximin Daia. In 311, Galerius died after issuing the Edict of Toleration (later appropriated by Constantine), allowing Christianity to become an acceptable cult within the empire. Constantine now moved against his brother-in-law Maxentius, defeating him at the Milvian Bridge. In the East, Licinius, Constantine's other brother-in-law, defeated Maximin Daia. These two conquerors ruled the empire together for the next twelve years. Diocletian's plan for political succession provided a concrete example of shared power for the next century.

AGE OF CONSTANTINE

Religious problems resurfaced in the West with Constantine's victory over Maxentius when Constantine had to deal with the Donatist controversy, concerning the actions of Christians during the last persecutions.[3] In the East, after Constantine defeated Licinius in 324, he had to wrestle with the Arian controversy concerning the nature of Christ. Constantine attempted to mark out his own program, both politically and religiously, as can be seen in his moving the capital from Rome to Byzantium in 324. Byzantium was renamed Constantinople ("City of Constantine") and dedicated as a Christian capital in 330. After Constantine's death and the ensuing political struggle, his son Constantius seized ultimate control of the empire. Needing help, Constantius installed his nephew Julian as Caesar to rule the West. The major foreign areas causing disturbances were the tribes on the Rhine, and Persia.

War with Persia erupted late in Constantius' rule and centered mainly on the siege and capture of Amida (in modern Iraq), the strategic city in the East and gateway to Roman Syria. After Julian's army proclaimed him emperor and Constantius' sudden death, Julian embarked on a pagan revival and a new Persian war. Unfortunately, his sudden and unexpected death forced Rome to make a disadvantageous treaty surrendering Galerius' conquest. After Julian's death the army chose Jovian, who then selected Valentinian as Caesar. When Jovian died in 365, Valentinian selected his brother Valens as emperor. Valentinian took the West and Valens the East, along lines of separation instituted by Diocletian.

The selection of Valentinian and Valens brought some stability and renewed vigor to the Roman state in the late fourth century. Archaeological remains indicate that Valentinian undertook an extensive military building program in the West, on the Rhine and Danube, thus restoring the frontiers. The military, too, underwent dramatic changes during the fourth century. Diocletian had broken up the large cavalry armies, and the military successfully maintained frontier security. Constantine, however, reintroduced the mobile cavalry armies. The division between cavalry and infantry armies worked well until the end of the fourth century. During the late fourth century Rome faced the growing problem of barbarians entering the empire and the army en masse. No longer entering as individuals, the tribes entered as complete groups under their own leaders, often without supervision by Roman commanders.

After Valentinian's death, his son Gratian succeeded him in the West while his uncle Valens continued to rule the East. In 376 the Visigoths produced trouble and entered the empire in the East not as individuals, but as an entire tribe. Unscrupulous bureaucrats charged them exorbitant prices for food. With famine approaching, the Visigoths became unsettled and they began to move en masse. With this action Valens decided to oust them from the empire. In 378, Valens, failing to wait for Gratian and his army, attacked the Visigoths at Adrianople (Document 10.A–B). The Visigoth cavalry routed and massacred the Roman legions, killing Valens.

Rome changed dramatically with the disaster at Adrianople, Valens' death, and Gratian's promotion of Theodosius in the East. Theodosius attempted to oust the Visigoths and, when that failed, he accepted them as part of his army. A fervent Catholic, Theodosius promoted the church, but also believed himself above the law, both civil and church. After committing a massacre at Thessalonica, Theodosius faced a new challenge in the person of Ambrose. As bishop of Milan, Ambrose used his ecclesiastical position to force Theodosius to do penance for the massacre (Document 6.B). In this act the church triumphed over secular law. Ambrose also used his position to force Theodosius to outlaw paganism. The conflict between Christianity and paganism had come full circle in less than a century.

COLLAPSE

For six months in 395, Theodosius combined and ruled both the East and West. After his death his sons took over, but the accession of his weak son Honorius in the West undermined Rome's political stability. Theodosius' German advisors, more concerned with their own tribes' advancement than with the preservation of Roman political unity, rose to power. Theodosius' general advisor and Vandal chieftain Stilicho now exerted strong influence upon the western emperor who moved the capital to Ravenna (northern Italy) in 402.

It was during Honorius' rule that the Visigoth chief Alaric successfully sacked Rome in 410. Honorius' nephew Valentinian III became emperor in 425 at the age of six and was guided by his mother Placidia. The family produced even more trouble when Honoria, Valentinian III's sister, asked Attila, the Hunnish chieftain, for help against her brother, the emperor. Attila and the Huns swept into the West, using Honoria's request as a pretext to gain power. Attila then devastated Gaul (Map 2). Aetius commanded the Roman army and although he defeated Attila at Troyes (in Gaul) in 451, Rome could not wipe Attila out. Attila then approached Rome only to turn away, supposedly by the authority of Pope Leo I. Attila died in 453 and the Huns disintegrated. Aetius was murdered by Valentinian in 455 for his rising popularity. Six months later, Aetius' retainers murdered Valentinian (Document 12.A–F). For the next 20 years the empire was ruled through a series of puppets controlled by Ricimir (Document 1.C), the Burgundian chieftain. He undermined

Roman power by giving power and lands to his tribesmen. By Ricimer's death in 472 the Western Empire had collapsed. During the fifth century Roman central power destabilized, and the various Germanic tribes migrated throughout the empire.

After the death of Alaric in 410 the Visigoths moved first into Gaul, and then into Spain in 415. They established their kingdom in southern Gaul and Spain, with their capital in Toulouse. During the 430s a group of Vandals, led by Gaiseric, arrived in North Africa and successfully took over the region. By 439, with his conquest of Carthage, Gaiseric controlled not only North Africa but the important grain trade. Gaiseric defeated a combined East/West naval invasion of North Africa, destroying the Roman fleet and, using his own navy to attack Italy, sacked Rome in 455. In Gaul, the arrival of the Merovingian Franks under Clovis defeated the Roman governor Syagrius, successor of Aetius, in 486 and established the Kingdom of the Franks. By 500 it is clear that the Roman Empire no longer existed.

There are numerous questions that need to be answered. Why did the West fall, but not the East? When did the West fall? What are the possible reasons for West's fall? In the studies that follow, the major assertions as to why Rome fell will be examined. These include a general decay in culture, economic and social declines, exterior and interior threats to the empire, and the religious question. This book ends with a recapitulation of the major hypotheses and whether a reason and date for Rome's fall can be asserted.

CHAPTER 1

LATE ROMAN CULTURE (250–500 C.E.)

ROMANIZATION

A society's cultural standing is often determined by popular perception; if considered superior, the society's history is often seen as outstanding. Likewise, if dismissed as inferior, its history is often said to be one of degradation. In addition, the assessment of a society's cultural cachet usually relies on the perceived characteristics of preceding and succeeding ages. According to popular belief, Roman culture reached its height during the early imperial age.

Early imperial Roman culture (14–235 C.E.) attempted to distinguish itself from the earlier Republican period or Eastern Hellenism, especially in the provinces. Such a process is called Romanization, defined as the merging of Roman, and, in essence, Hellenistic culture, with local customs, crafts, and themes, or the fusion of the Classical world with non-Classical regions.

Romanization occurred most profoundly in the West, because the East exported Hellenism to Rome during the late Republic. The Romans then exported their culture into the West where they fused with local culture such as the Gallic religion or Punic (African) architecture. During the early empire it is clear that Rome (i.e., Italy) took the lead in the practice of Romanization, with many regions receiving Roman culture unwillingly, as a form of cultural imperialism. Roman soldiers, bureaucrats, and colonists arrived in newly conquered western "barbarian" lands bringing with them Roman-Italian culture, building Roman administrative cities and villas, and imposing Roman cultural ideas on the indigenous populations. As a means of social, economic, and political advancement local elites adopted and imitated Roman culture. Finally, this adoption produced a local hybridization of Roman themes, crafts, and customs fitting the native one, producing Romanization. During the late empire the reverse happened when the provincial regions, due to their sons becoming emperors, senators and nobles transferred their periphery form of Roman culture, which was different from the classical arts, but not necessarily inferior, to Italy, the empire's center.

Since the Renaissance (1350–1600) many artists, critics, and scholars have argued that late Roman society produced artistic and cultural stagnation or even decline. Unfortunately, this attitude dismisses the rich material developed during the end of paganism[1] and the rise of Christianity. The conflict and compromise between these two religious philosophies produced some of the most important pieces of art in the West, namely, the mosaics which adorn churches with both pagan and Christian themes and the important literary and artistic creations that glorified both paganism and Christianity.

Literature and art are the two main sources of transmittable culture, and to understand the history and culture of the late empire, it is crucial to understand the varied sources of Late Roman life. Cultural and literary sources are intertwined, with each reflecting the rich complexities of the Late Roman period. This chapter will survey the different types of literature and art during this 200-year period.

LITERATURE

Literary sources, meant for contemporary publication, have usually survived in medieval manuscripts. Although literature is often viewed only in the form of histories, plays, or novels, expanding the perspective of what constitutes literature allows for consideration of many other forms of writing not normally considered "literature." These forms of literature help provide a more complete picture of an individual, event, or place, as seen in the life of Diocletian or the division between the rich and poor and the cities and countryside. Some examples of Late Roman literary sources discussed below are panegyrics, legal codices, biographies, chronographies, histories, geographies, and theological works.

Poetry continued to be written as in the Classical age, still an important vehicle both for expressing personal feelings, as in Ausonius' tender memorial to his wife, who died 36 years earlier (Document 1.B), and for marking historical events or forces, as in his ode to the Moselle River (Document 13.B). Surviving late-third-century–early-fourth-century Gallic (modern France) Latin *panegyrics* (Document 13.A), or praises, written mainly for Maximian and Constantius, glorified the Tetrarchs. In addition to their sanctioned views of the emperors and their policies, they provide many historical details of the wars in Gaul and Britain, and how contemporaries viewed these events and the emperor's role in them. In panegyrics emperors are portrayed as semidivine, creating a theological basis for the institution of the emperor. Later Latin panegyrics to Constantine and Theodosius continued this trend, substituting Christianity for the earlier gods Jupiter and Hercules. In the East the Greek historian Eusebius (c. 330) delivered a series of panegyrics to Constantine the Great, glorifying the emperor and praising his adoption of Christianity.

A counterpart to panegyric is *vituperatio*, or denigration best seen in the Christian Lactantius' *The Death of the Persecutors*, where persecuting Tetrarchs Diocletian, Maximian, and Galerius are denigrated (Document 5.A). Thus, to Lactantius, the Tetrarchs' deaths, Galerius' of a painful illness, Maximian's of suicide, and Diocletian's of insanity, were fitting ends to their miserable and destructive lives.

Late Roman history produced the two great *legal codes* of antiquity, the Theodosian (Documents 5.C–E, 6.A) and Justinian law codes.[2] These codes transmitted the rich Roman law and procedure through medieval Europe into the modern age. Louisiana still uses Roman law, via the Napoleonic codes, continuing ancient Roman legal traditions. The Theodosian code collected imperial edicts from emperors after Diocletian to Theodosius II, while the Justinian code compiled imperial actions relating to private matters, usually in the form of rescripts, in which emperors provided responses to citizens' petitions. These codes provide valuable insight into legal, social, and economic problems, such as taxation, inheritance, and civil suits. Still, history is not only reported by panegyrics or laws enacted; it is also contained in contemporary biographies, the tabloids of history.

Fourth-century imperial *biographies* generally present the emperors' lives in a didactic fashion, as a tool to teach readers morals. Although not as favorable as panegyrics, they nevertheless contain contemporary sentiments about good and bad emperors, either glorifying good emperors, like Constantine, or denigrating bad ones, such as Carinus. This method invoked the use of the emperor's moral qualities, good or bad, in determining if the state prospered or declined. Authors took as their model the first-century C.E. author Suetonius' *Lives of the Twelve Caesars*, about the sensational and scurrilous lives of the first twelve emperors. One major work, *Lives of the Later Caesars*, a collection of biographies from Hadrian through Carinus written in the fourth century, presents few tangible historical facts, but includes moralistic, racy, and slanderous stories of emperors. Other histories written by Aurelius Victor and Eutropius (Document 1.A) are recognizable as biographies, also sensationalizing the emperors' lives; nevertheless, they contain some useful information concerning imperial reforms and how the nobility viewed the later-fourth-century emperors.

Chronicles (Documents 11.C–E, 12.E) are similar to biographies, discussing the emperors chronologically, giving selected highlights of their rule, and present the information chronologically without necessarily telling a complete story. Important chronicles include John Malalas' *Chronicle*, which discusses the emperors' physical appearances, reforms, and general policies; the *Consuls of Constantinople*, which presents the lists of consuls and important events; the *Easter Chronicle*, with a list of Easter celebrations; and Eusebius' chronicle, transmitted through Jerome's Latin chronicle, presenting the important events of a particular year. Later historians used these works, often without checking their accuracy or thinking about the motives of the original author. Such poor scholarship caused skewed portraits of the emperors.

Analogous to the chronicles were the *notitiae*, or provincial lists, providing valuable information about provincial reorganization. From the fifth century the *List of Offices* (Document 7.A) gives the bureaucratic posts, legions, other military units, and provinces. A seventh-century manuscript contains the Verona List, detailing the division of the empire into dioceses and provinces, and dates from the early fourth century. Such documents continue to show the idea of imperial unity. Based on official archives, they suggest a powerful and influential empire, at least on paper.

Historical works continued the earlier traditions and provide the most important historical data. Many of these works took polemical positions either defending or condemning Christianity. Eusebius' *Ecclesiastical History* (Document 5.B), written during the 330s, covers the period down to Constantine's victory accommodating and praising the rise of Christianity, while his *Martyrs of Palestine* details the history and suffering of Christians in Palestine during the last great persecution. Writing in Latin a century later, Orosius argued that he planned to dispute the pagan view that Christianity caused the empire's decline. The Greek pagan historian Zosimus wrote the *New Histories*, condemning the Christian emperors Constantine and Theodosius, but glorifying the pagan ruler Julian and his pagan senators. Modern scholars have questioned Zosimus' value as a source because he criticized Christianity; nevertheless, he does give a plausible non-Christian perspective.

Perhaps the greatest historical work is by the pagan Latin author Ammianus Marcellinus (Document 10.A), who wrote a history of Rome from 100 to 378 C.E., of which only the last 30 years survive and which is reminiscent of earlier historians Livy and Tacitus. The surviving part concentrates on the Persian wars, Julian's rise to power, and ends with the disaster at Adrianople. Ammianus views Julian as one of the greatest Roman emperors, and perceives his subsequent war as noble.

The late empire continued to exist within a unified geographical region, and *geographical treatises* (Document 13.B), with their Classical roots, present useful economic and sociological data about the Late Roman Empire. The Latin *An Examination of the Entire World* lists the provinces, with their particular products and customs, from the Far East westward and provides useful information about ports, chief cities, and the level of imperial prosperity. A contemporary Greek work is Eusebius' *Place Names (Onomasticon)*, which presents the geography of early-fourth-century Palestine based on the Hebrew Bible, and was meant to help Christians understand the geography of Palestine.

Christianity, in turn, created *theological works* to justify and explain itself, beginning in the second century. In the fourth century, Arnobius, originally a pagan North African rhetorician, converted to Christianity, and to prove that his conversion was real, wrote a work criticizing pagan religions. He argued that the problems in the world were not due to Christianity, but had always existed, and were diminished by Christ's birth. Arnobius presents a view of humankind as ignorant and knowing little about the universe. Arnobius further argued that God did not make man since God made only good, and that the soul was not immortal. Arnobius did not know, or for that matter, care to answer where man came from; to him men existed to spread evil. Arnobius' view that the soul is not immortal reminds one of Gnosticism, and often went against some of the church's own ideas. Arnobius also suggested that it was better to believe in God, because if He did not exist then nothing was lost, but if He did exist, then one might ensure salvation through one's belief.

Lactantius, a contemporary of Arnobius, wrote his *Divine Institutes* to appeal to the educated Roman, quoting extensively from earlier Latin writers, and placing Christianity in both the realm of philosophy and religion. Lactantius argued that humans have a duty to do what is good, for God punishes the wicked and rewards the good, and he attempted to qualify the idea of good, suggesting that a good deed done to receive an earthly reward is not a good deed. He denounced all killings, including capital punishment and war, asserting that wars, including those on behalf of one's own country, violated God's law.

The greatest Christian writers of the age, Jerome (Documents 10.C, 11.A) and Augustine, wrote at the end of the fourth century, after Christianity's legalization and triumph. Both wrote against Christian heresies and discussed how individuals ought to live. Jerome immersed himself in literature and his works indicate his training in the classics. Knowing Hebrew and Greek, he based his Latin translation of the Bible, the Vulgate, on Hebrew rather than on Greek. Jerome explored ideas in the Bible, and his works justified and explained Christianity by using examples from the Hebrew Bible, while his letters espoused mainstream Christian beliefs and provide a valuable portrait of the life and culture of his day. Although a great scholar and champion of monasticism, Jerome was not necessarily a great thinker; he attacked heresies and supported the official church line without understanding the theological debates that gave rise to these dogmas.

The second great writer, Augustine, argued, especially in *The City of God*, that Christianity did not destroy Rome, but rather succeeded this decadent empire. *The City of God* also presented the Catholic opposition to Donatism (see Chapter 3 on Religion). His autobiography, *The Confessions*, showed the journey of an elite provincial, born of a pagan father and Christian mother, who explored a variety of religions. Augustine had studied Manichaeanism, whose followers argued that they were the only true Christians; and they believed that the Catholic Church was corrupt and that they discovered the ideas of good versus evil. After becoming dissatisfied with the Manichaeans' philosophical limits, Augustine studied Neo-Platonism, discovering the joy of philosophy and the arguments concerning good and evil. He then began to study under Ambrose, which allowed Augustine to use Neo-Platonist ideas of philosophy and apply them to Christianity.

DOCUMENTARY SOURCES

While literary sources confirm, support, or question the understanding of Late Roman history, *documentary evidence*, both written and material objects, provide a useful check on literary sources. These documents present a cultural record of the late empire, indicating that individuals continued the traditional record keeping, accounts, and letters of the Classical age. There are two types of documents: *public* and *private*. Public documents are laws (Documents 5.C–E, 6.A), decrees (Documents 5.A, 13.A), resolutions (Document 4.E), treaties, administrative records (Document 7.A–B), official letters (Document 5.B), petitions (Document 4.E), and dedicatory pieces. Private documents are business records and accounts, memoranda, and individual legal documents such as wills, contracts, agreements, divorce deeds, private letters (Document 2.A–F) and sepulchral inscriptions. Law codes, listed above as literary sources, thus bridge the gap between literary and documentary works.

Documentary sources are usually transmitted through material objects such as inscriptions, papyri, lead, wood, statues, and ostraca, rather than through traditional manuscripts. The amount of documentary evidence for the late empire is staggering and important, especially when compared to the number of surviving literary documents from the same period.

Extensive *epigraphic material* (inscriptions), including honorary, dedicatory, and imperial, points to imperial popularity, patronage, and importance continuing earlier imperial forms (Figure 6b). The importance of inscriptions is best seen in Diocletian's economic reforms, his price edict and coinage decree. The price edict, perhaps the most famous Tetrarchic inscription, clearly shows Diocletian's attempt to control the market, while the coinage decree points to the emperors' attempt to adjust the internal monetary system without physically changing the coin. Neither act could be well documented if not for these inscriptions. Epigraphic evidence can provide important sources for imperial policy. Inscriptions (Documents 4.E, 13.A) are generally divided into two major types: honorary and regulatory. Honorific inscriptions, often with statues or sculptural friezes, commemorated someone or something, such as a battle, an office, a career, or someone's generosity. These inscriptions were set up by the emperor, his agents, or a city, and often detailed a law for a territory or even the entire empire. Regulatory inscriptions, such as Diocletian's price edict (Document 13.A) can indicate a specific problem and the measures taken by an official to correct it.

Papyri (Documents 2.F–G, 3.A, 7.B), analogous to inscriptions, provide not only imperial decrees, but the most information on Roman daily life. Like inscriptions, papyri are often fragmentary and isolated, but their sheer volume, providing numerous tax returns, census declarations, land leases, bills of sale, and accounts showing tax reforms, price regulations, military positions, and numerous other imperial policies, provide raw data for analysis dealing with the economic and social conditions. Many of these are private documents that offer a rich portrait of life on the periphery of the Roman Empire, especially from the province of Egypt. These private documents also provide information about certain social changes. The two most important changes were the change in landholding patterns toward large estates and the continuing involvement or intrusion of the state in the lives of the private citizen.

ARCHAEOLOGY

Archaeological evidence documents imperial building activities, pointing to a revival in municipal life during the late third–early fourth centuries; sculpture and other art pieces promoted the propaganda and the image of the emperors. Not only does archaeology help date and reveal general trends in Roman history, it is also the most important material primary source for understanding the living standard of the ordinary inhabitant of the Roman Empire.

Numismatics, the study of coins and medals, is a final major source of data for the ancient historian and overlaps with archaeological material, since many coins come from archaeological sites. Coin hoards may illustrate changes in metal content, circulation patterns, attitudes, and general disturbances, and may show the general value placed on coins during specific eras. Site finds, individual coin losses, help provide a correlation to the hoards in circulation patterns, help date archaeological sites, and provide insight into the relative value placed on certain coins, since individual losses tend to be the least valued. In addition to being money, coins also displayed messages, and can thus be seen as a means of spreading propaganda (Figure 1a). Imperial ideology and portraiture indicate how the emperors wished to be seen.

Thus, a combination of the foregoing sources allow researchers to create a fuller picture of Diocletian such as given in the biography, which shows how he campaigned against Rome's enemies, produced a price edict, undertook a land census, and attempted to stamp out Christianity. Each of these acts is known from a variety of sources complementing one another. Likewise, the divisions between the rich and the poor and the cities and the countryside are known from letters and papyri, reinforced by the archaeological remains of villas, as well as coin hoards showing disruption and economic turmoil, and the representation of familiar scenes in art.

ART

Art is perhaps the most important cultural manifestation of an era or a society. Just as in the approach to literature, one common view is that art during the late imperial period "declined." So, whereas Roman sculpture had by and large continued the trend begun in Archaic Greece of depicting the body more and more realistically, artists of the later empire moved away from these "naturalistic" artistic conventions, seen in the second century, producing a decline in the fourth century. The two styles are best seen in the Arch of Constantine in Rome (c. 315), which contains reused sculpture from Hadrian and fourth century additions (Figure 2). Rather than, or in addition to, assuming that these later images represent a decline, they can be viewed more neutrally as representing different concepts about what art is and how it might reflect the culture. The Hadrianic roundels are impressive, with clearly defined portraits of the emperor and other citizens, whereas the two scenes of Constantine's visit in Rome, such as the *adlocutio*, showing the emperor addressing the people, portray the individuals in an undifferentiated manner. This concept of nondifferentiation is reminiscent of Diocletian's Tetrarchy and the famous sculptural group in Venice where there is no difference between Diocletian and Maximian or Galerius and Constantius, except for the junior emperors' lack of facial hair. The statues are cubist and nondistinct. Judging from these representations one may assume that the later empire did, in fact, decline. However, examination of other art pieces offers somewhat different ideas, such as the continual distinction in sculpture, seen in the colossal statue of Constantine. The sarcophagus of Helena is reminiscent of sculpture during Marcus Aurelius' era. The mosaics that populate the late Roman villas are as intricate and stylized as those from first-century Pompeii, indicating that a decline did not exist (Figure 3). Later mosaics from Ravenna show the full flowering of this particular art form with the union of classical workmanship and Christian idealism.

Art for personal viewing provides a major source for ancient art works and their social meanings (Figure 4). The houses of the elite were not just private living quarters; they were also public places (Document 3.B) where one entertained his equals and, hopefully his superiors, and doled out beneficence to his clients. Living spaces were decorated with paintings on the walls and ceilings and mosaic floors, depicting all aspects of life. An owner might have sculptures indicating his wealth and beliefs, as well as furniture, glassware, and silverware (Figure 5). The more important an individual was the more lavish the art he collected (Figures 6a–6b). This personal art not only indicated a man's stature, it also attempted to connect the individual with the larger society. Visitors would undoubtedly be familiar with all of these portrayals and find them pleasing. For his clients the presentation of these artistic pieces indicated the patron's position and power. The patron overawed his client. This same type of presentation continued from the private to the public arena.

Entering into the city, an individual viewed public, or civic, art describing familiar scenes such as the circus, as well as drivers and workers, and how the nobility sponsored them for the public (Figure 7). These pieces of art, often funerary, allowed individuals to make a connection between the event, the person depicted, and the ideas of patronage where the nobility advertised their munificence. This public arena extended to religion, daily life, and the military, with art works showing individuals sacrificing (Figure 8), visiting the baths, and working in the fields, and military representations. Indeed, all individuals would have seen artwork that in some way represented themselves and their social position.

Art reflected imperial ceremony and propaganda. The splendor of the emperor, wearing his silk purple garments and pearled shoes, clearly marked him not as a human equal, but as a god, further highlighted by the *adventus* or the emperor's ceremonial arrival in a city invoking a ceremony and a parade; a social and political event. The emperor's presence, especially in cities other than the capital, profoundly altered an inhabitant's life. In addition to the increased tax burdens to supply the imperial retinue, a citizen could expect to see this divine person and perhaps enjoy gifts or donatives (Figure 1a). This imperial presence existed even when the emperor was not physically present, as in the case of his statue or image. The ultimate form of artistic ceremony dealt with the emperor's deification after his death, the apotheosis, a ceremony going back to the late republic, and presented in art and literature. The artistic depiction shows the emperor or in some cases a nobleman as he lived, then a panel or scene showing his cremation with eagles being released to take the spirit to the gods, and a final depiction of the new god in heaven. This ceremony joined religion, art, and the populace together to produce a religious basis for their rule.

This idea began during the late republic when Augustus honored and, more importantly, used his adopted father's name, Julius Caesar, to establish precedents for an absolute military dictatorship. Although Augustus distanced himself and chastised Caesar's desire for kingship, by the late third century emperors openly portrayed themselves as semidivine rulers. Beginning with "bad" rulers like Caligula, Nero, and Domitian, and moving to "good" leaders such as Aurelian, Diocletian, and Constantine, emperors portrayed themselves on coins not as a god, but as a great leader bringing protection, gifts, and progress to the people. Late-antiquity historians likewise viewed many emperors not merely as great individuals, but as semidivine. This view increased after the disastrous third century when emperors consolidated power. With the late third century and into Constantine's age the emperor now was a "God" or "Dominus et Deus" (Lord and God). With the adoption of Christianity, the emperor became semidivine, what Julius Caesar was accused of aspiring to, and the reason for his death.

Imperial art, however, has the greatest impact not only on the ancient citizens but on modern society in the institution of propaganda, seen on coins, statues, relief, and buildings (Figure 9). The most striking case is when an individual emperor or noble was condemned, the *damnatio*, where the name is erased and statues destroyed. Enacted by the senate, it officially made the individual and his acts outlawed. Although not forgotten, the *damnatio* purposely attempted to make the individual's memory worse than forgotten. In addition, imperial propaganda tied religion to art, best seen in late imperial statues, and the increased use of the Egyptian stone porphyry. Porphyry is a hard stone with a purple coloring, the sign of imperial power, and when used clearly indicated that the individual was the emperor. The second aspect of imperial art concerned the look of the emperor, again best seen on statues. Emperors up to and including Diocletian wore beards. In fact, the Tetrarchic statues normally show the senior emperors with beards and the junior emperors clean shaven. Constantine abandoned this idea by reintroducing the clean-shaven look, probably to distance himself from his predecessors. This clean-shaven look continued with his sons and relatives until Julian, a pagan, reintroduced the bearded look (Figure 11). It is clear that Julian decided to break with the precedent established by Constantine. After Julian's death, emperors returned to the clean-shaven look.

Throughout the late empire statues and relief works continued to show traditional Classical images and styles. Many of these works could be mistakenly dated from the second century due to theme, style, and workmanship. The most important form of Classical art for the late empire is its architecture seen in the arches, basilicas, and baths. These three forms continued the earlier precedents, but larger and grander, further supporting the idea that late antiquity contained a rich Classical culture. There existed numerous arches from the late third and fourth centuries such as the Arch of Constantine and the New Arch of Diocletian (now in fragments), commemorating not only military victories but the successful end of a war (Figure 9). Perhaps the most interesting arch is Constantine's, the first time an arch was constructed commemorating victory of one Roman over another, a far cry from Augustus' commemoration of Actium (31 B.C.E.) celebrating his victory over the foreigner Cleopatra, displayed on coins, statues, and in literature, but not over the Roman Antony. Contemporary is the basilica of Maxentius (310 C.E.) in the Roman Forum which completed the evolution of the Republican basilica in an even more grand style and size. As Christianity became more prominent, and ultimately official, the basilica moved from a legal and commercial building to a religious edifice, thereby replacing the pagan temple. The baths of Diocletian in Rome (307 C.E.) became the largest bath structure in the Roman world. These monumental achievements attest that Roman culture maintained its vitality, which continued in the new capital in Constantinople for the next millennium, possessing the same types of structures found in the city of Rome, but using the Christian motif.

Finally, religion was represented artistically. The worship of Isis, Serapis, and, above all, Mithras became more and more important. The worship of Mithras is perhaps the most interesting since the sculpture and relief work of Mithras killing the bull is not a cult statue, unlike those of Isis or Serapis. Instead these images of Mithras were merely representations of an event which occurred, similar to the concept of the Christian icons showing the Annunciation, Birth, Crucifixion, Resurrection, and Ascension of Christ. Unlike cult statues to Isis, Serapis, Jupiter, or other pagan gods which were worshipped, these images of Mithras or Christian events were not worshipped. Unlike Mithraism, which had a secret and underground meeting place, Christianity had its own architecture, the churches. Constantine began the institution of imperial patronage for churches building St. Peter's, St. Paul's, the Lateran, and Sta. Croce in Gerusalemme. These imperial churches, normally outside the city, not only glorified Christ but the emperor. The popes also began the construction of churches in Rome, especially after Alaric's sack in 410, such as Sta. Maria Maggiore and Sta. Sabina. Outside of Rome the mausoleum of Galla Placidia in Ravenna continued this trend of imperial patronage for Christianity.

The union of culture and society occurred with the festival. As these public festivals celebrated religious events, military victories, imperial birthdays, and accessions; they promoted the grandeur of the empire. Tied to the traditional state cults and the worship of the emperor, the festivals with their associated games allowed for popular public celebrations. These would continue into the Medieval Age with the Christian festivals and celebrations.

Late Roman culture was therefore a vibrant and continuing function of the Roman period, producing its own culture, which contained new elements and ideas that would transmit Roman ideology into the Medieval Age through literature and art.

CHAPTER 2

SOCIETY AND ECONOMICS IN LATE ANTIQUITY

SOCIETY

Late Roman society was based on rigid class separation, originally exist-ing between patricians and plebeians (similar to modern upper and lower classes), based upon one's birth. During the third century, avenues for ad-vancement opened up, allowing more movement into the upper class, with certain individuals now designated as clarissime, meaning "the best." Thus Roman society maintained the traditional separation of classes, but allowed new members to join the upper classes. A second sep-aration existed within Roman law; this was between the rich and poor. The class of *honestores* (honored individuals) included everyone above peasants, who were afforded more rights in Roman law. The peasants, who numbered roughly 90 percent of society, were designated as *humiliores* (humble individuals), and rose to the status of *honestores* by en-tering the army.

During his term of service, a soldier, based on his abilities, connec-tions, and luck, could rise through military ranks, and hence through so-ciety, perhaps becoming an equestrian or a senator. By collecting his yearly donatives, extortions, and retirement bonuses, a soldier might even be able to retire with enough money to purchase land, respectability, and importance. The army, then, allowed for social mobility and served as a means to escape poor peasantry conditions.

The Late Roman army contained preexisting units, although often re-duced in size. The infantry or cohorts remained the legionary tactical units, theoretically consisting of 480 men commanded by a centurion. The cavalry units, *ala*, consisted of units of 512 or a larger unit of 768 men. Mixed units, composed of infantry and cavalry, had 120 cavalry and 600 infantry or a larger unit of 240 cavalry and 760 infantry. Special units originated during the third century and included the *numeri, equites, exploratores*, and *cunei*. The *numeri*, composed of local indigenous units, were similar to the cavalry *ala*, while the *equites* (cavalry) were often identified from particular regions such as the *Mauri* or Moorish light cavalry, the *Illyrici* (Illyrian) cavalry from the Danube, and the eastern mounted archers. The *exploratores*, mounted scouts, provided reconnaissance. The *cunei* or *cunei equitum* developed in the third century after the *numeri*, and were stationed on the Danube. There also existed the camel units used only in the East. The elite units consisted of the *equites singulares Augusti* or the old imperial mounted guard, and the *equites legionis (equites stablesiani)*, mounted legionaries. The legions, still the elite units, had a theoretical strength of 5,000 men, but were consistently reduced when men were needed elsewhere. Traditionally, when units were needed for campaign, instead of entire legions being transferred, units called *vexillationes* numbering up to 1,000 strong were sent. These units were then later renamed by Constantine into new mobile cavalry forces and legions. Soldiers could also rise from the legions to the cavalry to an elite unit thereby increasing their own status. The greatest social force in the late empire therefore became the army.

Equestrians, part of the upper class, were originally businessmen under the republic and early empire, and increased in importance during the third century. Emperors, distrustful of the senate, tapped the equestrians for administrative duties as provincial governors, commanders, and bureaucratic officials. By Diocletian and Constantine's era equestrians controlled most of the bureaucracy and military commands. Upon completing their offices they were usually accorded senatorial rank, still attractive because of its traditional honored position.

Humiliores, the peasants, continued to carry the brunt of the work throughout the late empire. By 350 c.e., laws were enacted to force peasants to remain where they were born, *coloni*, "tied to the soil"; such a system was the precursor of medieval serfdom. Many of these laws were aimed at specific places where depopulation seems to have occurred. By keeping the peasants located in their place of origin, the state attempted to maintain the status quo in regard to collection of taxes, compulsory work, and recruitment. Peasants were also required to enter their father's trade, producing a caste system. These individuals had some legal rights, while beneath them, the slaves, lacking any liberty or rights, could be bought and sold as property.

A second distinction between individuals was based upon gender. In the annals of Western patriarchal history, women have been controlled by men politically, socially, economically, and legally. Rome was no different. Although some women in the late empire owned slaves and property, entered into business agreements, signed contracts, and had a great deal of economic independence, most women, practically speaking, remained under the control of men, even when the ancient custom of *manus* had ceased. Whereas men could advance in social standing through the military, women had to rely on marriage. Many noblewomen were forced to marry due to political or social circumstances, rather than for love, while peasant women often had more discretion in choosing their future partners. Divorce became easier for women after the emperor Augustus, although during the late empire Christian emperors attempted to curtail the practice. After the success of Christianity, some Christian women became driving forces in new religious communities; for example, the Roman aristocrat Melania became Jerome's patron, helping him to establish a monastery in the East. As with any imperial house, women often ruled de facto over their husbands, brothers, or sons. Honoria, Pulcheria, and Constantia all exerted strong influence in political matters. Some of these women provided great benefits to Rome, while others occasionally caused disturbances, leading to war and disruption.

Society did not stagnate during the late empire. Individuals occasionally rose from the peasantry to the nobility. Women, while dominated by men, did have some opportunities. Although the majority of the population lived in the countryside, cities still held the cradle of Roman society.

CITIES

Cities provided the social, cultural, and intellectual life of the Roman Empire with their amphitheatres, schools, temples, baths, and theaters. In large cities with extensive amounts of land and money to outfit teams, chariot races were held in the Circus (Document 2.A–E; Figure 10), an oblong-shaped circuit with tight end curves, similar to a U shape (Figure 7). These races allowed the inhabitants to gamble and cheer for their favorite teams, providing emotional release, much as modern sports still do. In the late empire the Circus factions in Constantinople became famous not only for races, but for political outlets. Different teams were supported by different social and political elements, such as the merchants, senators, the emperor or his wife, and were thus identified with their parties. The Circus then allowed city dwellers a way to express their political opinion without fear of reprisal. This phenomenon still exits in many countries like Turkey, Brazil, and Nigeria. The Circus therefore provided both political and social outlets for society.

Whereas the Circus did not exist in every city, amphitheatres or arenas where games and contests took place existed throughout the empire, especially in the West. Such contests can be divided into gladiatorial battles (Document 2.F–G) and wild beast hunts. These events provided the city's inhabitants with an outlet similar to that provided by the Circus, although it was much bloodier. Gladiatorial combat continued into the Christian empire, for the citizenry's thirst for blood and gore could not be quickly diminished.

Cities also possessed schools for the teaching of certain professions, including philosophers, grammarians, and orators, who might advocate for individuals or their city. Other students became record keepers, providing cities with scribes and letter writers, still in high demand since the majority of the population was illiterate. Egypt provides evidence of an active letter-writing society, in which illiterate individuals paid scribes to write letters for them. These letters were usually carried to other cities by friends, slaves, or acquaintances. This epistolary practice seemed to occur in all levels of society, allowing people to keep in touch with friends, family, and business partners (Document 3.A).

Temples acted as repositories of a city's treasure, at least until their despoilment under Christianity. Temples and later Christian churches allowed cities to maintain their regional, social, and religious position. These sites allowed the congregation to hear about important events. Under Christianity the importance of sermons increased, where heretical or opposition sects and even emperors were attacked, as occurred in Ambrose's attack on Theodosius the Great for his massacre of 7,000 citizens in Thessalonica (modern Greece). Ambrose's fierce sermon forced Theodosius to recant and do penance for his sin (Document 6.B).

Cities also possessed theatres where Greek and Latin plays were performed and where speakers may have read their own works. There exists a rich collection of speeches, in this case panegyrics or praises, in Latin from the West, and Greek from the East. Such panegyrics were read aloud, usually in front of an emperor or governor, praising these individuals on their rule and/or the benefit of Rome to the region. The theatres continued to produce works as they had for nearly a millennium. Rome, followed by Constantinople, consumed the lion's share of commodities and imported goods in the empire. Rome had endured for over a millennium and, by the fourth century, had achieved its greatest mass, both in terms of size and number, with a complex infrastructure.

From the Augustan age onward, Rome's population ranged from 500,000 to 800,000, with most inhabitants living in small apartments or tenements. According to a fourth-century *notitiae*, Rome had 26,000 *insulae* (apartment houses) and 1,700 *domus* (houses) in the city. Debate on what an *insula* was continues, although it originally meant a tenement house several stories high. This view definitely holds for Ostia, Rome's port, where archaeological remains from the second to fourth centuries indicate the existence of four- to six-story-high apartment houses. Rome undoubtedly had these, but the term *insula* may have also meant more than just tenements. Evidence suggests that the *insula* included old atrium-style houses, now subdivided into boarding rooms. These houses could easily have held 10 to 20 apartments in one to three stories, housing 50 to 80 people.

The state distributed supplies to its citizens to keep the population of Rome peaceful. In addition to the grain dole instituted centuries earlier, emperors added new commodities, including wine, oil, pork, and finally, instead of grain, bread. Rome was not the only city to have a grain dole: Alexandria, Constantinople, and even the medium-sized town Oxyrhynchus in central Egypt had such grain doles. In addition to these commodities, aqueducts supplied Rome with an immense volume of fresh water for the city's fountains, baths, and private homes. The aqueduct represents one of Rome's greatest achievements, allowing for the transport of huge quantities of fresh water over hundreds of miles, and enabling cities to flourish. Because of the aqueducts, which totaled eleven in Rome by the late empire, the city had fresh water to sustain a population approaching 1 million. When Gaiseric besieged the city in 455 he captured it only after cutting the aqueducts. Rome would never have this amount of fresh running water until the early twentieth century.

The baths, a Roman staple, became its hallmark, especially in the West. During the late empire the bath complex in Rome reached its height, as witnessed with the baths of Diocletian. Baths were available to everyone, regardless of their status, including slaves. The entrance fee was minimal, probably only 1 *denarius*, when the daily wage of a farm worker or manual laborer was 25 *denarii*. Both men and women visited the baths, although at different times during the day, and, depending on their means, probably visited an average of four to five days a week. If one did not have a slave to watch over one's possessions, one could pay to have a locker, although thievery often occurred. After an optional exercise, a bather proceeded into a warm room where oil was used to cleanse the skin, moved on to a hot room, and then into a steam room, allowing the skin and pores to be open, where the oil with the accumulation of dirt was scraped off with a bronze strigil or scraper. Finally, the visitor plunged into a cold swimming pool to close the pores, a process that completed the bath. Diocletian's baths completed the transformation from mere hygienic and therapeutic centers into mini-cities with exercise rooms, libraries, shops, restaurants, and social areas, providing citizens with further relaxation and pleasure.

The city of Rome had grown in size, complexity, and wealth, while the government had been transformed from the old imperial senate to a local governing board. After legalization the Christian church became more important, with the pope acting not only as a spiritual leader, but a political leader as well. By the end of the fourth century Rome possessed several great Christian churches or basilicas. These churches showed the prestige and power of the new favored religion.

VILLAS

The countryside, meanwhile, was dotted with villas (Document 3.A–B). Originally agricultural units, villas often become places of refuge for their owners (Document 8.A–B). During the early empire wealthy individuals went there when they wished to retire from the hectic, noisy, and smelly city. Over time, villas became not only centers of production but places to hide from civil and foreign disturbances. Beginning in the mid-third century, villas were fortified with walls and defensive towers enclosing a courtyard. While they could not necessarily hold out from a full scale attack, they seem to have been able to prevail against bands of marauders. Out of town, and presumably away from troops, wealthy villa owners may have avoided paying certain obligations and taxes to cities and the army.

Rustic estates or villas continued to dominate the rural economic life by providing markets, employment, and industries such as cloth making, wine and olive presses, and specialty shops. Some of these villas were fortified against local and foreign troubles. They tended to be in frontier regions or areas easily accessible by land or water routes. Ultimately, with their fortified position and their economic wealth, these villas became the precursors to medieval mansions or castles. Other villas continued to be nonfortified and were usually located in more secure or isolated regions. An excellent comparison of the style and function of these two types can be seen in two contemporary villas, one at Split (modern Croatia), for the retired emperor Diocletian and, if correctly dated, the Piazza Armerina in Sicily, supposedly owned by Diocletian's colleague Maximian, often called a "hunting" villa because of its mosaics. Three imposing walls, each with a gate, surrounded Diocletian's villa, while the sea fronted the fourth wall. The layout is reminiscent of a military encampment, and the villa was divided in half with the private area near the sea wall, with apartments, a reception hall, and bath complex, and a public area toward the eastern wall, which had a temple, mausoleum, and reception area. The converse was the Piazza Armerina, stylistically reminiscent of Hadrian's villa at Tivoli outside Rome (130 C.E.), having a monumental entryway with a bath complex off it, leading to a basilica-style reception hall with private quarters off to one side. Although it presents a scene of a rambling estate, the procession leads the visitor to this grand reception hall where interspersed here and there mosaics of hunting, gladiatorial, and racing scenes exist. This "hunting" villa in the mountains of Sicily provided its owner with a private, relaxing avenue of serenity. The two contemporary villas are very different, one a military fortress, the other a leisure resort, but both provided places of refuge.

ECONOMY

The late empire's economic history indicates a movement from a unified market economy to regional markets. This occurred mainly due to political and military events, and resulted in regional chauvinism and unrest. In particular, a rise in the number of isolated and fortified luxurious villas and estates took place at the same time the importance of the local city diminished, due to the same political and military uncertainties that made villa life so attractive.

The traditional Greco-Roman city flourished during the Tetrarchy and the Constantinian age. To force the city elite to maintain connections to the city, the state made local communities responsible for taxes. Diocletian introduced extensive economic reforms aimed at regularizing the collection of taxes from agriculture and the population. The agricultural tax, really an income tax, was collected as a percentage from the yield, based on the quality and the type of land. The state divided land into public and private, which paid different rates, and divided arable land into good and marginal, again with different tax rates. Because 75 to 80 percent of the population engaged in agriculture, the state received the majority of its income from agricultural taxes. The state produced a standard taxation schedule for five-year increments. With this schedule was a census, not only on the quality and type of land, but on the number of inhabitants of a community.

Associated with this census was the poll tax or head tax, originally collected from the rural, but not the urban, population. This tax also varied based on the person's age, sex, and dwelling place. Some provinces collected the tax on all individuals over a certain age, others only on men, and others on males of all ages. This local variation allowed Rome to maintain local traditions while still meeting government expectations. In addition to these taxes, the government also published expectations for its military requirements, such as clothing, metal work, transport, and others. The Praetorian Prefects, financial officers, sent these requirements to the governors who, in turn, assessed each region or city in the form of another tax. Under Constantine, a tax on commerce was added, which brought a considerable amount of revenue into the treasury.

The market economy continued throughout the third and fourth centuries, providing trade and communication. These markets existed in both the cities and the rural regions. In the East (where the information is more complete), there existed over 900 cities while in the West, Gaul had 114 cities and eight *castra* or large military camps, Britain about twenty-eight cities, and Africa probably contained 650 towns producing for the empire about 3,000 city markets along with innumerable small villages, hamlets, and collections of huts. In addition, there were numerous imperial and private estates of immense size such as in the East, about forty to fifty large imperial estates existed. Emperors even attempted to increase the number of cities by turning some towns into cities, probably with tax exemptions. A generous number, therefore, for economic areas: cities, villages, estates, and markets totaled perhaps 5,000, far too many for the central government to oversee. This forced the central government, through the local councils, *boule*, and governors, to oversee these urban markets. Local officials policed the marketplace and, if necessary, acted to carry out the central government's orders, collecting custom dues and enforcing regulations (Document 7.B). In contrast to the urban markets, the rural markets continued to be the periodic markets, meeting every seven to fifteen days, where the inhabitants of the countryside traditionally traveled to the nearest village, military post, or villa to buy, sell, and communicate. These periodic markets, probably spaced at an average 15-mile radius, could handle the needs of most of the rural population. Nearly three-fourths of all trade probably took place in these periodic markets and local villages. Merchants would also travel about in search of markets, sometimes paying taxes or dues to the government.

The neighboring countryside, then, supplied the markets with local produce. The farmers harvested the crops and transported them to the city's depot. The total amount of taxes probably amounted to 40 percent of an individual's proceeds. Taxpayers would receive a certificate attesting to the amount and purity of their produce. Here the local farmers either paid the *annona* (taxes) directly to the state via the town's ten commissioners, the *dekaprotoi*, or if they were tenant farmers, to their landlords, who then supplied the state. This grain was transported to a central receiving point for that part of the territory. If produce came from the hinterland, a camel, mule, or wagon would be employed. The state used the *cursus publicus* (public roads), especially wagons, to transport grain to the main emporium. Such carts traveled at a rate of about two miles per hour, stopping each night at a government post or *mansiones* for new oxen, mules, or repairs, near the periodic markets and villages where the government had a known place for tax collection. If the city did not collect enough taxes, the overseers, wealthy individuals who acted as tax collectors, had to make up the difference from their personal funds. Once at a receiving point, ideally on a waterway, the grain was transported to the main port of the province or diocese. Again receipts would be given attesting to purity and quantity. From there, the state grain shippers, the *navicularii*, transported the grain to the army, to Rome, or to areas in need of supplies.

Markets and collection points complemented each other so that trade and tax collections proceeded more easily. Water transport was always preferred over land since it was cheaper, safer, and faster. Egypt, where cropland was no further than 10 miles from the Nile, provides the best example for this collection system, which was similar throughout the empire. The commissariat ordered grain to be transported to Alexandria, which was to be pure wheat with no earth or barley contaminants. Receipts showed the amounts paid, and prevented fraud, established liability, and in the case of purity prevented deception by the exporting countries and the receiver from making fraudulent claims.

The markets, then, formed the necessary link between producer and consumer. For the large estate owner, a market meant an easily accessible area to sell his surplus and hire temporary labor. Markets allowed local inhabitants to buy and sell produce and to obtain information. Markets supplied the state with a center for the collection of taxes and information, for disseminating government policy, and for policing the population.

DEATH OF A TOWN

Late Roman literature has numerous references to deserted lands and failing villages. These references were often in relation to cruel administrators or corrupt officials (Document 8.A–B). Without statistics and other reports an assessment of the literary evidence is difficult, but papyri from Egypt provide valuable insight to some particular cases. Theadelphia (central Egypt) provides one such example, witnessed in the archives of Aurelius Sakaon, one of its inhabitants, where the town collapsed and disappeared by the mid- to late fourth century. But was this town's death caused by imperial actions, heavy tax rates instituted by Diocletian or Constantine as some believe, or by other events?

Situated on a hill at the far end of the local territory, Theadelphia relied on an irrigation canal for water and survival. At the beginning of the fourth century, the central government assessed Theadelphia for a total of about 500 acres. The amount of land actually under cultivation was less than this, about 300, but the village was taxed as if it still had 500 productive acres.

One document shows a governor inquiring if the canal had been tampered with by the villagers of a nearby town, who were accused by Theadelphia of carrying stones off, and another town accused of blocking a feeder canal leading to Theadelphia. This irrigation problem kept surfacing and ultimately destroyed the village. This archive shows the other events of small-town life. In 280 someone is accused of stealing 60 sheep, a seemingly common offense. Sakaon had 16 goats stolen in 318. Documents show that during the early fourth century Theadelphia thrived without any hint of problems. Houses were bought and sold, leases on sheep and goats with taxes assessed on them continued. But by June 3, 320, a hearing took place before the provincial governor during which inhabitants of Theadelphia claimed that their village was deserted (only three people are claimed) because the channel had been dammed up with dirt.

Although probably an exaggeration, the village suffered from desertion and economic decline due to a blocked water channel by another village, which they did not deny as apparently in an earlier report. Theadelphia asked the governor to help reduce its taxes and clear the channel. To accomplish this task the residents asked that the nearby city of Hermopolis take over control of the village and contribute the land dues so the residents could keep occupying their lands. Their petition is striking for a few other reasons. The inspectors seem not to have the authority or the power to unblock or force the unblocking of the channel. And someone in Theadelphia either knew the law, or knew someone who did since they point to an earlier law and edict allowing poorer villages to be attached to richer ones. But why did the village ultimately die?

This region, the Fayum district, had over 5,000 acres of arable land and supported numerous estates during the third century. A vibrant commerce and trade existed with Alexandria and beyond with the large estates acting as commercial centers. One such estate was that of Appianus and his family during the mid-third century. His daughter, Diodora, continued to own vast tracts, and the family, in fact, had helped construct an irrigation canal, probably the one mentioned in the numerous Sakaon petitions. She held land at least till June 8, 276, and then her land was controlled by the imperial treasury at least by 289. The reason why the land was lost is unclear, but possibly it was political unrest. It is also possible that unrest brought ruin not only to her family but other families as well. Appianus' family decline, whether political or just economic, might have also ruined Theadelphia by withdrawing a powerful magnate's support; then the village could not defend itself from other villages with powerful families. Although commerce continued, it became local, and

Theadelphia continued to decline with a loss of population, arable land, and wealth.

What is obvious is that by the time of Diocletian the village of Theadelphia was already declining, perhaps even dead, and that his policies did not ruin the village, for it was already ruined. The final blow to Sakaon occurs in 342 when the village's grain land is nearly gone and all that remains is land for pasture. Sakaon has paid a wheat tax, but another resident has now stolen 82 sheep. This is the final indignation: no arable land; taxes required on the land; cattle stolen, and no one cares. As remarked in the literary sources, the death of a town and wasteland has occurred. Does this mean that Rome lost taxes on the 500 acres? Not really, because the water stolen was undoubtedly used for agriculture elsewhere and probably allowed others to increase their productivity or bring more land under cultivation, perhaps even benefiting the central government more. But this was probably small solace for Theadelphia. The death of an obscure Egyptian town might indicate that the empire as a whole was collapsing. This assessment, however, does not recognize that the other towns might have increased their productivity. This case study shows that Late Roman society was continually changing, leading to a different environment, but not necessarily an environment of decline. As with modern society, where some regions lose populations and manufacturing while others gain them, so too it was with late Rome.

CHAPTER 3

RELIGIOUS CONFLICT IN CHRISTIAN ROME

The Late Roman world saw a fierce fight between the gods of old and a new fanatical offshoot of Judaism known as Christianity, a monotheistic belief in one god, which not only fought for survival against paganism, which was polytheistic—belief in many gods—but for preeminence over Judaism. This religious struggle could not produce a compromise: One group, polytheism or paganism, which tended to religious tolerance, argued that all must worship or at least allow others to worship their chief deities, while the second, monotheistic Christianity, took a more exclusionary path and argued for the primacy of its own deity.

This titanic struggle influenced the Roman Empire religiously as well as politically. Both sides argued that the other side had betrayed the empire. Pagans asserted that Christianity had allowed the Germanic invasions, while Christians countered that paganism had deprived the empire of moral virtue. Christian apologists maintained that problems in the Roman Empire were caused by many things, but not by the existence of Christ or his adherents. During the struggle the Roman Empire hung between the old and the new.

PAGANISM

Paganism existed as a state function where citizens worshipped their city's gods to assure the city's welfare. For example, Rome historically worshipped Jupiter by performing sacrifices at his temple and thereby ensured his protection. These sacrifices were very ritualistic, with the priest following a formulaic prayer and then slaughtering the animal to examine its liver and entrails for imperfections (meaning the gods were angry) or purity (the gods favored them). If the sacrifices were performed correctly, the gods would favor Rome, thus serving the interests of the public, rather than the individual worshipper. Thus, Roman paganism was initially concerned with civic, rather than individual, salvation. Over time, however, a shift toward private salvation occurred, creating more interest in the mystery religions. Originally developed in Greece during the fifth century B.C.E., mystery religions underwent resurgence during the Roman Empire, attempting to fill the void in paganism with personal fulfillment. Ancestor worship and agricultural rites, such as for Bona Dea, continued into the late empire bridging public and private sentiments. As time continued the mystery religions became more important in society.

The mystery religions promoted individual salvation through enlightenment rather than the Olympic belief of eternal suffering in Hades. After initiation, one could discover the correct path to salvation and communion with the gods. In addition to their comforting message, these religions became attractive since individuals could belong to more than one mystery religion, essentially hedging their bets religiously. Rites to Demeter, Isis, Mithras, and Serapis did not abandon the old state or city gods, but rather supplemented them. Such rites, popular among all social classes, were often disseminated by the army, as in the case of Mithras, which argued for a duality, a world with good and evil. Originally Indian, the religion found a stronghold in Persia where Mithras searched for goodness fighting for the god Ahura-Mazda against the dark side, embodied in the evil god Ahriman. Mithras' labors involved two deeds, wrestling with the Sun, thus becoming its friend, and capturing and sacrificing a bull to bring about a renewal in agriculture (Figure 8). The image of the Mithraean labors can be seen in many sculptures, especially from the Western Empire. As this rite spread westward the importance it placed upon the Sun increased.

The connection between the Sun god and the army, through Mithras, fostered the worship of Sol Invictus, the Unconquered Sun, under Emperor Aurelian, especially in the army. The rise of these new religions within the army potentially allowed for society to have a new state religion. Aurelian may have attempted to produce a new state religion based upon the rites of Sol Invictus, which Maxentius may have used to counter Constantine's newfound favoring of Christianity. Maxentius failed to triumph with Sol Invictus against Constantine's Christianity at the Milvian Bridge, ending the official political avocation of Sol Invictus; however, the rites persisted. But a new monotheistic religion prevailed.

CHRISTIANITY

Monotheistic Judaism had been given the right to exist without interference before the reign of Julius Caesar.[1] This right, however, did not mean that Rome considered Judaism valid or as compelling as its own religion. During the early empire emperors expelled Jews from Rome to keep them from accruing power or influence. In Alexandria, the Jews and Hellenes (Greeks) often engaged in violent religious riots, necessitating direct, and costly, Roman intervention. Furthermore, Jewish nationalism provoked several rebellions, the most famous of which occurred in 66 C.E. and was put down by Vespasian and his son Titus, who destroyed Jerusalem and its temple in 70 C.E. A second great revolt under Hadrian in 132 C.E. led to the Diaspora or expulsion of the Jews from Palestine, with Jerusalem becoming a Roman colony.

Christianity grew up in this contentious climate. Originally an offshoot of Judaism, Christianity allowed gentiles to become followers without men undergoing painful circumcision (i.e., convert first to Judaism, and then to Christianity). This "renegade" religion soon spread beyond Palestine, both geographically and ethnically. The Jewish rebellion of 66 C.E. created the decisive break between Judaism and Christianity, when Christians openly divorced themselves from Judaism so as not to be branded as traitors to Rome.

Breaking from Judaism, however, caused problems, since the Romans argued that an individual either worshipped the Roman gods or was a Jew, as Judaism was the only monotheistic religion Rome sanctioned. Christians argued that they were not Jewish, so Rome expected them to do pagan sacrifice. When Christians refused such sacrifice, saying that they worshipped only one god, Rome classified them as Jewish, which Christians found inaccurate and offensive. Roman officials, skeptical of Judaism, now viewed Christians with even more suspicion. Rome, therefore, did not recognize Christianity as a separate and viable religion, apart from Judaism, and viewed Christianity as seditious nonbelievers, or atheists, and not as adherents to another mystery religion.

Christianity, unlike the mystery religions, however, was exclusive; one could not hedge one's bet by worshipping Christ as well as other gods.

Christian exclusivity, though a source of problems with the empire, be-came its greatest asset, since individuals clearly understood their religion's expectations. In addition, one's social and economic position did not matter in this religion. Unlike mystery religions, Christians did not pay an entrance fee, so one was not forced into a gradation of salvation. Christianity instead appealed to, and held the promise of salvation for, believers from all economic classes and social groups. The upper class could continue to own slaves, control patrons, and increase their wealth. Slaves and the poor were offered the hope of eternal salvation and hap-piness where they could be equal, or even superior, to their masters. Christianity promised salvation to all who fulfilled its few simple re-quirements: Believe in only one God; follow the moral tenets of the Ten Commandments; believe that Jesus is the Messiah, the Savior.

Early Christianity appealed especially to the lower classes, which nat-urally made Roman officials even more suspicious, since the memory of Spartacus and his great slave revolt of 73–71 B.C.E. remained a firm part of the Roman psyche. Additionally, Rome always distrusted groups that met privately, fearing that they would foment revolution; for example, Rome outlawed a volunteer fire department because its members met pri-vately.[2] Fearing revolution, Rome believed that these volunteer fire-fighters would meet and talk, and would soon begin to discuss their dissent about their government. Soon, then, they would rebel against the empire. Christianity was seen with similar skepticism.

PERSECUTIONS

Rome outlawed Christianity in the middle of the first century. During the next century, the Antonine Age, Rome left Christianity to its own devices, with occasional local repression, or persecution. This mild cen-sure changed during the chaotic and tumultuous third century when em-perors looked to deflect problems away from their leadership and increasingly blamed Christians for all the disasters that befell Rome. Roman officials soon became violent in their attempts to force Chris-tians back into the pagan polytheistic fold. By the 240s, Rome attempted to require universal sacrifice where an individual would sprinkle incense onto a fire and say a prescribed prayer (Document 4.C). The importance of this act was the ritual observance of form and prayers, and not the sub-stance of belief. Rome demanded the outward sign of sacrifice, but did not require that individuals believe in the theology of paganism. Compulsory pagan sacrifice, however, was anathema to Christianity. When Rome demanded this compulsory and now public sacrifice, Christians were easily identified and persecuted.

Under Decius and then Valerian, this mid-century persecution produced the first universal Roman attack on Christianity. However, when Valerian was captured by the Persians, the state and Christianity entered into an uneasy peace, and, by the late third–early fourth century, Christians had enjoyed some 50 years of peace and prosperity until Diocletian, Galerius, and Maximin Daia (Document 4.E) carried out the last persecutions. Ultimately, however, Christianity survived and within five centuries of its foundation it had eradicated public paganism.

When the Romans persecuted the Christians their modus operandi was first to force Christians to make sacrifices. If one refused, the Romans would attempt to force the Christians to curse their God. Indeed, the Romans thought that cursing the name Jesus would destroy him, since they held to the religious idea that cursing a name had magical powers. When Christians refused to sacrifice, or to recant, the government tortured them, in the hope of achieving several results. First, they might force the individual to recant, curse Christ, and become pagan. Rome had some successes, since the Christian church soon established severe punishments for those who lapsed, or committed apostasy. The second desired result of torture was to convince marginal Christians that it was not worth fighting the empire. Many Christians may have acquiesced, committed apostasy, or even fled into the wilds to avoid torture, which the church allowed as an acceptable means to avoid persecution. A third desired result was to appease the pagan mob. It is clear that Romans blamed Christianity for many of the state's problems. By torturing, and allowing public spectacles, Rome hoped to placate the mob it had aroused. The psychology of mass hatred is nothing new; the Romans were able to whip up support for their own policies.

These persecutions attempted to destroy Christianity, but, in fact, it survived and thrived. Indeed, many Christians believed that the long peace between Valerian and Diocletian had sapped the fervor from Christianity, making Christians "soft." Some Christians, including Cyprian in the 260s, believed that Christianity had been seduced by wealth and worldly goods, becoming more interested in securing its place in society than in the afterlife. The persecutions reinvigorated Christians, allowing them to imitate Christ by dying for their faith. Many of the executed willingly chose martyrdom over fleeing, hiding, or apostasy. Indeed, the church had to remind Christians that voluntary martyrdom (i.e., seeking out death) was not virtuous, and would not be rewarded.

Persecutions varied in severity from region to region. In the West the persecutions were not as violent or as protracted as in the East except in Africa and Spain, where authorities actively sought to persecute Christians. In the East the persecutions continued until 313 C.E. The emperors Galerius and Maximin Daia believed that Christianity was a disease to be cut out. Galerius' pagan priestess mother Romula, once offended by a Christian, instilled her hatred into him and perhaps into Maximin, her grandson, and Galerius' nephew. Christianity triumphed when Galerius, dying from a painful illness, issued his Edict of Toleration (Document 5.A). Christians pointed to God's wrath as Galerius' just reward.

Of course, the end of the persecutions did not end Christianity's troubles, for internal fighting arose, in which the church turned to the state for help. The church, using the state, also attacked paganism. Two clear examples show how the new religion sought aid from the state for its internal problems, Donatism and Arianism.

DONATISM

During the persecutions in North Africa there arose particular cases surrounding individuals, "traditor" (traitor), handing over sacred texts (the Bible, letters from early officials, etc.) to pagan Roman officials (Document 4.D). After the persecutions some Christians argued that a local bishop, Felix, was a "traditor," and that his acts, including the sacraments of Baptism, Marriage, and Holy Orders (ordination of priests) as well as consecrating a new bishop, were invalid. A new bishop, Caecilian, was consecrated by three bishops, one of whom was the accused bishop Felix. Majorinus opposed Caecilian and was consecrated bishop after the Numidian bishops deposed Caecilian. Caecilian's accusers based their position upon the rumor that Felix had been a "traditor," arguing that since Felix was guilty of such a mortal sin, his sacraments, specifically his consecration of Caecilian, were invalid. The controversy then settled on two questions. Was Felix a traditor, and were the sacraments valid if he was? The supporters of Caecilian, the Catholics, argued that the sacraments were valid regardless of Felix's guilt, and that Felix was innocent anyway.

Both groups appealed to Constantine, the new emperor who, through his counsel, Bishop Ossius of Cordova (Spain), sided with Caecilian. Majorinus soon died and Donatus, who supplied the movement's name, took up the cause. In 313 the Donatists again appealed to the emperor, asking that the bishops of Gaul, who had not been persecuted, and therefore did not have a vested interest in the outcome, decide the matter.

Constantine delegated the matter to Miltiades of Rome, a bishop from Africa who decided in favor of Caecilian. In August of 314 the Council of Arles, composed of Gallic bishops, also decided in favor of Caecilian, expressing their disgust at the Donatists' violence. With Felix's acquittal of being a "traditor" in 314, the matter should have ended. The Donatists, however, continued to argue that the Catholic bishops and priests were not entitled to their offices. Setting up counter bishops and priests, the two sides fought continuously for two centuries, each saying that the others' original founders were "traditors." Within a short time many North African regions were partisans of one side or the other, with some cities having both groups of priests and bishops (Document 6.A).

But why did the Council rule against the Donatists? Their decision may lie with Roman law. One duty of a priest was to sanctify a marriage. As the new religion, now free from the constraints of persecution, began to grow and obtain a favored position in Constantine's new government, the church validated marriages. In Roman law, marriage was a civil issue to determine the legitimacy of one's heirs. A child was legitimate, and able to inherit, only if its parents were married to each other at the time of its birth. If a couple's priest was not valid, and the sacrament of Marriage was not valid, then the offspring of this invalid marriage could be viewed as illegitimate, having no legal standing to inherit property. Even if the couple were then "remarried" the original children would still be illegitimate. Thus, councilors to Constantine and bishops may have foreseen the tremendous problems associated with backing the Donatists. Further, if these priests were deemed invalid, all of the marriages, baptisms, and other rites they had performed would be invalidated, undermining the new religion and its recently gained political position.

The Donatists' refusal to accept the ruling led to continual fighting within the church. Constantine, growing impatient over the situation, attempted to compel the Donatists to accept his decision by sending in officials to arrest them. This led to a new persecution, that of Christian against Christian; Constantine ended his overt attacks on the Donatists by 321, allowing the Donatists to gain ground and even claim victory in the matter.

During the 390s all of this changed due to political turmoil and the rise of one of the Orthodoxy's greatest champions, Augustine of Hippo (Tunisia). From 393 to 398 the Donatists supported Gildo, a local military commander, who rebelled against Theodosius and Honorius, thereby losing official support. Appealing to the emperor Honorius, the Catholics successfully revived legislation against the Donatists, who lost power over the next 10 years. At the same time, Augustine produced a solid theological argument against Donatism; his analysis remains the basis of Catholic theology in its premise that the sacrament is sacrosanct or valid, regardless of the grace of the minister who bestows it. In other words, the fact that a priest is guilty of a serious sin does not invalidate the sacraments he has bestowed upon the faithful. Augustine and his theological argument reinvigorated the Catholic movement curtailing the Donatists. The movement was further diminished by the arrival of the Arian Vandals in the 430s, which persecuted both Orthodox and Donatist. Finally, in the eighth century, Islamic forces extinguished Donatism.

ARIANISM

In the East, a different controversy, concerning God's nature, arose. Orthodox, or Catholic, theology maintained that Jesus and God the Father are co-eternal, of one nature. Around 320, Arius, a priest in Egypt, preached that Jesus, being the Son, must have come after God the Father; therefore, he could not be considered co-eternal. Arius' analysis seemed logical to many Christians and pagans, for how can a son be equal in age, and therefore power, to his father? Finding many adherents in the East, Arius won over bishops including Eusebius of Nicomedia (Turkey) and Eusebius of Caesarea (Palestine), the great church historian. His argument, however, went against the Orthodox views espoused by Athanasius in Alexandria. For the next few years Arius successfully promoted his cause throughout the East, splitting the Eastern church.

Constantine was drawn into the controversy after defeating Licinius in 324. Calling the Council of Nicaea (Turkey), composed mainly of Eastern bishops, Arius and Athanasius presented their cases before the emperor and bishops. Outnumbered, Arius was attacked by Athanasius, who used his great oratorical skill to undermine Arius' argument. The result was the Nicene Creed, reaffirming the Catholic view that God, the Father, and Jesus, the Son, are co-eternal.

But the controversy raged on with Arius preaching under the protection of Constantine's advisor, Eusebius, the Bishop of Nicomedia. While affirming the Nicene Creed, Constantine at first refused to curtail Arius and his followers, perhaps because of his failures with the Donatists in Africa. Constantine eventually condemned Arius, sending him into exile in Illyria late in 325, and exiling Arius' ally, Eusebius of Nicomedia, to Gaul, from 325 to 328. Upon his return, Eusebius pursued the Arian cause first as advisor to Constantine and then, after 337, as the bishop of Constantinople, securing Arius' recall in 337. Athanasius was, at the same time, fighting another heresy, the Melitian Schism, which centered on how to readmit Christians who had fled or committed apostasy during Diocletian's persecutions; he could not protect himself, and after being condemned and stripped of his See he was exiled to Trier (in Gaul) in 335. Arius returned from exile after Athanasius' deposition, and was restored to his old position, but died before reentering Alexandria; his followers claimed he was murdered. Arius' movement, however, did not die, as his followers preached his message, especially in the North, and converted the Goths and Vandals. For his part, Eusebius of Nicomedia influenced Constantius, the emperor's son and future ruler in the East, using the controversy to maintain the independence of the Eastern church from Rome.

With Constantine's death, the eastern Arian emperor Constantius persecuted many Orthodox bishops. In the West, however, the exiled Athanasius found protection with the Catholic emperor Constans, Constantius' brother. Civil war nearly erupted between the Catholic and Arian emperors until Constantius allowed Athanasius to return to his See in Alexandria in 341. With the murder of Constans in 350, Constantius became emperor of a united empire, once again attacking Athanasius and the Catholics in both the East and West, and forcing Athanasius to flee into the Egyptian desert in 356. For a short time the radical Arians held power, but, upon Constantius' death, all of this changed with the rule of the pagan Julian, who had no partisan interest in these struggles, but who allowed the exiles removed by Constantius to return to their posts. Julian profited by the continuing struggle between the Arians and Catholics since it distracted many Christian leaders from his pro-pagan policies.

After Julian's death and the return of a Christian emperor, Jovian, the Arians remained strong in the East, not because of their position, but because of the divisions in their opposition. This situation changed in the 370s, with Basil of Caesarea in Cappadocia, who sought to reunite the various Eastern groups. Further, with the accession of Gratian and Theodosius I, both of whom strictly followed the Orthodox Nicene Creed, the Arians lost their political and official strength. The struggle between Arianism and Orthodox Christianity had weakened the church and the East which impacted Late Roman society. The Arians' greatest impact occurred in Africa where the devout and avid Arian Vandal kings Genseric, Huneric, and Thrasamund persecuted the Catholics and Donatists for nearly a century (428–523). Although many of the other tribes in the West were Arians they did not produce the same ferocity as the Vandals.

By the sixth century, Catholicism had supplanted Arianism but their struggle profoundly affected the empire. Not only did the beginning of the split between East and West occur, both theological and political, but many in the West now viewed the East with suspicion since the Arians converted the barbarians. The East also viewed the West with suspicion since the pope and others had asserted the Western supremacy over all other bishops.

PAGAN PHILOSOPHY

The brief interlude of Julian provides an opportunity to examine the ideas of Neo-Platonism. Arising during the third century, Neo-Platonism attempted to unify the ideas of Plato and the mystery religions, Neo-Pythagoreans and Christianity. The great spokesmen for Neo-Platonism were Plotinus, his student Porphyry, and his follower Iambilicus. Each believed differently, but nevertheless brought about a revival of Platonic ideology. In his *Enneads* Plotinus refuted Aristotle and his ideas of rationalism and argued for theurgy where mysticism guided the soul to enlightenment. Porphyry attempted to instill the ideas of Aristotle, creating a new system of Hellenic philosophy. Iambilicus argued for Neo-Pythagoreans and the union of mysticism. All of these ideas attempted to provide a new philosophical justification for paganism. Although Julian attempted a philosophical revival of paganism, it was ineffective since so many of the government officials were Christian and Julian reigned for too brief a time. If this philosophical view had started in the 150s paganism might have remained viable.

Christianity and paganism's final major struggle concerned the Altar (or gold statue) of Nike (Victory) housed in the senate at Rome. The statue, originally set up by Octavian (Augustus) in 29 B.C.E., promoted the idea that the emperor received his power from the gods, anathema to Christians. Beginning with Constantine, Christianity officially challenged paganism ultimately leading to the statue's removal. At first Christianity was given equal status and its buildings restored. Then followed attacks against pagan astrologers and soothsayers. Christians were favored by being given special tax exemptions for priests, although these were curtailed (Document 5.B–E). Constantius II ordered the statue removed in 357. Julian subsequently ordered it returned, and it stayed until 383 when Gratian ordered it removed again. This order culminated in the final debate between Symmachus (an ardent pagan and senator), who argued for its return since it was the basis of Roman rule, and his kinsman Ambrose, bishop of Milan (Italy), who successfully persuaded the emperor to prevent its reestablishment. The statue returned briefly to the Senate House from 393 to 394 when Eugenius, a Christian who was in need of the pagan senators' support, restored it. In 394, after his victory over Eugenius, Theodosius ordered the statue removed for good, but even as late as 402 when Prudentius wrote his work *Against Symmachus* (an attack on the pagan Symmachus who wanted the statue returned), the controversy was still current. Ultimately, the statue was melted down to pay Alaric his booty in 410. The triumph over the statue (Altar) of Victory marked Christianity's victory over paganism. In less than a century Christianity had gone from a persecuted sect to the official religion of the empire. But paganism, nevertheless, still existed in many rural areas and was continually practiced for centuries.

Christianity's response during this time centered on the both public and private worship. Publicly, the official triumph of Christianity over paganism made Christianity the dominant religion, but privately many individuals still clung to their pagan ways. Christianity now attempted to bridge this gap. One example can be seen in the celebration of Christmas. The emperor Aurelian had commemorated the god Sol Invictus' (the Unconquered Sun) feast day as December 25. Christianity attempted to supplant this feast by introducing this date as Christ's birthday, first attested around 336. The connection between the two in fact rested on the idea of Sol, the Sun god and the birth of Christ, the son of justice. The feast celebrating Christmas on December 25 soon spread throughout the West and in the 380s reached the East. By 439 the date was universally accepted as Christ's birthday and not the feast day of Sol Invictus. Christianity thus appropriated a pagan feast day to bring harmony among the masses.

Another response to paganism was the development of monasticism seen in two distinct types, the anchorite and cenobite. The anchorite had as its founder Anthony, who had wandered into the Egyptian desert in search of solitude, finding it originally in a village, then in a tomb in the mountainside near the Nile River, and finally in an abandoned desert fort. Then a small community arose around him, forcing him to move toward the Red Sea, where another monastery later developed. These monks, living apart from society, believed in solitude as an escape from worldly things. The cenobite, founded in Egypt by Pachomius, on the other hand lived in a community supported by the local clergy who often worked lands held by all. Originally, these communities were exclusively male, but ultimately produced sister societies for women. This type of monastic order provided an alternative to the corruption of the city life and produced a contemplative space. These monasteries spread beyond Egypt to Arabia, Palestine, and Asia Minor. In the West monasteries developed differently when Benedict established a space for refuge from the world in southern Italy at Monte Cassino. Benedict united the two types where individuals lived in a community, helping each other and society, but created a contemplative society. Western monasteries promoted working in society, while Eastern communities fled society.

Most individuals, however, did not enter monasteries or become priests, living instead as individuals trying to search for some meaning to life. To accomplish and enhance this search, the church promoted devotions to individual Christians, martyrs, saints, and celebrated sites. After the legalization of Christianity, many Christians outside Palestine and Rome undertook pilgrimages to see the important places. These trips, usually to the Holy Land or Rome, allowed individuals to commemorate Christ and/or the early apostles and martyrs, and gave rise to a series of geographical works or guides for pilgrims such as itineraries and Eusebius' work on *Biblical Places*. One of the most famous pilgrimages was undertaken by Helen, mother of Constantine, to Palestine where she "discovered" relics of the true cross, and deposited them in Rome. Still on display at San Croce in Jerusalem, these relics allowed individuals to venerate Christ and others. Such pilgrimages continued throughout this period and well into the future, providing not only religious introspection but economic opportunities for all.

The religious development during the late Roman Empire produced a series of debates and conflicts dividing Christianity for centuries. These debates, often political and theological, reflected the divergent views of Christians after the persecutions. The history of Christianity during this time was not monolithic in structure or ideology, but instead developed like many of the other movements, changing society over time. Christianity in many ways contributed to the fall of the empire, but not in the view of eighteenth-century historian Gibbon, who argued that Christianity usurped political power from a morally decaying state. Rather, Christianity showed that forces other than political caused people to contemplate and seek change.

CHAPTER 4

ENEMIES OF ROME

One hypothesis is that Rome's end came about in part due to its enemies, traditionally viewed as the Germanic tribes which, by 476, had carved out kingdoms in the West. However, this is only part of the story. Rome's enemies included not only external threats, but internal forces which together caused its decline and fall.

FOREIGN THREATS

East

Rome faced both Eastern and Western external threats. Because of the geographical conditions in the East, namely, deserts and high mountains, Rome did not face a continuous stream of invaders or a highly organized attack from local tribes. Rome's greatest concern remained the Sassinid Persians, especially over Armenia, but their organized threat could be tempered with diplomacy.

Sassinids. The Sassinid Persians, claiming their ancestry from the original sixth-century B.C.E. Persian kingdom of Cyrus and Darius, forced Rome to expend a tremendous amount of energy and resources countering them. Shapur or Sapor I (241–272), defeated the Roman emperor Valerian in 260, sacked Antioch, and established a powerful presence in the East. In 309 his grandson Shapur II (309–379) inaugurated the golden age of the Persians, even forcing Rome, after Julian's debacle in 363, to make a humiliating peace.

Persian and Roman problems occurred in Armenia, a mountainous buffer state between them in what is now Turkey. With Galerius' success in 297–298, Rome dictated conditions, and forced Persia to acquiesce to them. This peace treaty did not require Persia to give up extensive amounts of land, but to cede strategic spots, which allowed Rome to maintain an easy defense against future Persian aggressions. This situation was reversed after Julian's death and Jovian's humiliation in 363. Persia continued to be a symbolic threat for the next 150 years, forcing Rome to divert energy, manpower, and supplies to the East; but peace existed between the two due to internal problems, mainly civil wars, in Persia.

Desert Tribes. The other major eastern group Rome faced was desert marauders in Syria, Arabia, Egypt, and North Africa. Although occasionally disrupting provinces, these tribes never constituted a major threat to the empire because of their disconnected geographical regions. Their disruptions usually occurred in the agricultural regions, around watering holes.

In Arabia the Saracens constantly raided the region east of the Jordan River. Although never presenting a serious threat to the empire, their rapid strikes forced Rome to place mobile, therefore more expensive, troops in the region. Control of roads and oases thus dictated Rome's defensive policy. Diocletian gave up southern Egyptian land to allied nomadic tribes in order to create a buffer zone against other tribes, notably the Blemmynes around the Nile at the first cataracts. In Libya, desert marauders raided Roman cities, especially after the 360s and into the fifth century, while in western North Africa, indigenous mountain tribes attacked Roman farms. Rome reacted by fortifying these farms and their rich agricultural lands. Thus, Rome had to commit forces to strike into the interior to reassert its control over the region.

West

Nomadic Tribes. Since the early empire many tribes east of the Rhine and north of the Danube moved westward toward Roman territory, pushed by new tribes, especially the Huns. During the early empire Rome allowed defeated individual remnants to enter Roman service under Roman commanders. During the third century emperors often accepted into the empire entire defeated tribes, while in the fourth century, Rome now accepted into the empire unconquered tribes as allies. Many of the tribes Rome faced in the late empire were remnants of earlier tribes who now coalesced. Their new power lay in their unification into larger political units, which provided new leadership and new opportunities to interact with the empire, either peacefully or militarily. To counter these united forces, Rome continued its previous policy of frontier raids and diplomacy. As the second century progressed, Rome created a frontier zone along the Rhine, allowing for its continual economic development. This development allowed for the region to advance from small tribes into a larger "national" tribe. The Romans believed the region was pacified, and they moved nearly half of their garrison to the Danube.

Franks. In the northern Rhine River delta, the Franks coalesced out of several early Germanic tribes into a single, formable foe during the mid-third century. By 300 C.E., Diocletian's colleague, Maximian (Document 1.A), successfully defeated the Franks, making them allies who provided troops under their own commanders serving as a formable buffer against other tribes. In the late fourth century Valentinian II, an ineffective and weak ruler, made the Frankish pagan general Arbogast his chief advisor. Arbogast then seized power in Gaul and executed Valentinian. In 394, Theodosius with his foreign allies, Goths, Alani, Huns, and others, commanded by the German chieftains Stilicho and Alaric, defeated Arbogast and his puppet emperor Eugenius. Arbogast had inaugurated the new era of barbarian kingmakers which continued during the next century. By the end of the fifth century Frankish power culminated under the chieftain Clovis, who converted to Orthodox Christianity, setting himself up as Christianity's protector against the Arian Visigoths, Ostrogoths, and Burgundians. With Clovis' rule Rome's power in Gaul ended.

Saxons. The Saxons, east of the Franks in Denmark, raided the English Channel during the third, fourth, and fifth centuries. When Rome abandoned Britain militarily in 410, the Saxons, along with the nearby tribes of Angles and Jutes, established a strong presence in Britain, and, within a century, effaced Rome's political, military, and cultural influence on that island.

Burgundians. Several tribes faced Rome south along the Rhine. The Marcommani, which had existed since Julius Caesar's time, gave way to the Alammani and the Burgundians. These new tribes incorporated elements of previous Germanic tribes in the mid-third century. By the fourth century many of their elements served as auxiliaries and allies in the Roman army. These tribes ultimately filled the gap between the Franks in Gaul and the Visigoths in Italy, holding the area between the Rhine and Danube Rivers. Aetius defeated the Burgundians in 437 and, in 443, allowed them to enter the empire as a federated tribe, settling in south-eastern France. Their presence created another foreign faction in the empire in the fifth century.

Sarmatians. Militarily, the Rhine became secondary to the Danube during the second century when new tribes exerted more pressure in part because of the formation of those "national" tribes to the North and West. Unable to negotiate with these new tribes, Rome created a military buffer zone on the frontiers. As it had on the Rhine, Rome broke the tribal powers in the late third and early fourth centuries; however, unlike the Rhine frontier, the Danube region did not have time to allow for the normal progression to settled, "national" tribes. Instead, the Roman frontier faced new threats from larger, more centralized tribes moving west.

Along the Danube the two major belligerent tribes which blended during the third century were the Carpi and Sarmatians, who forced Rome to expend a considerable amount of time and resources in skirmishes against them. After defeating them at the end of the third century, the Romans allowed them to enter the empire. On entering Rome's service, the tribes were commanded by their own leaders, rather than Romans, perhaps indicating that these tribes were not entirely defeated, or that Rome needed more recruits, or both. By the mid-fourth century these Danube tribes faced pressure from new tribes, the Goths, moving west through the steppes of Russia. From the Far East, the Mongols, or Huns, pushed the Goths, divided into Visigoths (Western Goths) and Ostrogoths (Eastern Goths), and the Vandals westward.

Visigoths. The Visigoths, defeated and forced west by the Huns in the 360s petitioned Rome for permission to enter the empire en masse. This resulted in continual troubles for the Romans for the next 100 years. The emperor Valens allowed the Visigoths to enter Thrace, but he provided no supplies for the starving and weakened tribe. Taking advantage, Valens moved his Roman legions against them at Adrianople. There, the Gothic tribe won, not by superior numbers, for they probably only had 25,000 men, but because of Rome's impetuous emperor, who recklessly attacked them without adequate reserves, thinking that they would be easy targets. After their victory, new emperor Theodosius used another tribe, the Vandals, and their chieftain Stilicho against the Visigoths, but being unable to destroy them, made peace with them in 382. Rome recognized their right for their own chieftains to rule them thereby producing a separate state within the Roman state.

Later the Visigoth king Alaric moved south, threatening Rome in 408, only to be bought off by the Roman emperor with a promise of 4,000 pounds of gold. This bribe was never paid. While Stilicho lived, he could deflect Alaric, but with his death in late 408, Alaric moved back across the Alps into Italy, and demanded his gold. Emperor Honorius refused and Alaric attacked Aquileia and Cremona. Picking up mercenaries and other tribes, he moved toward Rome, besieging the city by cutting off food and destroying the aqueducts. Rome then agreed to pay 5,000 pounds of gold, 30,000 pounds of silver, 4,000 silk tunics, and 3,000 pounds of pepper. When Alaric was then attacked by forces from Honorius in early 410, he argued that the treaty had been violated and, in 410, he sacked the city of Rome. This was the first time in 800 years a foreign enemy entered Rome in triumph (Document 11.A–F).

Alaric's sack and devastation of Rome destroyed the city's infrastructure and wealth. Honorius' half-sister Galla Placidia and thousands of other prisoners were taken. Moving south, Alaric soon died of a fever and his body was buried in a secret place under the Busento River. Alaric's brother-in-law Ataulf agreed to leave Italy if Placidia was given to him in marriage. Honorius refused, but Placidia agreed, and Ataulf marched out of Italy. Moving into Gaul to fight against the Vandals, the Visigoths made Toulouse their capital. Ataulf was assassinated in 415 and Placidia, who loved him, desired to remain a widow, but Honorius married her to his general Constantius. Their son, Valentinian III, guided by Placidia, ruled Rome for 25 years. The Visigoths ultimately settled in Spain after pushing the Vandals out. They remained until the Islamic conquest of the eighth century, having proven that the Roman army could be defeated, and that the city of Rome was no longer impregnable. Their descendents would lead the re-conquest of Spain against the Moors beginning in the eighth century.

Vandals. The Vandals, existing since the late first century in what is modern-day Poland, had moved into Hungary by the late third and early fourth centuries. After the Visigoths defeated them, their remnants received permission from Constantine to enter the empire en masse, settling and thriving in Pannonia, and serving the Romans as auxiliaries. Their leader Stilicho led the Vandals during the reigns of Theodosius and his son Honorius. Constantly at odds with the Visigoth chief Alaric, Stilicho, who had married into the house of Theodosius, controlled the West. When Theodosius died, Alaric invaded the Balkans. Stilicho led his Vandals against the Visigoths, trapping them and making peace with them upon hearing of a rebellion in Africa. Four years later, Stilicho, after stripping the Western garrisons, again faced Alaric and his Visigoths in the West. The two chieftains fought on Easter in 402, and Alaric retreated toward an undefended Rome, which was saved from conquest by bribes. The Vandals, with the Alani and Suevi, invaded a defenseless Gaul in the late fourth century. They then made an arc beginning at the Rhine, moving northwest toward the English Channel then south into Aquitaine, and finally east into Narbonne. Such devastation had not been seen in Gaul since the time of Julius Caesar, nearly five centuries earlier. One group under Radagaisus and 200,000 Alani, Quadi, Ostrogoths, and Vandals, entered northern Italy, where Stilicho, with a small force, defeated them and brought Radagaisus, in chains, to Honorius. Honorius' chancellor Olympius, who distrusted and feared Stilicho, convinced the emperor that Stilicho was planning a coup. In 408, Honorius condemned and executed Stilicho.

A second group of Vandals and Suevi, 100,000 strong, moved westward. They entered Spain in 409, where they held control until the Visigoths, paid by the imperial government, attacked and forced the Suevi to retreat into northwestern Spain, and the Vandals to retreat to Andalusia. The Vandals remained there until 429, when the governor of Africa, Boniface, invited them in. The Vandal king Gaiseric invaded Africa and, with 80,000 men, women, and children, established a kingdom, displacing the Orthodox Christians and the Donatists. Building a great fleet, Gaiseric ravaged the western Mediterranean until he was bought off by the emperor in Ravenna in the 440s. After the death of Valentinian III the Vandals attacked Italy, ravaging it far worse than Alaric ever had. By the 450s the Vandals had made Rome a third-class city. These conquests further weakened the West by removing the rich province of Africa from Roman control. Without its revenue, especially its grain, Rome could no longer feed and supply its army or the city of Rome (Document 12.A–F).

Huns. Moving west during the fourth century, the Huns led by Attila in 433, ruled a loose conglomeration of Germanic tribes from the Don to the Rhine. Psychology was one of Attila's greatest weapons. He allowed, and perhaps even fabricated, stories of Hunnish cruelty against Christians in order to create a general fear in the Roman world of Huns as the "scourge of God."

Not given to luxury or ostentatious behavior, Attila established his log house Palace at Buda (modern Budapest Hungary). By 440 he held the most powerful position within Western Europe, with both Western and Eastern emperors, Theodosius II and Valentinian III, paying him tribute to not attack their empires. When the East refused to pay, he crossed the Danube in 441 capturing Sirmium, Naissus (Nis), Singidunum (Belgrade), and Serdicca (Sophia). Although Theodosius' army was defeated, Constantinople was saved in part by its great walls, and in part by its tribute being raised to 2,100 pounds of gold instead of 700. With these attacks the region lost its importance in commerce, trade, and industry for nearly 500 years.

Attila turned his attention to the West where infighting between Valentinian III and his sister Honoria gave him an excuse for intervention. Honoria had sent him her ring with a plea for aid, to which Attila responded with a pronouncement that he accepted her request for marriage. This was not what she had in mind, but Attila demanded the Western Empire as her dowry. When his demands were refused, as he perhaps knew they would be, Attila declared war on Valentinian, and attacked. Moving across the Rhine into Germany and Gaul, Attila destroyed Trier and Metz. This invasion prompted Roman and Germanic tribes, all Christian, to form an alliance against this pagan invader. Theodoric I, king of the Visigoths, and Aetius, the Roman commander, joined forces and met the Huns at Troyes where over 150,000 men, including Theodoric, are supposed to have died. Although defeated, Attila retired in ease since the Romans were too exhausted to pursue him.

Attila then invaded Italy, where he destroyed Aquileia, seized Verona and Vicenza, and allowed Padua and Milan to buy their safety. Pope Leo I met Attila when he turned toward Rome. Historians do not know what happened during this meeting; however, Attila turned north and returned to modern Hungary, where he died shortly thereafter, having choked on a broken blood vessel in his throat during his wedding night. The Huns became disorganized and their empire dissolved within a few years. The Huns effectively forced Rome to spread its forces thin and give up control of crucial areas. Valentinian III, who feared and distrusted Aetius, executed the general because of his failure to defeat Attila. A few months later Valentinian was assassinated by two of Aetius' retainers, another impact of the Huns.

Ostrogoths. The central figure now became Ricimer, a German who made and unmade emperors (Document 1.C). He supported the Germanic tribes as they became federates in the Roman Empire. With Ricimer's death in 472, the Germans under Odoacer became more powerful in Italy. In 476, Odoacer removed the last emperor, Romulus Augustus(ulus), and instead of naming a successor, ruled as Germanic king. The Ostrogoths, enhanced by their resurgence under Theodoric the Great, deposed Odoacer and controlled Italy. Theodoric's triumph brought an end to Roman rule in the West. Clearly, the empire's external threats were important, but often their power came from elements within the empire, its internal enemies.

INTERNAL THREATS

Bureaucrats

Rome's internal enemies may be classified as greed, jealousy, and apathy, exemplified by bureaucrats, magnates (often senators), church officials, and peasants. Bureaucrats (Document 7.A) professed service to the empire, but given the nature of bureaucratic life, they became its enemy. Roman bureaucracy had always been greedy and jealous. Numerous laws attempted to eliminate bureaucratic corruption, but the problem was ongoing. Why?

First, bureaucrats charged for their services, which did not guarantee that a petition would be approved, or even heard; it merely meant that the bureaucrat would not ignore it completely. Only after continual bribery did one's petition move on. Worse yet, one not only had to bribe a single bureaucrat, but the whole bureaucracy. Such greed gave bureaucrats an incentive to be slow and indecisive. With numerous levels of bureaucracy to bribe, a petitioner had to be rich and powerful for his case to move rapidly.

Second, the bureaucrats became jealous and protective of their position. Eager to ingratiate themselves into an emperor's party, they protected their position from rivals to ensure a continual source of income and power (Document 8.A). When Constantine split the military command into frontier and cavalry forces, the move resulted in fighting between military leaders and bureaucrats. The emperor's advisors also attempted to maintain their influence by attacking their rivals, as seen in the attacks on Stilicho and Aetius. Civil discord resulted, and military advisors were quick to use force to purge rival bureaucrats, while civilian advisors used their control of supplies to force mutinies. Ineffective emperors, easily swayed by whomever held their favor, oversaw a decline in their own power.

Third, the bureaucracy never controlled itself, resulting in uncontrolled growth and fragmentation, especially when the empire had two or more emperors, each with their own bureaucracy. This, of course, led to continual fighting between the separate bureaucracies over finite resources. The importance of the imperial bureaucracy increased and became more involved in every aspect of the empire. Given the personal weaknesses of the emperors, the imperial bureaucracy often controlled the empire's politics.

In most other areas the bureaucracies proved apathetic to society. This apathy allowed other elements of society, most noticeably the wealthy and powerful magnates, to attack the structure of the empire.

Magnates

Powerful magnates owned landed estates, or latifundia, worked by slaves and *coloni*, free peasants tied to an area (Document 3.B). Large estates had always existed but they became more and more politically important during the late empire. In the West, these estates or villas became local regional focal points controlling economic markets, the labor pool, industry, and political power.

Villas originated as investment property for absentee landowners, usually senators, who, by law and custom, had to invest in land. During the early empire, 14 to 180 c.e., senators controlled villas, but, with time, more and more of the local elite purchased land and estates. Many of these owners began to usurp power from local cities and towns, and, since owners could bribe military officers, they exerted pressure on local garrisons for support. Owners also exercised more and more control over the local economy by controlling what was planted, especially cash crops, as well as labor contracts.

During the chaotic third century villas had become focal points in resistance, often fortified, both against external foes and internal rebellions. Thus, peasants looked to the local landowners for protection, abandoning their support of the city, which now seemed ineffective and powerless. Villas therefore replaced cities as the central point of the West.

This growth and transformation again took part because of greed, jealousy, and apathy. Landowners abandoned service to the empire and concentrated on acquiring more land and power for themselves. This power grab extended to the acquisition of labor, not of slaves but of free *coloni*, giving landowners a pool of free individuals who could exert influence in the cities and could even be used for armed resistance or bullying. Such *coloni* were more dependent upon the landowners than upon the state.

Landowners were also often jealous of each other, fostering political infighting. The political infighting between magnates and the provincial bureaucracies for the favor of the governors, armies, and imperial officials led to separatism, which created a more insular philosophy among the local inhabitants, who no longer felt direct loyalty to faraway Rome.

Because of their separatism and greed, magnates became more apathetic and defiant toward the central government. During the Germanic invasions magnates realized that their own safety and power lay in independence or collusion with the nearby tribal leaders, rather than with distant Rome.

The Church

Some church officials also constituted an internal threat to the Roman Empire. Like magnates and bureaucrats, church officials could also be greedy, as when Christians despoiled rich pagan temples, and when they requested tax breaks (Document 5.C–E). After Christianity was legalized, the church went on the offensive, politically, religiously, and economically. By the end of the fourth century paganism had been outlawed and its treasures taken to benefit the church. At the same time Constantine and other emperors gave tax breaks to those who became priests or entered religious service. This prompted many individuals to claim they were religious officials, creating potential problems for the empire's tax revenue. As a result, emperors cancelled some of these incentives. The church also realized that many entering religious life were not properly trained or held ideas contrary to traditional church teachings, causing heresies and the development of sects. This, in turn, often led bishops to attack each other over jurisdiction and doctrine. Jealousy between church officials, politicians, and bureaucrats often centered on whomever directly influenced the emperor or imperial officials, and led to civil strife.

Because Christianity believed that the world would end soon, apathy arose among many church leaders in regard to the empire's survival. They argued that since the end of the world was fast approaching, the church did not need to worry about which emperor led them. When it became clear that the end of the world was not going to occur, the church changed, becoming more and more temporal and secular. By then, however, the empire had already collapsed.

Peasants

While most peasants were poor and generally disenfranchised, their importance should not be underestimated, since they represented at least 70 percent of the empire's population. Perhaps their most destructive attribute was their apathy, their acceptance of whatever changes occurred around them. One can hardly blame them, since they were trying merely to survive; however, their passivity allowed a small group of foreigners, the Germanic tribes, to seize power (Document 8.B).

The Emperor

Foreign and internal enemies help explain the Fall of the Roman Empire, especially in the West, but they were not the final or only reason for this fall. Rome could have beaten back its enemies, and could have rooted out abuses. The greatest weakness, however, lay not in foreign enemies or internal threats, but rather in the emperors themselves.

The imperial household must ultimately be held responsible for the Western collapse, at least militarily and politically. That is not to say that any one emperor is at fault; rather, it was the collective imperial philosophical leadership. With few exceptions, imperial power resided with the army, which made and unmade emperors. During the chaotic third century the army realized and exploited its power, mainly to enrich it with donatives, or bonuses. Through his reforms Diocletian gained temporary control of the army. Lacking sons, Diocletian produced a system of adoption and marriage to transmit imperial power. This system failed when Constantine, backed by an army, seized power beginning in 306. Constantine then returned the empire to dynastic succession, which continued to be the norm, and produced some stability. This system had disastrous effects during the house of Theodosius, especially with Honorius and Valentinian III. The successors of Constantine and Theodosius permitted family intrigue to hamstring the empire, allowing the rise of powerful generals and bureaucrats. Dynastic succession did not guarantee that the best individual ruled. Throughout its history Rome never solved the problem of competent successors, which contributed to the empire's instability.

A second problem produced by the emperors in the third century and accelerated during the fourth and fifth centuries was the division of the empire. The emperors originally made the division to carry out military tasks and win back separatist and re-conquered breakaway regions. During the time of Constantine and Theodosius' successors this division became more dynastic and formalized. No longer was there an idea that the empire was united; instead, there were two parallel states, often not cooperating with each other.

ALLIES

One may deduce from this discussion that Rome was besieged from within and without. This is somewhat true, but there were also many who helped the empire. First, many of the tribes eagerly desired to enter the empire, not as conquerors, but as people seeking more prospects for themselves. These tribesmen and their leaders became the backbone of the new army. Although many later joined separatist movements, the tribes consistently professed their loyalty to the concept of Rome.

A second friend of the empire was the church, which provided a political and religious justification for the rule of the emperors. In addition, the church became the voice of opposition against the Germanic tribes who were Arians or pagan, especially during the fifth century. Church leaders, such as Leo I, successfully prevented or lessened the effects of attacks on the city of Rome, its churches, and its people. To the church, the fall of the empire could result in the fall of the church and its power.

This is best seen in Africa, where the Arian Vandals confiscated the lands of Catholics and Donatists.

Cities were a third friend, allowing for continual transmission of Classical heritage and economic power. Cities viewed foreign tribes as possible destroyers of their philosophical leadership of Classical civilization, which rallied many cities to the idea of Rome and its empire. Other imperial friends were tribes desiring to remain outside the empire, but yet willing to engage in commerce and provide mercenaries for the empire, allowing the empire to use them as a counterweight against many of the tribes who invaded it. The Roman Empire had a variety of enemies and friends who often changed roles and continually disrupted the fabric of Roman society and power.

CHAPTER 5

WHY AND WHEN ROME FELL

WHY

The preceding chapters examined various factors in Rome's decline and fall. Rome clearly evolved over time; however, many of these changes were not healthful to the empire. Indeed, some changes led to its decline and fall, although historians differ as to which ones proved fatal. Comparing and contrasting the various hypotheses or why such a powerful empire collapsed upon itself is instructive.

Some historians suggest that Rome's collapse came about with a decline in the quality and quantity of its soldiers. On the surface this may make sense, since successful invasions during the fifth century indicate the attackers overwhelmed and outmatched Rome. However, the Western armies did not suffer the sorts of crushing defeats that plagued the Eastern armies. Therefore, the army was not uniformly weak, and was, in fact, quite successful on some fronts. For example, Valens' disaster at Adrianople (see Chapter 4) was an Eastern, not a Western, defeat. Had Valens waited for his nephew's army, he probably would have won the engagement. Indeed, Valentinian in the West had restored and strengthened the military's defenses. The Visigoth invasion was not caused by the insecurity of the Rhine region, but rather by the political maneuvering of Theodosius the Great; and, the Huns' successful invasion was aided, in part, by incompetent Eastern military policy. As for the army being outmatched, Aetius clearly showed Western Roman superiority in both Italy and Gaul. If there was any military inferiority, in size or competence, it falls to the East, especially in such disastrous decisions as sending the fleet against Gaiseric in 441.

The second argument for a military collapse was the West's geographical position. While the Caucasus and Black Sea, and Constantinople's
strategic location sheltered the East from barbarian invasions, the West
had no such natural defenses. Thus, the argument that the West fell because of its geographical vulnerability to invasion seems attractive and
sensible. But Rome's Eastern neighbor, Persia, constituted a more serious
threat to Roman boundaries than did any force in the North, and Rome
expended much energy and manpower in the East. Nevertheless, the
West had the long boundary drawn upon the Rhine and Danube Rivers
which provided a weak natural barrier. Unlike Constantinople and its
narrow land mass, there existed no secondary line of defense for Gaul,
and only a weak one for Italy, the Alps. While it is true that the Germanic tribes ultimately extinguished the Roman rulers, they did not do
so with the sword, and the Fall of Rome cannot be fully explained as
being the result of military incompetence.

A second hypothesis, closely associated with the military, is that the
West lacked competent political leaders, although the East did not. Indeed, one might argue, all the Western emperors after Theodosius were
utter failures, and the incompetent rule of Honorius probably accelerated
the West's fall more than any other factor. This hypothesis is convenient
until critically examined. For instance, until the reign of Justin, all of the
Eastern emperors were as dismal as their Western counterparts. Not as
inept as Honorius, Theodosius II still did not inspire great confidence.
More importantly, incompetent leaders were not unique to this period.
Caligula, Nero, Commodus, Elagabalus, numerous third-century leaders,
Constantius II, and even Julian failed miserably, and the empire endured,
despite their blunders. The factor that marks this period is that a con-
fluence of poor leaders and non-Roman advisors rendered the political
climate dangerous in ways it had not previously been. Had these later advisors been "traditional" Romans, the state might have persevered, but
many of these "traditional" Romans were worse than the Germans, and
always had been, as was discussed in Chapter 4.

A third hypothesis was that the real political problem, succession, was
not unique to this period but to all dynasties. Rome never established an
efficient, stable, and beneficial means of succession. Diocletian attempted
to solve this problem by adoption, as had the Antonines a century and
a half earlier, but Constantine and a strong prejudice in favor of dynastic rule overrode this sensible plan. The problem of dynastic succession,

evident since Augustus, constantly plagued Rome, and likely caused some weakness. However, even here, the same problem existed in the East, continuing for the next millennium, until Constantinople fell. Thus, poor leadership and issues of succession cannot be singled out as the cause of the Roman Empire's collapse.

A fourth hypothesis has political problems pitting the new governing class against the old. This is perhaps best seen in the differences in religion. The new governing class in the West, especially among the German advisors, tended to be Arian Christians, a fact which brought them into conflict with the Catholic populace and the emperor. Furthermore, the Roman senate, still influenced by paganism, seemed always to be causing troubles for Christian leaders. This difficult religious and political situation, then, has been postulated as one of the major reason for Rome's decline. This conflict, inside and outside of Christianity, weakened and divided the empire. From its origin, Christianity was an intolerant, monotheistic religion inside a tolerant, often apathetic, polytheistic society. Because its adherents were persecuted, Christianity developed a sense of determination and superiority in regard to its "unenlightened" oppressors. When Constantine converted to Christianity, Christians believed that they had been vindicated, and, by the end of the fourth century, this once abject religion was itself persecuting adherents of the old religions. Furthermore, conflicts within Christianity, namely, over the Donatists and Arians (see Chapter 3), produced mutual hatred and violence. Although Constantine tried to address this problem with edicts, enticements, threats, and force, the opposing forces refused to accommodate each other.

With Arian missionaries in the North, many Germanic tribes became ardent Arians. Their fervor manifested itself in the West with their arrival in the empire and their subsequent conflict with Orthodox Christianity. Such change was unobtrusive in Spain or Gaul, but elsewhere, especially in North Africa, religious intolerance produced severe disruption and hardship. Religious conflict, then, had a profound effect on the empire, as can be seen clearly in the West during the fifth century, when pagan, Orthodox, Arian, and Donatist factions all struggled for control of the region's religious and political fate.

The East, nevertheless, had its share of religious dissent. Arianism was still strong and, although ultimately broken by 400, continually influenced the region. In addition, the ongoing struggle between the Orthodox Patriarch and the pope, and numerous heretical sects, still raged. The skirmishes of these groups sapped the empire's energy at the precise time when strength was needed to tackle foreign threats, economic troubles, and internal succession. Thus, to argue that the West had more religious problems than the East is not accurate. Religious unrest, then, cannot be the deciding factor in Rome's fall.

A fifth hypothesis for Rome's fall concerns society. Society itself underwent extensive changes during this period. Beginning with the reign of Constantine, sons were required by law to succeed their fathers in whatever trade he pursued. It is difficult to know how many people followed this law, since it was laid down in only a few legal edicts. Furthermore, at this point most individuals willingly pursued their father's occupation, a phenomenon that occurred well into the nineteenth and twentieth centuries; thus, the law itself may simply have codified reality, rather than create it. At the same time, individuals were subject to a sharp distinction between the status of *honestores* and *humiliores* (see Chapter 2). Although this might seem a danger, leading one group to abuse the other, such social hierarchies had always existed in Rome, and, while offensive to more democratic sensibilities, were simply a part of life.

A sixth possible explanation concerns Late Roman economics. Economically, the gap between rich and poor increased as the empire began its decline. The middle class seems to have disappeared, while the division between the upper and lower classes grew. While this hypothesis for Rome's fall is widely accepted, the evidence supporting it is tenuous. What probably occurred is the disappearance of one constituency and the rise of another, rather than the death of an economic class.

One area where change occurred was in the growing unwillingness of local elites to get involved in politics. This phenomenon is typically witnessed in the growth of villas farther from cities, and may point to several changes in society. First, local leaders may have become more nervous about their safety, due to foreign threats or internal tensions. This hypothesis is reinforced by the existence of fortified villas, suggesting that their owners were, quite literally, walling themselves away from "outsiders." Second, local individuals may have decided to withdraw from public life for economic reasons. Their disinclination to lead may have been caused by forced exactions, confiscations, business concerns, tax pressures, or general economic fears, which made protecting one's own interests seem more prudent than looking out for the interests of others.

A final reason may have been political, with individuals fearing to back the wrong candidate or general, lest their standing, or even their city, suffer. This idea assumes that the growth in villas in the third through the fifth centuries was indicative of a concerted retreat from political engagement; however, the evidence for this assumption is inconclusive.

Society did indeed change, but the biggest recorded changes took place only at the top, and resulted from political, economic, military, and religious upheavals. Such social change does not mean that the entire society declined, or that the West was vulnerable to a fall.

The third and fourth centuries' economic problems have often been viewed as reasons for Rome's fall. Again changes, and even problems, existed in Rome's economy. On the one hand, prices in *denarii* changed dramatically over time, but if compared to gold over time, they changed relatively little. What, in fact, had changed was the accounting system, which makes it difficult for historians to come to any firm conclusions about the values of coins, and the effects of inflation.

Other changes in the economy did occur. For example, some marginal lands and cities declined in this period, reducing the amount of agricultural production. This reduced amount may have been significant, but the wild claims that immense expanses of fields became vacant should be dismissed. Nevertheless, a continuing and accelerated concentration of wealth and labor in the hands of a few arose. The continual growth of large estates occurred, but again, this is not unique to this age and should not be seen as peculiar.

A major shift in the economy concerns the growth of Christianity. The church gained more and more land, usually from confiscated pagan temple lands. At the same time the state gave the church tax exemptions on land and people, encouraging some individuals to enter the religious life or start religious communities simply for the tax break.

Diocletian's regulation of taxes produced the biggest change in the economy with the creation of a national budget requiring provinces to collect a set amount of taxes, which allowed for a more planned economy, and produced a more efficient estimation of expenditures and revenue. Did these changes cause Rome's decline? If anything the economic changes helped preserve the empire. If these changes had not occurred, the state might not have had enough resources to continue the empire.

Finally, culture changed during this period, with provinces becoming more romanized and in so changing, they altered the direction of art and literature, producing a new culture which continued after Rome's fall (see Chapter 1).

It is necessary to dismiss some popular, but ill-considered hypotheses about the reasons for Rome's fall. During the early twentieth century it was argued that racization, the mixing of the different ethnic groups, destroyed the empire. There is no scientific evidence supporting this view, which is propagated by some individuals, groups, and countries who argue for racial inferiority. Furthermore, the evidence used by some studies has been shown to be inaccurate.

Another common idea is that lead poisoning is to blame for the Fall of Rome. The theory is that the use of lead water pipes caused lead poisoning, producing sterility and/or mental retardation in the Roman citizenry. The theory gained prominence in the 1970s, when scientists proved that leaded paint chips caused severe and irreversible problems in those children who had consumed them. Since lead poisoning is known to harm a person's brain and overall health, this hypothesis that lead pipes in Rome caused its fall sounds plausible; however, if the theory were true then the problems would have been manifested earlier. Lead pipes had been used for centuries and to suddenly claim that the fall occurred in the fifth century due to an accumulation of lead in people's bodies is unrealistic, especially since these same, supposedly fatal, lead pipes were used until the modern age. For these reasons and others, this theory has now been generally discredited.

Another hypothesis is that moral decay somehow caused the Fall of the Roman Empire. This hypothesis asserts that the empire fell because of the sensual pleasures engaged in by the nobility. Again this theory does not take into account the fact that excessive, self-indulgent sensual practices had existed in Rome since the middle republic, as far back as 200 B.C.E. Moral decadence is one of the most frequent allegations hurled by detractors who wish to explain the decline of a city or a nation. This moralist view should be discounted because it is ill-argued and because one can always say that a previous society was morally decadent in some way.

Thus, in looking at the causes of Rome's decline and fall, there are many possibilities, but each one can be discounted, diminished or refuted with the observation that the same things occurred in the East, without such dire consequences. Therefore, the reasons for Rome's fall are perhaps elusive. Some have suggested that it may be more profitable to look at *when* Rome fell and in doing so explain *why* Rome fell.

WHEN DID ROME FALL?

When Rome fell is therefore complicated by what caused Rome's "fall." The two ideas are linked depending upon what "fall" means. Several dates can be advanced for Rome's "fall" and why it fell.

The year 284 has often been seen as the fall of the empire, with Diocletian's accession. Popular understanding is that Diocletian created such a radical transformation of the empire that his reign initiated the Dominate, a military dictatorship. Unlike the first and second centuries C.E., when society was more fluid, this new era produced a more structured and rigid society, akin to the military camp. During the twentieth century this theory became popular as more nations experienced democratic governments as opposed to monarchies and repressive regimes. The major drawback to this concept is that first, the Principate had never really existed, other than a military dictatorship. Since Augustus, the emperor ruled the empire as a military dictator. While some emperors were more successful than others in disguising this fact, it does not mean that the dictatorship did not exist. Another reason for giving Diocletian's reign as the end of Rome is that the capital now resided with the emperor. Again this is attractive, since the seat of power is often viewed as the empire. The problem again with this proposal is that the capital had not resided in Rome since the beginning of the third century. Most of the emperors during the past century had been on the frontier fighting, and so the end of the empire would have then occurred earlier. Furthermore, during the fourth and fifth centuries the emperors would reside in their respective capitals, Constantinople and Ravenna.

What made Diocletian's reign unique was his length of rule. For the first time since Antoninus Pius (137–161), an emperor had ruled for over 20 years. This length of service undoubtedly changed Roman society. In addition, Diocletian carried out numerous reforms needed by the state; thus, the advent of his rule might easily be seen as a watershed date for Rome. Indeed, Diocletian's reign was of singular importance to Rome; however, the emperor's reign preserved, rather than destroyed, Rome's strength and influence.

Other scholars suggest that the date of Rome's decline was 312 when the Christian Constantine successfully defeated Maxentius and unified the West under Christian control. At the same time Licinius, likewise professing Christianity, defeated the persecuting Maximin Daia in the

East and the two victors, united by family ties, ruled the empire together. In addition, both emperors issued the Edict of Toleration (Document 5.A), which recognized Christianity as a valid religion. The year 312 is, then, attractive based on the concept of a new dynasty and the recognition of a new religion. The major drawbacks in hypothesizing this date are several. First, the change in leadership was not new, and few at the time granted the victory to Christianity. Furthermore, this change in leadership was, at best, a tenuous one. In 316, Constantine and Licinius came to blows in the Balkans, with Constantine winning and Licinius agreeing to surrender the region. In 324, Constantine again defeated Licinius and, by 325, was in sole control of the empire again. Furthermore, the filial relationship between the two emperors did not create a harmonious state of affairs; indeed Constantine executed his brother-in-law Licinius. Additionally, the recognition of Christianity represented by the Edict of Toleration was not really the result of Constantine or Licinius; indeed, Galerius, as he lay dying, issued the Edict in hopes that the Christian god would be appeased and save him from his disease. Constantine and Licinius then reissued the Edict in their names to further their cause against Maxentius and Maximin Daia. Constantine's conversion to Christianity at the Milvian Bridge in Rome where he used the Chi Rho sign again has been argued as a change. But again, his conversion was not necessarily seen as a universal endorsement for the new religion.

Another year suggested for the Fall of Rome is 337, when Constantine died and his sons carried out their purge of the imperial family. Those who assert that Rome fell in 337 suggest that this purge created hostility among its survivors leading to a series of disasters for the empire. The first of these disasters was the ongoing conflict between Constantius II, who was Arian, and his brother Constans, who was Catholic. The two men struggled mightily over religious issues. Furthermore, with the death of Constans, Constantius installed his nephew Julian, who rebelled against him and seized power.

Julian attempted to reverse the religious trend of the past half century. His ultimate debacle and death in Persia shifted the balance of power in the East away from Rome. Thus, the family of Constantine may be seen as a complete disaster for the fate of Rome. While it is true that these disasters did occur, the civil wars erupting over the control of the empire were not unique to the house of Constantine. In addition, the purge carried out by Constantine's sons was not unique; the same violence occurred under Claudius, Nero, Hadrian, and the Severi. What was unique was the speed with which these sons undertook their purge. The favoring of Christianity has something to commend itself, for during this time an increase in legislation against paganism and, more important, legislation in favor of Christianity began, putting Christianity and paganism on equal legal footing.

A case could be made for the end of Rome in 378 with the battle of Adrianople (Document 10.A–B). Here the Eastern legions under Valens were routed by the Visigoth cavalry. This attack and destruction showed that the once invincible legions could be beaten. This scenario, however, is only half true. First, Valens' defeat came about through impetuous actions and failing to wait for reinforcements. Second, Rome had suffered defeats earlier, in 9 C.E. under Augustus, during Domitian's reign, and during the third century. What is different is that the Romans did not regroup and tenaciously counter the Visigoths. Instead, Theodosius, sent by Gratian, allowed and in many ways fostered the Visigoths by using them to enlarge his army and move west.

Adrianople has the makings of the disaster for Rome. A great military defeat could be said to indicate the end of military and political life. But actions after the battle clearly show that Rome and the Germans did not view it as the end. What is clear, though, is that Rome decided not to expel the Visigoths and other Germans since it had already relied upon them to fill the army. The battle rather shows the rashness of an emperor, Valens, and the shortsightedness of a future usurper, Emperor Theodosius.

The house of Theodosius looms large in determining a possible date for the Fall of Rome. Theodosius himself could be said to enact the end with his restatement and issuing of new laws banning paganism in 394. Theodosius, at the urging of Ambrose, formally declared paganism outlawed, ending the traditional Roman religion and as such producing a new Roman Empire, one that was Christian. An example of the impact was the debate and final removal of Augustus' Altar of Victory from the Roman Senate House under Theodosius, which commemorated Rome's past by honoring the pagan goddess of Victory. For some pagan senators, including Ambrose's own relatives, this meant the end of the Roman Empire.

This view, used by many who claim that Christianity caused the end of Rome, argues that the vast majority of the population would have been motivated and impacted by this act. In reality, most of society probably did not take great notice. While the nobility may have greatly objected, individual citizens would not have altered their lives that much. It would be inaccurate to state that the majority of the people who were still pagan simply stopped their worship. Indeed, many individuals continued their traditional religious rites. The end of official, state-sponsored paganism merely brought to a conclusion a process begun nearly 75 years earlier when Rome's emperors moved from one religious philosophy, paganism or polytheism, to another, Christianity or monotheism. The end of paganism had more to do with the political fighting between the emperor, the Bishop of Milan, and the senate.

Under Theodosius' successor Honorius, a more serious calamity befell Rome, one which might clearly signal its death, the sack of the city of Rome itself in 410 (Document 11.A–F). For the first time in 800 years foreigners had taken the city. The sack showed that the emperors in Ravenna or Constantinople had no power to stop the city's collapse or plunder. Alaric's sack of Rome clearly marked an end of an era, as Jerome and others indicated. The sack instilled a psychological trauma throughout the empire. It was not just Rome, but the empire, that was lost. But even in this hour of gloom certain assumptions should be questioned. First, the city had been witness to numerous attacks, many more disastrous than Alaric's, including Marius' and Sulla's seizures under the republic, the Sullan Proscriptions, the Second Triumvirate and its renewed proscriptions, the civil war after Nero, the numerous emperors in the third century, and Constantine's arrival after the Milvian Bridge. While it is true that this was the first "foreign" conquest, individuals during these earlier Roman occupations may have had it worse. But Rome recovered its ability and in fact over 30 years later successfully stood firm against another invader, Attila, who mysteriously fled before attacking the city. Rome was not so lucky against Gaiseric in 455.

The year 455 saw Gaiseric and his Vandals arrive and systematically plunder the city (Document 12.A–F). In this instance the city could not be saved, although the pope negotiated that its inhabitants and churches be spared. The sack might be seen as the end of Rome since the city would not really recover. Its aqueducts cut and the city reduced to possible starvation showed how powerless the city and empire had become. Worse yet, there appeared to be no one willing to help Rome. Unlike

410, though, when the capital was still fresh in everyone's mind, the sack of 455 was now seen as just another calamity without real comment.

The final date, 476, still holds allure for the historian. Like the battle of Adrianople, the year 476 corresponds to a clear act, Odoacer dismissing the young emperor and telling the Eastern emperor that the West did not need a new emperor. But again, this was merely the last nail; Rome had already fallen. So when did the West fall?

In returning to the analogy of an elderly patient who has died of a stroke, and about whom a life history has been completed, there are similarities between his fate and that of the Roman Empire. Like the patient who has smoked and abused alcohol, Rome too suffered from abuses, some self-inflicted (religious disputes, social changes, and economic problems), while others were external. Like the patient suffering stress or illnesses, Rome had belligerent neighbors and diseases. Constantine can be likened to Rome's first cigarette, or first night of drunken carousing. Although the consequences of Constantine's actions were not immediate, he nevertheless sowed the seeds of Rome's destruction. First, he abandoned Diocletian's mode of succession and adoption for dynastic rule. Unfortunately, his rash temper made him listen to the charges against Crispus, his son and capable general, whom he executed in 326. The charge seems to have been related to Constantius' wife Fausta, Crispus' stepmother. Shortly after Crispus' death, she herself was executed. It is tempting to see the two events entangled. Perhaps she accused Crispus to promote her three children, and after Crispus' death, Constantine learned the truth and exacted revenge. Of his three children their succession would produce political and religious discord. In retrospect, the dynastic succession was a failure.

The second way Constantine undermined the empire was through his religious policy. While he may have been a sincere Christian, it is also clear that he used Christianity as a political tool. By promoting this religion he separated himself from previous emperors and the aristocracy. He also gathered around him a new group loyal to him through this new religion. In addition, Constantine attempted to solve the two religious problems, Donatism and Arianism, as if they were political or legal issues. After hearings and attempts to find common ground failed, Constantine ordered a military attack. In this fashion these Christian groups now were persecuted. Although Constantine could point to a legal success for Orthodoxy, his solutions produced discord. Furthermore, Constantine held no theological training and his attempt to get personally and politically involved set the dangerous precedent for future emperors.

A third way Constantine harmed the health of the empire was through his economic policies. Here he abandoned the minting of an abundant silver coinage and large stable bronze coins, instead reverting to the third-century policy of minting abundant smaller bronze coins which produced a series of inflationary decades during the 330s to 360s. Constantine's tax policies also moved toward granting exemptions for Christians and introducing an onerous tax on merchants. He tied the peasant to the soil (*coloni*) and forced children to follow in the footsteps of their fathers. Taken as a whole the economic policies of Constantine produced a disaster.

His fourth policy was the creation of a large, mobile army based in the interior in cities. His policy promoted a dual class system in the military with superior mobile forces in the interior and inferior infantry on the frontier, weakening the army and frontier zones. This collection of a large number of mobile troops, well paid and supplied, gave future generals the means and resources to rebel. His policy on the frontiers, especially the Rhine and Danube, made it easier for enemy troops to cross over. He furthermore increased the practice of allowing whole groups of foreign barbarians to enter into the army together under their own leaders, thereby weakening the command structure.

Finally, in 324, Constantine announced his plan to move the capital from Rome to Byzantium, now renamed Constantinople (Document 9.A), producing a psychological blow for the empire. No longer was the nominal capital in the Latin West, but now in the Greek East. Furthermore, this capital was to be Christian, without the temples of the old Roman gods. The movement of the capital would be akin to moving the U.S. capital from Washington, D.C., to Lincoln, Nebraska.

Thus, in looking at a date for Rome's fall, 324 should come to the forefront, when all of these events coalesced in the reign of Constantine. Rome's future in 324 looked bright, just as when sixteen-year-old youths smoke their first cigarette and drink their first beer. Who could tell what lay in store?

CHAPTER 6

CONCLUSION

Fifteen hundred years after the fact, the Decline and Fall of Rome is captivating due to the difficulty of determining its cause(s). Rome's decline ended seven centuries of political, economic, and cultural unity in the Mediterranean and northwest Europe, which had produced the world's largest empire to that date. In the West the once unified political empire's breakup produced a series of small Germanic kingdoms, a constricted economic system, and the triumph of the Latin Christian church. With Rome's vanished military might, the Germanic tribes created more competitive regional military and political kingdoms with smaller territories within the old Roman provinces. These kingdoms, identified with their chieftains, looked upon their power and dominions as personal property to be disposed of as they wished. Succession, in which multiple sons each inherited portions of the kingdoms, accelerated the pace of fragmentation. The concept of one dominion had now vanished and, by the Carolingian period (800 c.e.), the kingdoms of France, Germany, Italy, and minor duchies now existed, but as the personal property of their rulers rather than as countries.

With the collapse of the central Roman imperial government, the central bureaucracy decreased in size and power. By the mid-sixth century Roman imperial bureaucracy remained only in Rome (Document 2.A–E), replaced in the rest of the empire by German tribal organization and later by a Catholic Church bureaucracy. Socially, the empire's collapse prompted continual class division. The middle class, once a significant element in Roman society, almost completely disappeared, and the gulf between the high and low classes widened. With the end of Roman conscription and its resulting social mobility, Roman class distinctions now grew more rigid, with little upward social mobility possible. Such class division ultimately led to the institution of serfdom, the roots of which can be traced to the late empire's institution of the *coloni*.

Economically, the empire's decline ended strong international commerce, hastening the rise of regional interaction. This change reduced the quantity and assortment of goods traded and the vitality of cities suffered. Trade items now included mainly rare or valuable items, with little of the bulk trade and organized corporations that had existed earlier. City sizes now decreased, with their population becoming mainly administrative and religious. In addition, economies became more self-sufficient and allowed for autarky or complete economic self-sufficiency. The use of coinage continued but it had a reduced status, and taxes were usually collected in kind. Thus, local manors often became centers of economic activity, as they had begun to do in the Late Roman period with villas.

The collapse of the Roman Empire accelerated the growth of monotheistic Christianity, officially displacing polytheism. Many viewed the collapse of Rome as divine intervention or as a justification for the end of paganism. This new era allowed the Christian church to create an empire for Christ, achieving its goal with Charlemagne, crowned Holy Roman Emperor by the pope in 800. The church acted as the protector of society and became the center for Roman prestige, power, and learning. A bulwark against the Arians and Germans, the Catholic Church made alliances with the East and, more importantly, the Franks under Clovis, who became Catholic. These alliances helped bring Justinian into Italian affairs in the 530s and brought the Franks into Italy by 800 c.e. The church also exercised temporal power, with the pope becoming the political leader of the city of Rome enhanced when the pope saved the city from complete destruction in 410 and 455. The church, through its monasteries, became the center of Classical learning after the Roman Empire fell, preserving its cultural heritage, language, literature, and art.

The Fall of Rome created not one, but two new cultures, the Latin Medieval West and the Greek Byzantine East. This in turn affected the development of Western and Eastern European history and culture differently, and the effects are still present in modern society. As time passed, the East and the West had grown apart, producing a split that began in 324 when Constantine moved the Roman capital to Constantinople. Ultimately, this separation produced a splitting of cultures, with the East producing the Byzantine state which left both the political and religious policies in the hands of the emperor. This policy led to serious political and religious problems, as witnessed by the Iconoclast Controversy, in which the emperors tried to force their own theology on the Eastern church by abolishing the use of icons in the ninth century.

While the year 476 evokes a romantic image of Odoacer returning the imperial standards to Constantinople, Rome's end is not so neat. In 488, shortly after Romulus Augustus(ulus)' "retirement," Theodoric, the Ostrogothic client king, bluffed and cajoled Odoacer to leave the safety of Ravenna. Then Theodoric executed Odoacer and reclaimed the Roman Empire for the East. Once again, an emperor ruled over Rome, addressing the senate as a partner in the same way Augustus had done five centuries earlier, as if no disaster had occurred. If this romantic legend is not accurate, can a firm date be ascertained? As seen in the earlier chapters, various dates have been proposed for the Fall of Rome from the foundation of Constantinople (324), the Battle of Adrianople (378), Alaric's sack of Rome (410), Gaiseric's ravages of Rome (455), to the deposition of Romulus Augustus(ulus) (476).

Popular wisdom holds that the Roman Empire collapsed in 476 when German tribes swept across the Rhine and destroyed the Roman state. But the empire did not fall, since the East continued, with the Latin West developing differently than the Greek East. The development of these two cultures indicates the stark distinction between the East and the West in the transmission of Rome's memory after its collapse, seemingly only a century after Theodosius had restored the empire. The collapse of the West and its memory can be summarized as producing a cascade of different events and policies.

First, the West had a longer frontier, consisting of the Rhine and Danube Rivers, whereas the East only had the lower Danube. Thus, the West more than the East had to expend more manpower and revenue to protect its frontier thereby depleting its resources. The Western Empire required more soldiers to protect its frontiers and it sought German tribes to fill this need. Since the West could not draw upon Eastern wealth to pay its mercenaries, it taxed its citizens for the revenue, giving rise to citizen apathy, tax evasion, and the West's ultimate financial and political collapse.

This simplistic analysis, while tempting, is not sufficient. Likewise, other individual reasons for the Fall of Rome, such as depopulation,

Christianity, land exhaustion, the rise of large estates, monarchy, the decline of the city, Christianity versus paganism, moral decay, apathy, tax policy, the bureaucracy, militarism, and incompetence of leaders have been espoused.[1] As seen in the previous chapters, the causes are interrelated, suggesting that Rome's fall is problematic. As shown, the Fall of Rome was not an instant event, but rather an accumulation of events, forces, and people. Imperial policies enacted, especially by Constantine and his family, Theodosius, and Valentinian III, produced weaknesses in the West, and often strengthened the East. The exact situation(s) are not important; however, how the emperors reacted to these situations and held on to power for nearly two more centuries is. The German tribes continued to espouse the ideas of Rome but in an altered fashion. These two centuries then from Constantine to Theodoric produced a cultural, religious, political, and economic change that moved the empire away from imperial pagan Rome to the Christian Germanic kingdoms.

Since all of the theories giving the cause or date for Rome's collapse have not produced definitive answers to the questions they purport to answer, perhaps more important is the next question. Why should the fall of Rome concern citizens in the twenty-first century? First, like Rome, most countries desire to make their mark on civilization. France, Japan, Germany, the Ottomans, Spain, Britain, Russia, China, the United States, and most other countries have attempted to expand their boundaries, increase their prestige, and influence others. In the nineteenth century, nations such as Britain, France, and Russia called themselves empires, often modeled on Rome. Therefore Rome's decline and fall became a concern since, like Rome, any nation could lose its influence, power, and luster. The empire's collapse served as a warning for other nations and empires. By trying to understand and explain Rome's fall, each nation might avoid the same "mistakes" and thereby "save" itself. Associated with Rome's fall is the fact that Rome's collapse shows an inability to accept that some things are not understandable; things must take place for a logical reason. But since there is no logical reason for the fall of such a powerful empire, a second question looms: What lessons can be learned from Rome's fall?

The most important lesson is humility: Any nation can fall, such as the Ottoman Empire or the Chinese Manchus dynasty, both of which fell in the early twentieth century after 500 years of rule. There are, of course, other lessons to learn from Rome's fall; even the ancient Romans argued that their society would collapse because of their decadence. This became a call for action in late antiquity to return to the idealized earlier days, when people supposedly behaved with more decorum and restraint. Modern societies also argue that they are corrupt and decadent. In America this ideology has been used to discredit the current culture. For years, the 1950s have been seen as an era of peace and propriety that gave way to the turbulent 1960s, Vietnam, the 1970s, and high inflation. Modern commentators too often forget that the 1950s also produced McCarthyism, discrimination, both racial and sexual, a climate of fear and mistrust, and economic stagnation. In the Middle East a resurgence of Islamic Fundamentalism has taken place, arguing that the decadent West has corrupted Islam. Unfortunately, as times have changed so has Islam. Islam was originally tolerant of other religions and society; however, some now view their religion in purely military, not religious, terms. Like Rome, modern societies look back to a golden age that never really existed. By concentrating on this false past, societies often ignore chances for productive change.

Another lesson to learn from the Fall of Rome is that autocratic governments lose the backing of their people. From its inception the Roman Empire ignored the role of citizens in the formation of their government. With the loss of real senatorial power under Augustus, no citizen group could challenge the imperial system. The army became the only group that could effect change, and this power was confined to the leadership, not the rank and file. Such a situation created even more problems as the professional army realized its importance to the empire and used it to its own advantage. Even now, the symbiotic relationship between armies and leaders often results in brutality and conformism. This takes citizens out of the decision-making processes, leading to their apathy or even their hatred of the government. When such governments are challenged through war, revolution, or popular political demonstration, their support often quickly evaporates.

A corollary lesson often espoused by commentators is that governments should not be economically oppressive to their citizens. The Roman Empire has often been accused of driving its population into the hands of the Germanic invaders because it levied high taxes and engaged in economically oppressive behavior. The selective evidence used could be applied to earlier or later periods. While economic and oppressive behavior produced some local rebellions, the late empire did not have an abundance of popular discontent or revolutions resulting from taxation.

A final lesson from the Fall of Rome concerns the role of incompetent leaders. Incompetence was often fueled by special interest groups attempting to ingratiate themselves to emperors and military leaders. Although the mass media did not exist during the Roman Empire, kowtowing to interest groups, like the army and wealthy, enabled certain individuals to succeed while more competent adversaries failed. As is often the case, form was more important than substance. These lessons clearly indicate that the scholarly and philosophical arguments concerning Rome's fall can be applied to similar situations in modern society. Indeed, with conflicting theories, causes, effects, and reasons the Decline and Fall of Rome shows that history is open to interpretation, exploration, and discussion.

But who benefited from Rome's fall? By examining the social and political groups from the bottom up, a fuller picture can be gained. The peasantry and poor clearly did not benefit from Rome's collapse. These individuals still paid taxes, worked the lands, and coped with constant attacks and demands. The urban poor clearly suffered, losing their grain dole, games, and, often, their personal safety. Above them the merchants clearly did not benefit from Rome's collapse. Without imperial protection, trade and commerce suffered, becoming more localized. Long-distance trade, with the potential of exotic items and fantastic rewards, diminished. As society changed, the market for rare or expensive merchandise for numerous wealthy patrons diminished while greater risks to the merchants accrued.

The elite may have benefited, positioned as local magnates controlling the regions politically, socially, and economically. By using their landed estates with military retainers the elites often became quite powerful, perhaps more so without imperial checks and balances. At the same time these individuals were often in danger, since without imperial protection large-scale invasions could destroy their property and power.

The church gained from the collapse of Rome, and promoted itself as the protector of society, often against the Arian Germanic chieftains. With the imperial collapse, the church became the most important organization in society. The German tribes also benefited from Rome's fall. As the new power they controlled the resources, population, and land.

Nevertheless, their divisions and wars never allowed the West to unite again for an extended period of time.

In essence, the winners and losers are again not the people but the ideals. The passing of Rome really meant the end of the culture and not just the political state. The Fall of Rome then extinguished the light that Maximus believed shined forth, giving the world hope. Although many would attempt to resurrect the old Roman Empire, it lay dead. The idea of Rome or *Romanitas*, however, has never been extinguished. The allure of Rome and its empire remains with us, with the continual fear of its end.

As Byron stated:

> While Stands the Coliseum, Rome shall stand;
> When fall the Coliseum, Rome shall fall
> And When Rome falls—The World.[2]

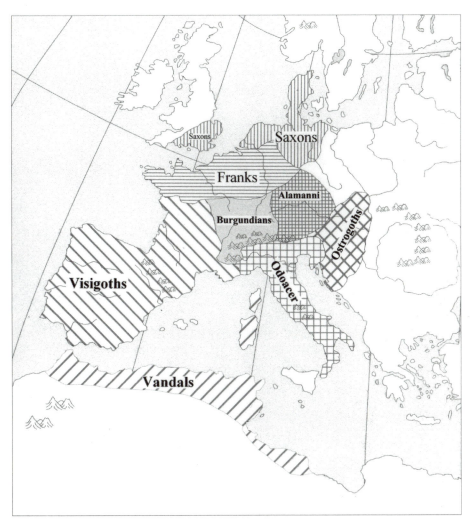

Map 1: Germanic kingdoms: 476.

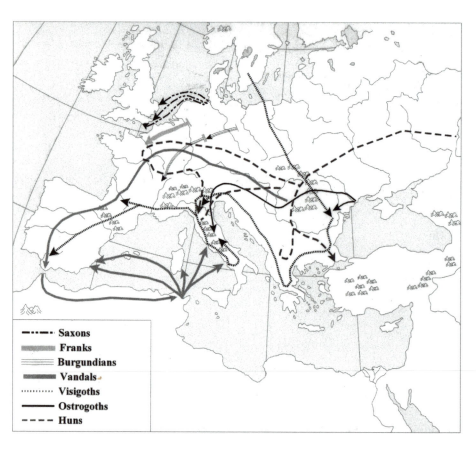

Map 2: German migrations to 500.

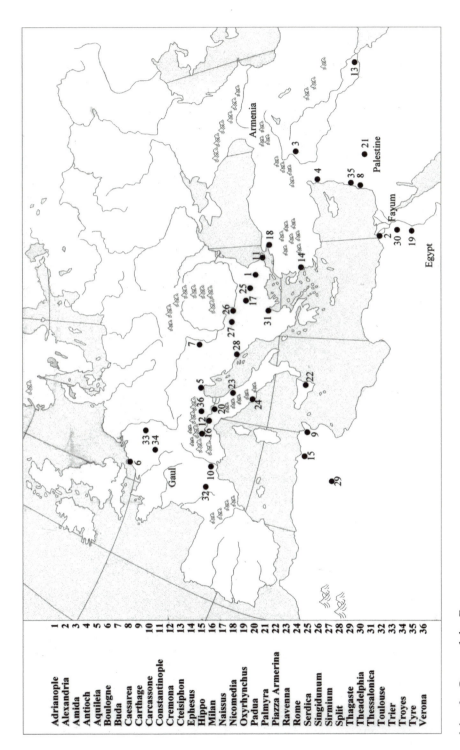

Adrianople	1
Alexandria	2
Amida	3
Antioch	4
Aquileia	5
Boulogne	6
Buda	7
Caesarea	8
Carthage	9
Carcassone	10
Constantinople	11
Cremona	12
Cteisiphon	13
Ephesus	14
Hippo	15
Milan	16
Naissus	17
Nicomedia	18
Oxyrhynchus	19
Padua	20
Palmyra	21
Piazza Armerina	22
Ravenna	23
Rome	24
Serdica	25
Singidunum	26
Sirmium	27
Split	28
Thagaste	29
Theadelphia	30
Thessalonica	31
Toulouse	32
Trier	33
Troyes	34
Tyre	35
Verona	36

Map 3: Cities of the Empire.

Figure 1a: Belt section with medallion and coin; gold and semiprecious stones, late fourth century. The Walters Art Museum, Baltimore.

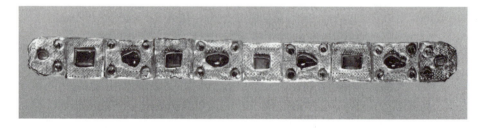

Figure 1b: Diadem, gold, amethysts, emeralds, fourth–fifth century. The Walters Art Museum, Baltimore.

Figure 2: Arch of Constantine with Hadrianic roundel (130 C.E.) on top and Constantinian frieze on bottom (315 C.E.). James W. Ermatinger.

Figure 3: Mosaic from Ostia Italy. James W. Ermatinger.

Figure 4: Portrait of a woman, tempera on wood, attributed to the St. Louis Painter (290–310 C.E.). The Saint Louis Art Museum. Gift of Mrs. Max A. Goldstein.

Figure 5: The Rubens Vase, gold, agnate, early fourth century. The Walters Art Museum, Baltimore.

Figure 6a: Gold bracelet, octagonal, alternating sides have inscriptions, 400 C.E. The Saint Louis Art Museum. Museum Purchase.

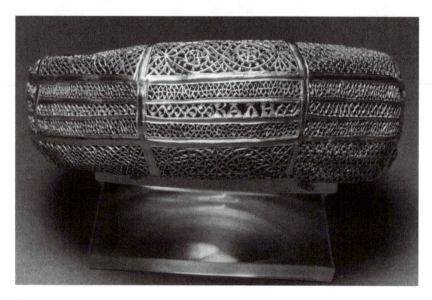

Figure 6b: Gold bracelet, inscription: translation "Dear soulmate wear this jewelry in all health." The Saint Louis Art Museum. Museum Purchase.

Figure 7: Intaglio circus with chariot race, red jasper. The Walters Art Museum, Baltimore.

Figure 8: Amulet with Mithra slaying the Bull, hematite, fourth–fifth century. The Walters Art Museum, Baltimore.

Figure 9: Arch of Constantine with Coliseum in background. James W. Ermatinger.

Figure 10: Circus of Maxentius, Rome, Italy. James W. Ermatinger.

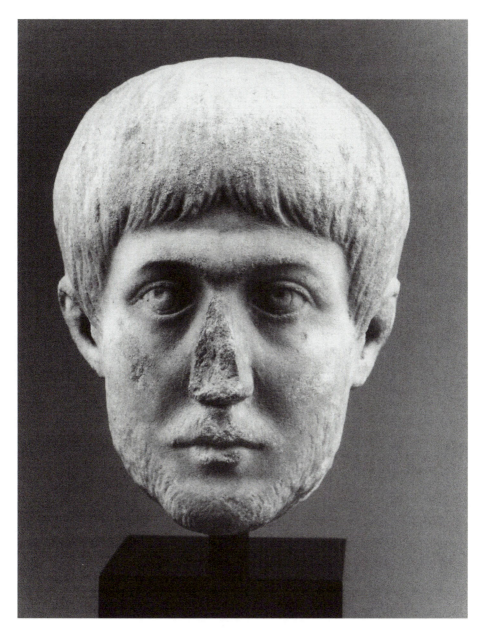

Figure 11: Head of a man, marble, fourth century. The Saint Louis Art Museum. Gift of Mr. and Mrs. Lester A. Crancer Jr., in honor of Sidney Goldstein. Museum Purchase, by exchange.

Figure 12: Pair of eagle fibulae, gold over bronze, semiprecious stones, meerschaum, Visigothic. The Walters Art Museum, Baltimore.

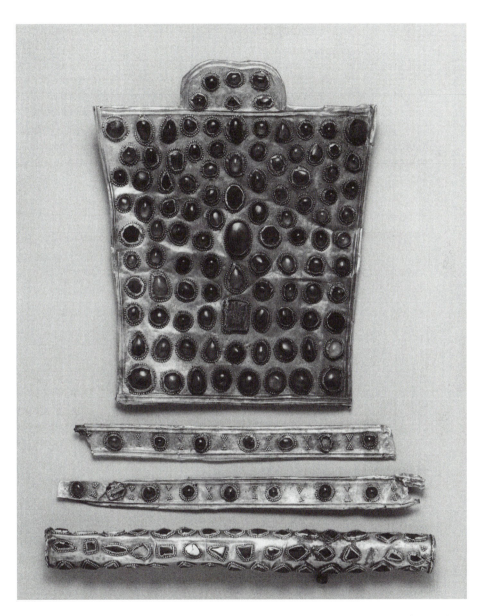

Figure 13: Horse trappings, gold, copper, bronze, gemstones, Hunnish. The Walters Art Museum, Baltimore.

BIOGRAPHIES:
PRINCIPAL
INDIVIDUALS IN
LATE ROME

Aetius (c. 400–454)

The Roman general Flavius Aetius, born of an Italian mother and a Scythian soldier about 400, became a hostage of Alaric and later Rugila, king of the Huns, where he learned the art of war and the importance of cavalry. Originally in the usurper Johannes' army (424), Aetius was pardoned after the former's execution. He became an advisor to Placidia and her son, the emperor Valentinian III. He ultimately supplanted Boniface, count of Africa, for supremacy of the army. Boniface then began a civil war with the Vandals as his allies, but died in battle after defeating Aetius in 432. Because of his defeat, Aetius retired briefly to the Hunnish camp, but in 433 took command of the Roman armies in the West with the Huns as his allies, defeating the Burgundians in 436.

In the 440s Aetius replaced Placidia as the major influence over Valentinian, becoming virtual leader of the West from 433 to 454. He continued to use the Huns to counter the Visigoths and Burgundians until the rise of Attila, leader of the Huns, in 451. Attila attacked Gaul, forcing Aetius to now rely on his old adversaries, the Visigoths and Burgundians, to fight against his former allies, the Huns. Aetius and his allies won a contested battle at Troyes in 452, but could not prevent Attila's invasion of Italy. After his success against Attila, Aetius returned to Ravenna where he attempted to persuade Valentinian to align their families closer. Aetius wished for his son to marry the emperor's daughter. Valentinian, in a fit of rage, stabbed and killed Aetius on September 21,

454, afterwards accusing him of treason. Valentinian, a weak ruler, was possibly influenced by the palace bureaucrats to move against Aetius. With Aetius' death the empire, in one swift blow, lost its protector. On March 16, 455, two of Aetius' body guards assassinated Valentinian on the Field of Mars (Campus Martius) in Rome in revenge.

Ambrose (c. 340–397)

Ambrose, like Augustine and Jerome, ranks as one of the great Latin Fathers of the Western church. Born the son of the Gallic praetorian prefect, Ambrose received a thorough training in law and philosophy. He became governor of Liguria (Northern Italy) and in 374 was made the bishop of Milan by popular acclamation, even though he had not yet been formally baptized.

Ambrose fought two major foes, paganism and Arianism. Advisor to emperors Valentinian I, Gratian, and Theodosius, he used his position as bishop to urge war against both paganism and Arianism. In 382 he convinced Gratian to remove the Altar of Victory, a golden statue of Nike, the goddess of Victory, from the Senate House where Augustus had placed it. His relative, the pagan philosopher Symmachus, wrote a series of hymns (letters) in an attempt to have the statue restored. Ambrose responded with his own letters and sermons arguing for its continual removal; he was victorious in 384. In 391, Ambrose convinced Theodosius to make a permanent end to paganism by closing all the pagan temples.

The powerful bishop, through his writings, especially *On Faith* and *On the Holy Spirit*, as well as through his sermons, fought against Arianism and defended the Nicene Creed. At the Council of Aquileia (Italy) in 381, Ambrose forced the emperor to remove several Arian bishops. When a Jewish synagogue burned down in northern Italy in 385, Ambrose and his followers occupied the site to prevent the Arian empress Justina from constructing an Arian church.

Ambrose completed Augustine's education and journey toward Christianity, culminating in Augustine's baptism on Easter of 387. Although not trained as a theologian, Ambrose defined in Latin the arguments of Christianity by using Greek theology and Neo-Platonism, and employed his Latin legal training to make Orthodox Catholic policy supreme in the West.

Ambrose used the Roman bureaucracy as well as his oratorical abilities to further the power of the church. He held sway over emperors, even forcing Theodosius to seek public penance after having massacred 7,000 citizens in Thessalonica in 390. Through his actions and writings Ambrose secured both the independence and dominance of the church over imperial control.

Arius (260–336)

Arius provoked one of the two great Christian schisms in early Christianity (the other being Donatism). Arius, a priest from Libya, was born about 260 and educated in Egypt, and began in 319 to argue that Jesus was from the Father and, as such, was not co-eternal with the Father. This view produced a theological debate within the church. His doctrine, Arianism, promoted *homoousia* whereby the Father was "superior," in opposition to the Orthodox view of *ousia*, "with" the Father. Arius was condemned at Alexandria but found supporters outside of Egypt. His popularity attracted individuals such as the historian Eusebius of Caesarea. In 325, Constantine sought to bring the two sides together by calling the Council of Nicaea. There, a young deacon named Athanasius eloquently and forcefully argued against Arius. The Council, refusing Eusebius' attempt to strike a middle road, condemned Arius for heresy. Exiled to the Balkans, Arius returned to Egypt after his friends encouraged Constantine to pardon him. Arius returned to Egypt but died on the way to Alexandria, allegedly murdered in a bath complex.

Athanasius (c. 296–373)

Athanasius, the greatest advocate for Orthodox Christianity against Arius, was born in 296 in Alexandria, probably of Greek non-Christian parents and received a Classical education. Converted to Christianity after the end of the great persecutions, Athanasius was influenced less by Origen, the greatest Christian thinker of the time, than were his contemporaries. A lector to his bishop Alexander, Athanasius attended the Nicaean Council probably as Alexander's secretary where he worked behind the scenes rather than in public, leading the opposition to Arius' position and refusing to compromise. His fierce opposition endeared him to the West, while many Eastern bishops considered him narrowminded and uncompromising.

Made bishop of Alexandria in 328, Athanasius engaged in a long battle with Arius and his allies over the nature of Christ. Athanasius promoted the Nicaean view that Christ was one nature with the Father, as opposed to Arius' view that Christ was subordinate to the Father. Never able to cultivate the imperial court as well as Arius, Athanasius and Constantine argued privately. Athanasius traveled extensively throughout Egypt trying to win over and suppress heretical sects, including the Arians. Arians outside of Egypt charged him with corruption at the Council of Tyre in 335. Athanasius appealed to Constantine, but his enemies maintained Athanasius had attempted to disrupt the Egyptian grain supply to Rome, and Constantine banished him to Trier in 335. When Constantine died, Athanasius was allowed to return to Alexandria, but the new Eastern emperor, Constantius II, an Arian, battled Athanasius publicly. Forced to flee to the West, Athanasius was restored to his See only after Constans, the Orthodox Western emperor and brother of Constantius, threatened war with the East in 346. Athanasius was deprived of imperial protection with the death of Constans, and once again forced into exile.

Athanasius returned to his See only after the new emperor, Julian, allowed those bishops exiled by Constantius to return from exile. Because Athanasius admired Antony and his institution of monasticism, he brought monasticism to the West. Narrowminded Athanasius was nevertheless a forceful orator, whose arguments formulated the ideas of modern Christianity. Athanasius died in 373.

Attila (c. 410–453)

Attila became king in 435 with his brother Bleda and attacked the East to force tribute. He killed his brother in 445 and assumed complete control of the Huns. An astute leader, capable of judging situations and patient, Attila made the Huns an efficient military force. During the late 430s and into the 440s he attacked the East after Theodosius II failed to pay his usual tribute. Stopped at Constantinople, Attila successfully besieged and took important cities in Pannonia, sacking Sirmium and Singidunum in 441, Serdica in 443, and Marcianopolis in 447. In 449 he received an invitation from Honoria, Valentinian III's sister, offering herself in marriage, so Attila claimed, and asking for his help against the emperor.

Attila's forces faced Aetius in 451 at Troyes, where Aetius now employed his old enemies, the Visigoths, against Attila. This gambit defeated the Huns, but, with his forces diminished and weakened, Aetius failed to wipe them out. Attila now turned toward Italy, and planned to move to the East since Marcian, the new Eastern emperor, had decided not to pay the tribute. Superstitious, Attila moved toward Rome where Pope Leo I negotiated with him and Attila mysteriously turned away. Legend had it that Attila had a dream forecasting his death as he neared Rome. A few days after turning away from Rome Attila died. Married many times, his last wife Ildico supposedly foretold his death on their wedding night. Leaderless, the Huns drifted across Roman borders and disintegrated.

Although astute, Attila's military abilities were more myth than reality. His greatest weapon was fear. Being pagan, the Huns alleged savagery against Christians, both Orthodox and Arian, which worked both for and against Attila; for him in that he could provoke fear, but against him since the Christians saw him as a common threat and united.

Augustine (354–430)

Augustine was born in Thagaste in Numidia (modern Algeria), the son of Patricius, a town official and a small landowner, and a Christian mother, Monica. He studied rhetoric at Carthage before traveling to Rome and ending up in Milan, where he befriended Ambrose.

After reading Cicero's *Hortenius* (now lost) at age eighteen, which inspired him to seek wisdom, Augustine studied Manichaeanism at Carthage. This Gnostic sect, however, proved intellectually and spiritually unsatisfactory and Augustine abandoned it in favor of skepticism. Augustine secured a position in Milan, and after hearing Ambrose's sermons he abandoned skepticism in favor of Christianity and Neo-Platonism.

Augustine returned to Thagaste where he withdrew from public life, living as a hermit from 388 to 391, and giving up public office and a marriage to his common-law wife of 15 years. He was forcibly ordained a priest at Hippo in 391, where he established a monastery. He also preached in church at the request of his bishop, even though this was not the African custom. In 395, Augustine was consecrated an assistant bishop, and, in 397, bishop, where he now studied theology. After becoming a bishop Augustine entered into a second career as a formidable preacher, promoting Catholic unity in Africa. Augustine preached and advocated unity, even forceful coercion, against Donatism in order to reunite Christendom. He preached against Pelagius and his definition of free will. He died August 28, 430, when the Vandals besieged Hippo.

Augustine's two greatest works were the *Confessions* and *City of God*. The *Confessions*, written in 397–400, was an autobiography, discussing his life down to 387. The work also shows the influence of Neo-Platonism on his life and his conversion to Christianity. His second work, *City of God* (413–426), produced a theological rebuttal to the charge that Christianity caused the sack of Rome in 410. Instead Augustine promoted the idea of the Eternal City, that is, the next world where the believers and nonbelievers would be separated. He wrote 93 works in 232 volumes, and well over 100 sermons and letters. With Jerome, Ambrose, and Gregory I, Augustine is hailed as one of the four fathers of the Catholic Church. His prominence is seen in medieval philosophy influencing thinkers such as Thomas Aquinas. Augustine attempted to resolve the issue of reason and faith. His conclusion was based on the idea that both were required in order to be a Christian. One needed to have reason to understand and have faith, and one needed faith to conduct reason. Having developed these ideas, Augustine began to explore the relationship between God and man. He argued against predestination, and developed the theology of redemption and actual grace.

Aurelian (c. 215–275)

Lucius Domitius Aurelian ruled Rome from 270 to 275. One of the soldier emperors from the Balkans, Aurelian successfully repelled the German Iuthungi and Vandals from northern Italy. Aurelian fought two wars against Zenobia, queen of Palmyra in 271 and 273, and captured her in the latter war. Palmyra was economically devastated by the war. Aurelian also campaigned against the Carpi on the Danube and in 274 he successfully defeated Tetricus who controlled Gaul. Aurelian effectively recovered the break-away provinces of Gaul and the East thereby preventing the total collapse of the empire. Aurelian began the defensive wall around Rome which ultimately encircled the city. He also undertook a coinage reform and instituted a change in the city of Rome's grain supply, supplying bread instead of raw grain. Aurelian supposedly instituted a distribution of pork and oil as well. He was assassinated in 275 by his generals while on campaign in the East.

Avitus (?–c. 456)

Avitus was father-in-law of Sidonius Apollinaris and emperor from 455–456. Eparchius Avitus espoused the case of the Gallo-Roman nobility and the Visigoths residing in Gaul. After making a treaty with the Visigoths in 439 he enlisted their help against Attila in 451. Avitus did not receive the support of the Italian nobles or their German allies, and while his Gothic allies were fighting in Spain, Ricimer defeated him in northern Italy at Placentia. He was subsequently made a bishop, apparently against his will. He died on a mission to Clermont.

Carausius (c. 250–293)

Carausius provides an excellent example of a secessionist typical in the third century. Like other secessionists he did not plan to establish an independent state. Rather, he desired to become emperor, and he styled himself as such.

Born in northern Belgium, Carausius learned a trade as a seafaring merchant. He entered the military and served with Maximian in Gaul in 285 against the Bagaudae. Carausius then served with distinction, effectively ending the Saxon pirates' menacing of the English Channel. Maximian accused him of allowing pirates to freely raid the northern Gallic coastline, seizing booty, and then capturing them on their return and keeping the stolen goods. Fearing execution, Carausius seized northern Gaul and the troops there supported him. He then won the support of the troops in Britain and made the island his major base.

Carausius consolidated his position in Britain and secured the region with his fleet. Maximian attempted to retake Britain by building a fleet. This invasion either failed or never took place, since several years later orators did not make reference to this invasion. Carausius did lose northern Gaul in 287, but regained it in 288–289. This blow to Maximian may have forced Diocletian to appoint Constantius as a junior partner or Caesar.

Carausius, calling himself emperor and controlling Britain, undertook a coinage reform, issuing pure silver coins before the central government under Diocletian undertook the same reform. Diocletian may have used Carausius' reform as a model for his own. He campaigned in northern Britain against the Picts and repaired Hadrian's Wall. He attempted to ingratiate himself with Maximian and Diocletian during the early 290s by assuming their praenomens (first names) Valerius and Aurelius. He issued coins with all their portraits with the legend Carausius and his brothers. The senior emperors did not reciprocate, although they may have made a tentative peace agreement. When Diocletian nominated Constantius as Caesar, Carausius abandoned this policy.

Constantius began a systematic reduction of cities controlled by Carausius of northern Gaul beginning in 292–293. Constantius' important siege and capture of Boulogne dealt a severe blow to Carausius. Although not present, the loss of Boulogne deprived Carausius of his most important naval base in northern Gaul. Carausius was assassinated by his lieutenant Allectus. Constantius now began to build his naval forces, but inland, since Allectus still controlled the English Channel. Constantius launched his invasion of Britain in a two-pronged front led by Asclepiodotus westward at the Isle of Wight, and Constantius northeast near the Thames estuary. Constantius' fleet was delayed by a storm but Asclepiodotus defeated and killed Allectus.

Carausius, and later Allectus, continued to identify themselves as emperors and viewed their dominion as the Roman Empire. The success of Carausius lay in his ability to be recognized as a Roman emperor by the people of Britain, and not as a secessionist. Carausius, and later Allectus, failed in their aims because the full weight of the empire was against them.

Constantine (285–337)

Constantine, born about 285 in Serdicca (in modern Serbia) to Constantius and his concubine Helena, grew up and was educated at Diocletian's imperial court. He served in Galerius' Persian campaign, perhaps as an aide. With the retirement of Maximian and Diocletian, Constantine became a hostage of Galerius. Escaping to the West, Constantine joined his father in Britain. When Constantius died, his troops hailed Constantine emperor. Galerius, forced to recognize him, allowed Constantine the title of Augustus. When Maxentius, with the help of his father Maximian, rebelled, Constantine at first supported him. To seal the relationship Constantine married Fausta, daughter of Maximian and sister of Maxentius. When Maximian quarreled with his son, he fled to Constantine and then tried to murder him, Constantine executed him in 310. In 312, Constantine, now in control of Britain, Gaul, and Spain, defeated Maxentius at the battle of the Milvian Bridge near Rome, winning the West, supposedly by invoking the name of Christ.

With the control of the West, Constantine made an alliance with Licinius in the East giving his sister as wife. Constantine began a series of reforms that transformed the army and the state. He separated the military command into two groups, the cavalry and the infantry. He placed the cavalry as mobile central reserves away from the frontier. He began his economic policies by reducing the weight of the gold *Solidus*, producing the standard for nearly 1,000 years. Constantine's greatest difficulty lay with the religious problems in North Africa with the Donatists where he backed the Catholic or Orthodox side against the Donatists.

Relations with Licinius began to sour in 316. Constantine defeated him in the Balkans, taking the lands west of the Hellespont. In 323, Constantine defeated Licinius and seized the remainder of the Roman Empire, executing him and his son. With this victory Constantine carried out reforms in the East. In 324, Constantine announced the moving of the capitol to Byzantium, now renamed Constantinople, officially founded in 330. This new capitol, completely Christian, superseded Rome. At the same time Constantine had to deal with the controversy of Arius and his followers. In 325, he assembled the Council of Nicaea which denounced Arius, despite Arius' still holding sway over many in the government.

In 326, Constantine executed his eldest son and heir designate, Crispus, and in 327 executed his own wife, Fausta, for adultery. The two events may be connected since Fausta may have attempted to supplant Crispus with her own children. Constantine attempted to formulate a policy in which his family would inherit his kingdom, but this failed. Although Constantine did not officially make Christianity the state religion, he did favor Christianity by granting lands and funds to the church. He ordered the Christian churches to be rebuilt by using funds from pagan temples. He granted tax exemptions to church officials and promoted churchmen into his bureaucracy. Although called upon to arbitrate religious controversies, he had little religious training and sought to make decisions that promoted imperial unity and peace rather than theological discernment. In 337, Constantine planned to march off to war against the Persians, but he fell ill and died.

Constantius II (317–361)

Born in Illyricum in 317, Constantius was named Caesar in 324, and in 333 given Antioch to administer. With Constantine's death in 337, a period of three months ensued where the empire was ruled in Constantine's name while his heirs decided what to do. Constantius II, the second son of Constantine and Fausta, with his older brother Constantine II and younger brother Constans, executed the remaining imperial family members, except the young brothers Gallus and Julian. Constantine II controlled Britain, Gaul, and Spain; Constans governed Italy, Africa, and the Balkans, while Constantius ruled the East where early in his rule he fought against Shapur II. In 340, Constantine attempted to oust Constans but was defeated and killed. The two remaining brothers ruled the East and the West uneasily, especially since Constantius was an Arian and Constans Orthodox.

Constantius, although deeply suspicious and superstitious, still promoted Arians into church leadership. Constantius campaigned against the Persians and the barbarians on the Danube. Constans, meanwhile, attempted to hold on to the West by ruling with an iron fist. When in 350 Magnentius rebelled, Constans' troops deserted him and Constans was killed trying to flee. His sister Constantina effectively divided the loyalty of the forces in the West by promoting Vetrano to the throne supporting Constantius. When Constantius invaded the Balkans, Vetrano resigned and retired. Constantius then defeated Magnentius at Mursa, winning a great battle over a larger force. Magnentius fled to Lyon where he committed suicide.

With his victory Constantius continued to campaign throughout the Roman world, in Gaul, on the Danube, and against the Persians. He defeated the Sarmatians and Quadi (after 350), and later in 359 attacked Mesopotamia. He realized, however, that he needed help so he promoted his cousin Gallus to the rank of Caesar. But Gallus became known for his harshness and was recalled and executed in 354. Constantius made a triumphant entry into Rome in 357, and then appointed Gallus' brother

Julian, who took over the West. When Constantius ordered Julian to send him troops to fight against Persia, the Gallic army proclaimed Julian its emperor. Constantius died of a fever en route to dealing with him on October 5, 361. Although given to paranoia and brutality, Constantius nevertheless displayed some aptitude for generalship.

Constantine the Great's successors, embodied by Constantius, failed to stabilize society and continually engaged in petty family squabbles. These wars depleted Roman resources and the strength of the frontier, while the continual religious strife promoted dissension and disunity.

Diocletian (c. 244–313)

Diocletian was born about 244 in Salona, Dalmatia, near modern Split (Croatia). He rose through the army ranks to become head of the protectors or officer corps for the emperor Carus when the latter invaded Persia in 283–284. With the death of Carus, Carus' son Numerian became emperor. Upon the army's return, Numerian's murder, traditionally blamed on his father-in-law Aper, the praetorian prefect, was discovered and the troops hailed Diocletian emperor in 284. Diocletian may, in fact, have had a hand in the murders of Carus and Numerian. In 285, Diocletian defeated Carinus, Carus' other son at the Margus River and became sole emperor. In 286, Diocletian appointed his friend and fellow general Maximian his co-emperor or Augusti. These two men then waged war throughout the empire, against the rebelling local peasants of Gaul, the Bagaudae, the Germans on the Rhine, Carausius, a usurper in Britain, the Carpi on the Danube, the Saracens in Arabia, and the Persians.

Needing more generals, Diocletian created the Tetrarchy or rule of four in 293. Here each Augusti received an assistant termed Caesar; Diocletian chose Galerius and Maximian Constantius. These generals waged war throughout the empire. Constantius defeated Carausius in Britain, Maximian campaigned in North Africa, Diocletian waged war on the Danube against the Sarmatians and Carpi, and later put down a second rebellion in Egypt in 297, while Galerius suppressed a rebellion in Egypt in 293, waged war on the Danube, and finally defeated the Persians in 298, producing a lasting peace.

Diocletian carried out numerous political and economic reforms. He accelerated and completed the process of dividing large provinces into smaller ones, including Italy. He closed the local mints, replacing them with a standardized mint system. He reformed the coinage, issuing large numbers of a gold coin called the *Solidus*, a pure silver coin called the *argenteus*, and a large bronze coin termed the *nummus*, which had a standard reverse type "Genio Populi Romani" or "Genius of the Roman People." In addition, Diocletian instituted a standardized tax reform, and the most controversial reform, the price edict or edict on maximum prices on goods and wages. Diocletian also carried out legal reforms and created a chancellery.

Diocletian attempted to eliminate Christianity beginning in 303 with the last of the great persecutions. At first his persecutions were confined to intimidation and the destruction of churches and sacred books. Ultimately, Diocletian issued orders that everyone in the empire perform sacrifice on pain of death. The persecutions were strongest in the East and North Africa.

In 305, after 21 years of rule, Diocletian decided to retire. Forcing his colleague Maximian to retire as well, the new Augusti Constantius and Galerius adopted Severus and Maximin Daia as Caesars, even though Maximian and Constantius had grown sons, Maxentius and Constantine. Diocletian retired to his fortress palace at Split. After Galerius' death in 311, Diocletian's wife Prisca and daughter Valeria were unable or unwilling to join him; Licinius executed them in 313. Diocletian, unable to save them, and distraught over his statues having been torn down with Maximian's attempted coup, either died or committed suicide in 313. He was declared a god, the last emperor to have such an act accorded to him.

Eusebius of Caesarea (c. 265–339)

Eusebius was born in Palestine, probably at Caesarea, around 265. Pamphilus, a student of Origen who had developed the scientific reasoning of Christianity, taught Eusebius. Eusebius venerated Pamphilus who perished in Diocletian's persecutions. During these persecutions Eusebius fled Palestine to Tyre and then Egypt where he was arrested and imprisoned. After the Edict of Toleration in 311, Eusebius returned to Palestine, and became bishop of Caesarea in 313.

One of Christianity's greatest writers, Eusebius wrote extensively on historical material, apologies, and biblical works. Some of his most important historical works are: the *Chronicon* or *Chronicle*, which, preserved in a Latin translation by Jerome, covers the history of the world from

Abraham to Constantine; the *Martyrs of Palestine*, originally a stand-alone work but later incorporated into his *Ecclesiastical History*, his greatest work, chronicling the history of Christianity down to 324. The work, edited several times, is important since it not only discuses the evolution of the church under the Roman Empire but preserves many important documents. Eusebius became a friend of Constantine and wrote several works in praise of the emperor. In 335, for his tricennial or 30-year celebration, Eusebius wrote an oration *In Praise of Constantine*, and in 337, after the emperor's death, wrote a panegyric, the *Life of Constantine*, where he promoted and praised the emperor's past even if it is sometimes unreliable. These early works indicate his breadth of knowledge in religious matters. His apologetic works included *Against Hierocles*, refuting the pagan theory that compared Jesus to Apollonius of Tyana, and the *Evangelical Preparation* and *Demonstration*, a discussion of the gospels. *The Preparation*, completely preserved, argued against paganism, showed the superiority of monotheism, and contradicted Greek philosophers and their errors. Parts of the *Demonstration* exist which argued against the Jewish charge that Christians corrupted their religion. Eusebius' surviving biblical works include the *Onomasticon* or *Biblical Place Names*, *On Easter*, detailing the date of its celebration, and fragments of biblical commentaries.

In 319, Eusebius followed the teachings of Arius. At the Council of Nicaea in 325, he attempted to form a compromise between the Arians and Orthodox Christians but failed. He finally signed onto the majority and condemned Arianism. Like other moderate Arians who joined the majority of Nicaea, he still hoped for a compromise. At the Council of Tyre he condemned the Orthodox Athanasius, giving weight to a charge that he still followed Arianism. Eusebius' fame and intellect influenced later Christian writers, most notably Jerome. He continued writing up to his death in 339.

Gaiseric (390–477)

Gaiseric, a Vandal king, the son of a slave woman, was Rome's greatest foe in the western Mediterranean during the fifth century. After his half-brother Gunderic's death, Gaiseric, said to be intelligent, austere, and an adept psychological "reader" of people, proved a capable leader. Gaiseric shrewdly used his forces to play Rome off the other tribes. Boniface, a close friend of Augustine in Africa, was sent to fight against the Vandals in Spain, but soon quarreled with other Roman generals. Boniface fought and defeated the Roman magister militum, but then refused an order to return to Ravenna. When declared an outlaw, Boniface invited Gaiseric into Africa from Spain in 429 to aid him but Gaiseric soon supplanted the Romans. During the next five years Gaieseric moved eastward taking Carthage in 439, and gained control of the grain supply to Rome and Constantinople. With his fleet he posed a danger to Italy.

In 455, Gaiseric attacked and plundered Rome, where he took the widow Empress Eudoxia and her two daughters back to Africa. The eldest married his son Huneric. Gaiseric attempted to influence the Western Empire's succession by having Olybrius, Eudoxia's second daughter's husband, on the Western throne. The Eastern emperor Leo decided to destroy Gaiseric with a three-pronged invasion using fleets and armies from both the East and the West landing in all parts of Africa. The Romans attempted to destroy his power and launched an invasion in 468 with disastrous results, due to Vandal fire ships, weather, and Roman ineptness. The military disaster bankrupted the Eastern Empire and the embarrassment indicated that Rome's power was deeply shaken.

Gaiseric promoted his Vandal chieftains by evicting Roman landowners, and replaced the Roman hierarchy, both political and economic, with a Vandal hierarchy. The old Roman social and political order died out, replaced by a Vandal government. To prevent rebellions Gaiseric destroyed city walls, and strengthened the Vandal army. As an Arian, Gaiseric persecuted Catholic and Donatist clergy, forcing many to flee, convert, or die. Gaiseric left a strong and united kingdom.

Galerius (c. 250–311)

Galerius became the archetypical example of the persecutor in later Christianity. Christian legend had Galerius' mother being a fervent pagan, insulted by a Christian, who then taught her children, especially Galerius, to hate Christians. Galerius was born in Dacia Ripensis, south of the Danube around 250 and rose through the military ranks to become Caesar or junior emperor in 293.

Galerius campaigned on the Danube River and in the East throughout his career. In 294, he arrived in Egypt where he put down a popular revolt. Galerius then returned to the Danube region and campaigned against the Sarmatians and Carpi. His greatest achievement occurred when the Persian king Narses attacked Armenia in 296, prompting Roman response. Galerius moved east from Antioch through the desert toward the Euphrates River. Narses attacked Galerius and, in a series of battles routed the junior emperor. Galerius returned to Antioch where Diocletian humiliated him by forcing him to walk for a mile beside him, while the senior emperor road in his cart and chastised him. Galerius collected a new army, mainly from the Danube region, and attacked Narses and the Persians in Armenia. Defeating Narses, Galerius even captured Narses' family. Galerius then proceeded to march down the Euphrates toward the Persian capital. Galerius wanted to move farther east in hopes of conquering the Persians, but Diocletian realized that an invasion of Persia would be disastrous, and prevented him. The peace treaty ceded small strategic regions that were geographically beneficial to Rome. This peace treaty remained until Julian's debacle.

According to Christians, Galerius now exerted undue influence over Diocletian. Galerius is portrayed as the instigator of Diocletian's persecutions, although the evidence is not conclusive or persuasive. When Diocletian retired in 305, Galerius became the most important member of the Second Tetrarchy, especially after his fellow senior partner, Constantius, died in 306. Galerius attempted to exert his influence in the West. His Caesar, Severus, however, was defeated and executed in Italy and Galerius then appointed Licinius. Galerius attempted to keep the Tetrarchic system from unraveling, but failed due to competition and personalities.

Galerius continued the persecutions until 311 when, suffering from a disease which he blamed on the Christian God, and realizing the persecutions had failed, he issued his Edict of Toleration. Galerius died shortly thereafter. Galerius' impact can be seen as the final gasp of official imperial paganism. Galerius' image had been denigrated the most by Christians. Because of this it is hard to present a well-balanced portrait. Like the other Tetrarchs, Galerius was an excellent soldier and general.

Gallienus (218–268)

Publius Licinius Egnatius Gallienus ruled as emperor from 253 to 268 when the Roman Empire nearly disintegrated. After the senate confirmed his father Valerian as emperor, Valerian raised his son to the rank of emperor and gave him command of the West while he moved to the East. Gallienus campaigned on the Rhine from 254 to 256, undertaking military reforms, the most important of which was the creation of a mobile cavalry army. When the Balkans had been overrun in 257 and his father defeated and captured by the Persians in 260, Gallienus was faced with the near dismemberment of the empire. In Gaul, the revolt of Postumus led to the Gallic Empire from 261 to 274; while in the East Odaenath, nominally an ally of Gallienus, now controlled the East from Palmyra; and in Egypt, a series of native rebellions deprived Italy of crucial grain supplies creating unrest. Economically, the silver coinage went from 15 percent to less than 2 percent. In 267, the Goths attacked again and Gallienus set out to deal with them. News arrived of a rebellion in Italy and upon returning he was assassinated by his generals, including Claudius II, the next emperor.

Gallus (325–354)

Flavius Claudius Constantius Gallus, son of Julius Constantius and elder brother of Julian, was born in 325. He and his brother escaped the massacre after Constantine's death and were imprisoned for six years with Julian in Cappadacia. Married to the emperor's sister, his cousin Constantia, Gallus was made Caesar in 351 by the emperor Constantius. Gallus moved to the East to Antioch to watch the Persians. His rule here was divisive when he attacked a Jewish uprising and conspiracies with severity. He moved to the West and attacked the usurper Magnentius. His rule was marked by brutality and paranoia, an outcome of his youth. Wrongly accused of treason, Gallus was executed by Constantius in 354.

Gratian (359–383)

Gratian (Flavius Gratianus), Valentinian's eldest son, was born in Sirmium in 359, and was designated by his father as heir in 367, something unusual due to his age. This was probably done to prevent infighting between the army and bureaucracy. Gratian was instructed by Ausonius, the Gallic rhetorician, and proclaimed emperor after his father's death in 375. Gratian, at age sixteen, had little experience as a warrior, and when his younger half-brother Valentinian II, aged four, was put forward as emperor by rival bureaucrats, Gratian accepted it. Grat-

ian controlled Gaul, Britain, and Spain, while the generals and bureaucrats in young Valentinian's name controlled Illyria, Africa, and Italy.
Gratian had to continually deal with the Alamanni and uncooperative
generals and bureaucrats. In February 378, Gratian defeated the Alamanni, and set out to help his uncle, Valens, in the East. He arrived too
late to prevent the disaster at Adrianople, but did recall Theodosius to
command the East. Educated by the poet Ausonius, he later fell under
the domination of Ambrose who badgered him to remove the Altar of
Victory from the Senate House. In 383, Magnus Maximus rebelled in
Britain and when Gratian arrived in Gaul, his army defected and he was
killed. His half-brother Valentinian II then ruled in name only until his
death in 392.

Honoria (417–?)

Honoria, sister of the emperor Valentinian III and daughter of Constantius III and Galla Placidia, was born in 417 and received the title of
Augusta in 425, after her brother's elevation. Honoria and her lover, her
steward Eugenius, were discovered and Eugenius executed. Valentinian
then betrothed Honoria to Flavius Herculanus against her will, prompting her to contact Attila the Hun for help by sending her ring. Attila
announced his acceptance of the marriage proposal, not what Honoria
had in mind, and attacked the West demanding Honoria and half the
empire as a dowry. Valentinian refused and the Huns retreated from Italy.
Her fate after this episode is unknown.

Hypatia (370–415)

Hypatia, daughter of the Alexandrian geometer and philosopher
Theon, became a famous mathematician and philosopher. Married to the
philosopher Isidorus, she taught Neo-Platonism while living in Alexandria during the reigns of Arcadius and Theodosius II. Her writings have
perished, but several ancient authors attest to her intellect and prominence.

Around 400, Hypatia became the head of the Platonist school in
Alexandria, lecturing on mathematics and philosophy. She followed the
teachings of Plotinus, the founder of Neo-Platonism (c. 280) and his follower Iambilichus (c. 300). The Neo-Platonists taught that the highest

level of intellect was beyond human thought or language, but by aiming at understanding and obtaining this goal and reaching different levels, one could find fulfillment. Hypatia, a charismatic teacher, because of her background in mathematics, placed more emphasis on a scientific method.

Due to her position as the leading pagan intellect, she became involved in a struggle between paganism and Christianity, as well as a political struggle between Orestes, the Roman prefect of Alexandria and Cyril, the bishop. Hypatia was a friend of Orestes and it appears that Cyril used her paganism as a tool against Orestes with the Alexandrian mob. The city traditionally had a habit of violence over philosophical schools and religion, and in the early fifth century violent riots erupted between pagans and Christians. According to one story, Hypatia was murdered by a fanatical sect of Christian monks loyal to Cyril, while another has her being murdered by a Christian mob. It is clear that her murder, dismemberment, and cremation occurred at the hands of Christians. Shortly after her murder many of the leading philosophers left Alexandria, contributing to its intellectual decline.

Her students included both pagans and Christians, such as Synesius, later bishop of Cyrene (Africa). Several of his letters to Hypatia survive, asking for advice and help in constructing an astrolabe and hydroscope, two ancient scientific instruments. She appears to have been well known throughout the Eastern Empire, for after her murder Emperor Theodosius even planned to punish the city, but was persuaded not to by an official who supposedly had been bribed.

Jerome (345–420)

Jerome, one of the four fathers of the Western Church, wrote extensively on biblical and historical scholarship. Born at Stridon near Aquileia in northern Italy and a student of Latin literature and rhetoric education in Rome, Jerome lived in a monastic community and then traveled to Gaul and back to Aquileia before going to Antioch in 374. Here Jerome reported that Christ condemned him, saying, "you are a Ciceronian, not a Christian," in reference to his love of Latin literature. For the next three years Jerome lived in the deserts of Syria.

Jerome traveled to Constantinople in 379 where he translated into Latin Eusebius' *World Chronicle* extending it to the year 378. In 383,

Jerome then traveled to Rome, where he became the secretary to Pope Damasus, who urged him to translate the Hebrew Old Testament and Greek New Testament into Latin. He now began this great task, which he completed in the East from 390 to 405. This work, his most famous, became known as the *Vulgate*, and became the Bible used in the West during the Medieval Age.

While at Rome Jerome became the spiritual advisor to Paula and her daughter Eustochium, supposedly a descendent of Rome's founder, the Trojan War hero Aeneas and the great Republican family, the Scipios. They became Jerome's patronesses, traveling with him to the Holy Land in 385 where they settled in Bethlehem, establishing monasteries. Jerome continued his work on the Bible, wrote commentaries on the books of the Bible, and engaged in theological discussions. In his works he praised Origen, although later condemned him, attacked Ambrose, and fought with his oldest friend Rufinus. In addition to the commentaries, Jerome wrote a work on illustrious men.

Working on the book of Ezekiel in 410, Jerome lamented the Fall of Rome. After this disaster many refugees fled to the East. One such refugee was Pelagius, a British-born monk, who argued that man was committed to sin, responsible for his actions, and reduced the need of divine grace. Jerome's opposition forced Pelagius to move to North Africa where he was condemned. On September 30, 420, Jerome died in Bethlehem.

Julian (331–363)

Julian, emperor from 355 to 363, was the last member of the house of Constantine, and Rome's final pagan emperor. The nephew of Constantine, born in 331 at Constantinople, his father Julius Constantius and other relatives were murdered when Constantine died in 337. Julian and his older half-brother Gallus were raised in Cappadocia, away from Constantinople. Although professing Christianity, Julian continued to study the ancient classics, especially Greek philosophy. He studied Neo-Platonism under Maximus of Ephesus and made a full conversion, albeit secretly, to paganism. Gallus became Constantius' Caesar and was later executed in 355, whereupon Julian, who had married Helena, Constantius' sister, became Caesar.

Constantius sent Julian to Gaul to deal with the Franks and Alamanni after their invasion into Gaul. He achieved success on the Rhine in 357. In 360, Constantius ordered the best troops from Gaul to be sent to the East to fight Persia. These troops mutinied and proclaimed Julian Augustus. Julian may have feared that like Gallus, this was a move to remove and execute him. While Julian marched east, Constantius, moving west, died of a fever in Asia Minor. Julian now became emperor.

Julian entered Constantinople and enacted a series of reforms: purged the palace staff, decreased taxes, reformed the finances, recalled exiled clergy, and preached religious toleration for both pagan and Christian. His reforms seemed to be aimed at rebuilding the cities hard hit by economic problems during the last generation.

Julian now embarked on a program to revive paganism. He ordered the pagan temples to be rebuilt. He reorganized the pagan priesthood with the emperor as its chief priest, and he attempted to unify all of paganism into a Neo-Platonist theology. Julian excluded Christians from teaching this new religion, now bitterly resented by Christians. Although said to be a persecutor, Julian merely sought to keep Christians from corrupting his new religion.

Julian made Antioch his camp to attack Persia in 363. A series of natural disasters and foolish policies by both Julian and the Christian town council led to strained relations. These problems can be seen in the works of Julian and Libanius, a local orator.

In 363, Julian launched the Persian expedition, which went well at first. The army drove deep into Persia but failed to take Ctesiphon, a key city and supply depot. Unable to maintain his supply line, Julian withdrew. As the army retreated Julian was killed in a skirmish. The army chose the Christian Jovian as emperor, who was now forced to make a humiliating peace treaty to save the army.

Julian was an accomplished writer and philosopher who may have, if he lived and had not undertaken the Persian war, revitalized the empire. His death ended the house of Constantine.

Maxentius (279–312)

Marcus Aurelius Valerius Maxentius ruled Italy and Africa from 306 to 312. The son of the emperor Maximian and Eutropia, Maxentius was married to Valeria Maximilla, the daughter of Galerius, but like Constantine was passed over in Diocletian's succession plans. Constantine, after the death of Constantius Chlorus, his father, became emperor prompting Maxentius on October 28, 306, to rebel in Rome, aided by the Praetorian Guard. The senior emperor Galerius opposed this move and sent the junior emperor Severus to crush the rebellion. Maxentius, aided by his father and troops loyal to his father, defeated and captured Severus, later killing him, and then defeated Galerius. Maxentius and Constantine allied themselves through a marriage with Fausta, Maxentius' sister. Maximian attempted to replace his son as emperor only to fail and flee to Constantine. Africa in 308 rebelled against Maxentius, cutting off the grain supply to Rome and forcing an expedition in 311 to recapture the province. In this expedition Carthage was devastated as punishment. Constantine now decided to move against Maxentius, invading Italy in 312 and winning battles at Segusis and Augusta Taurinorum. Maxentius made one more attempt to defeat Constantine outside Rome at the Milvian Bridge but was defeated and in his retreat, fell into the Tiber River and drowned. Although contemporary Christians condemned his rule as a tyranny, the evidence indicates that he tolerated Christians.

Maximian (c. 240–310)

Marcus Aurelius Valerius Maximianus was born to a poor family about 240 in Sirmium. He entered the army and rose through the ranks and in 286 Diocletian made him co-Augusti. Given the task of controlling and winning back the West, Maximian staunchly supported Diocletian's policy. He campaigned against the Germans and Franks and at first recovered northern Gaul from Carausius. After failing to recover Britain, Diocletian appointed Constantius Chlorus as Maximian's junior emperor and gave him the task of recovering Britain while Maximian campaigned in North Africa. When Diocletian retired in 305, Maximian was likewise forced to retire. He promoted his son Maxentius as emperor in 307, making an alliance with Constantine through marriage with his daughter Fausta. But when father and son quarreled, Maximian fled to his son-in-law Constantine in 308. Maximian attempted a coup against Constantine in 310 but was betrayed by his daughter Fausta. Constantine then probably executed him.

Placidia (388–450)

Daughter of Galla and Theodosius the Great, Galla Placidia was born about 388 in the East. After the death of her mother, Placidia was raised by Serena, cousin of Theodosius, and her husband Stilicho, the great general. In 394 she arrived in Milan where her father was staying and witnessed his death in 395. She was in Rome when Alaric attacked in 408 and seems to have sanctioned the execution of Serena. Staying there when Alaric attacked again in 410, she was captured by the Visigoths. In 414, Placidia married Alaric's brother-in-law Ataulf in Narbonne, Gaul. This wedding may have been an attempt to create a union between the Visigoths and Romans, in much the same way as Stilicho (Vandals) and Serena's. Placidia bore a son, Theodosius, but he soon died, ending any hope of a political union. In 416, Athaulf was murdered and Placidia, after enduring several months in a degraded fashion by the new Visigoth king Singeric, was ultimately sold back to the Romans by Wallia who had murdered Singeric.

Placidia returned to her half-brother Honorius who forced her to marry his general, Constantius III. Although she married him reluctantly, they had two children, a daughter and a son, the future Emperor Valentinian III. In 421, Constantius became co-emperor and Placidia Augusta. When Constantius died later in the year, she quarreled with her brother Honorius and fled with her children to the East to her nephew, Emperor Theodosius II. With the death of Honorius and the defeat of the usurper Johannes, the Eastern Empire recognized the claim of Placidia's son Valentinian, who was now installed by the Eastern army.

Placidia now became regent to her son, ruling the empire for the first twelve years. An early struggle arose between Boniface in Africa, whom Placidia supported, and Aetius. After the death of Boniface, Placidia reluctantly supported Aetius and his command. Aetius would ultimately supplant Placidia, who now retired. Placidia was a patron to the church, constructing and repairing churches in Rome and Ravenna. One structure, the mausoleum of Galla Placidia in Ravenna, may have originally been a church. She died on November 27, 450.

Pulcheria (399–453)

Daughter of the Eastern emperor Arcadius and Eudoxia, Aelia Pulcheria and her three siblings were left orphaned with their father's death in 408. Being the eldest, she took over the training of her brother, the new emperor, Theodosius II. In 412, at the age of fifteen, she convinced the emperor to dismiss Antiochus, the powerful chamberlain. The following year Pulcheria formally announced her vow of celibacy, encouraging her two sisters to follow suit to avoid potential threats to Theodosius and her own rule. This vow gave her prestige as a pious woman whose only interests lay in the church and state. She continued this vow even when 37 years later she married the emperor Marcian. In July of 414 she had Theodosius declare her Augusta, giving her virtual equality with the emperor.

Her power soon rested with the religious authorities. Being pro-Orthodox, she championed the ideas of the Nicaean Creed and instituted laws against pagans, Jews, and heretics. Pagans were banned from serving in the military and holding public office, which removed potentially powerful rivals. Her actions against the Jews were severe: she forbade the building of new synagogues, and even approved the destruction of some older ones. Pulcheria organized the Council of Ephesus in 431 which condemned Nestorianism (the belief that there were two separate persons in Jesus, a divine and a human), leading to the banishment of her rival Nestorius, the patriarch of Constantinople. She likewise organized the Council of Chalcedon in 451 which reaffirmed the Orthodox cause.

Pulcheria continually exerted control over Theodosius throughout his rule. In 421 she chose Eudocia as his wife. A recent convert, Eudocia bore Theodosius three children, but only their daughter Licinia survived to maturity. Pulcheria and Eudocia struggled for control over Theodosius, with Pulcheria winning when Eudocia was accused of and condemned for adultery. Eudocia was exiled to Jerusalem. After this time Theodosius began to exert more control over his destiny.

Pulcheria did not interfere in the military and administrative life of the empire; she relied on competent officials to handle these affairs. When Theodosius died in 450, Pulcheria married Marcian, an able and powerful senator who became emperor. This marriage was more for an ease of transition of power than love. Pulcheria died in 453, willing all of her possessions to the poor.

Ricimer (?–472)

Ricimer was born to a Suevian woman and a Gothic king, as magister militum (master of the soldiers). Flavius Ricimer ruled the West through puppet emperors, notably Libius Severus and Anthemius, since he was not able to actually assume the emperorship because of his German origins. In 456 he defeated a Vandal fleet; with this victory he was promoted to magister militum, overthrew the emperor Avitus, and placed Majorian on the throne.

Ricimer in 461 removed Majorian and replaced him with Libius Severus even though the emperor in Constantinople objected. This independence by Ricimer allowed Severus to remain emperor. Ricimer defended Italy against Gaiseric, king of the Vandals. In 465 he removed Severus and ruled the empire himself till 467 when Anthemius was appointed. To ensure his continual position and control he married Anthemius' daughter Alypia.

He distrusted the Eastern emperor and refused to take part in the invasion of Vandal Africa in 467. Anthemius attempted to increase his own independence, which led to a temporary break in 470. Reconciled in 472, Ricimer then executed Anthemius and put a new candidate on the throne. However, Ricimer died shortly thereafter.

Ricimer perhaps more than any other individual destroyed the West by his continual placing and removing of emperors who were ineffective and weak. He forced emperors to give up large tracts of land to his followers and allies. He ruled through them, weakening the empire.

Sidonius Apollinaris (432–480)

Sidonius Apollinaris was born in Lugdunum (Lyon) Gaul in 432 to a senatorial family and received a traditional Classical education. Although his family background was not spectacular, he married Papianilia, daughter of Avitus, a powerful official in Gaul. When Avitus became emperor in 456, Sidonius delivered a panegyric for him in Rome, and a golden statue of Sidonius was placed in the Forum of Trajan. With Avitus' fall, Sidonius left Rome and returned to Gaul. Sidonius became Count of Auvergne in 461, but resigned and went into retirement a year later.

Sidonius delivered a second panegyric to the new emperor Majorian in 458 at Ludgunum, and held some unknown office in Rome until 461 when he again returned to Gaul. He led a delegation to the new emperor and delivered in 468 yet a third panegyric to Anthemius, which led to Sidonius' becoming Prefecture of Rome. Sidonius returned to Auvergne in 469 and was elected Bishop of Clermont by popular acclamation. This act was not an uncommon practice, even though Sidonius did not have theological training. This nevertheless did not stop him from being involved in both ecclesiastical and civil affairs. As bishop, Sidonius attempted to protect the region from the Goths in 471–474. He came into conflict with the Gothic king Euric, and was exiled to Carcassonne in 474. Reconciled with the king, Sidonius returned 2 years later where he took over his See again, but his exile had weakened him and he died in 480.

Perhaps most importantly, Sidonius left behind a collection of letters. Unlike Symmachus, Sidonius' letters detailed a rich assortment of life in the fifth century. These letters provide a vivid account of the society, economy, and religion of fifth-century Gaul. They clearly show that the concept of Romanization or the ideals of Rome continued throughout the fifth century.

Sidonius' career provides an excellent example of the life of a Christian senator from Gaul. He included among his acquaintances emperors, kings, the poet Ausonius, and other important individuals, both Roman and German.

Stilicho (?–408)

Master of the Soldiers, Flavius Stilicho effectively ruled the West during the reign of Honorius, son of Theodosius the Great. The son of a Vandal soldier and Roman lady, Stilicho advanced through the military. In 383 he became ambassador to Persia. He served under Theodosius I successfully as Master of Households (*comes domesticorum*) where he amassed power and prestige from 385 to 392; then Master of the Troops in Thrace in 392, and general against Eugenius. In 394, Theodosius made him Master of the Soldiers in the West and guardian for Theodosius' younger son Honorius. His ties to Theodosius were made even closer with a marriage in 385 to Serena, Theodosius' niece.

Stilicho's power increased more after Theodosius' death in 395, when he declared himself guardian for both Honorius and his elder brother Arcadius. He centralized the Western bureaucracy under his control and nearly annihilated Alaric and the Visigoths. Arcadius declared him an enemy of the state in 397, prompting Gildo in Africa to rebel. After Gildo's defeat in 398, Stilicho increased his control in the West by holding the consulship in 405.

Successful on the battlefield, he defeated Alaric in 401 at Pollentia. In 406, using Alaric and the Visigoths as allies, he defeated the Burgundian Radagisus. He then elevated Alaric to Master of the Soldiers and planned to march east to take the Balkans away from Arcadius. A rebellion in Gaul, however, thwarted his plans, and with the rebellion Alaric demanded 4,000 pounds of gold from Rome which Stilicho forced the senate to pay. After Arcadius' death in 408 Stilicho desired to control Constantinople but was accused of wanting his own son to be put on the throne. Weakened by Alaric's double dealing, Stilicho was arrested and executed on August 22, 408. Both Stilicho and his wife Serena had remained unpopular at both Rome and Constantinople. Their daughters Maria and Thermantia were married to Honorius.

Stilicho's reputation was generally damaged by his dealings with Alaric. Alaric's siege and capture of Rome in 408 and 410 further blackened Stilicho since he had not only allowed the Visigoths to survive but had promoted Alaric. Stilicho nevertheless was a capable general who defeated the invading barbarians. As an avid Christian he further promoted Christianity at the expense of paganism.

Theodoric the Great (c. 454–526)

Theodoric the Great was an Ostrogoth who at the age of eight, became a Roman hostage in Constantinople and received a Classical education. At the age of eighteen he returned to the Ostrogoths where he became leader of part of the tribe. He was made consul and master of the soldiers by the emperor in 484. Theodoric then marched against Odoacer in Italy, forcing him to surrender in 493. Ruling Italy, Theodoric attempted to fuse the Ostrogoths and Romans with the help of ministers like Cassiodorus. He attempted to unite the regions of the West giving aid to the Franks against the Visigoths, and maintaining that the Roman Empire in the West still continued. To the Goths he ruled as king, while to the Romans he was a patrician. Being an Arian, he tried to help the Arians in the East, and he intervened in the election of the pope. His health declined after he realized he could not bring about reconciliation of the various religious problems. He died in August of 526.

Theodosius I (346–395)

Theodosius I was born in Cauca, Spain, about 346; Theodosius the Great, known as Flavius Theodosius, was the son of Count Theodosius, who had previously and successfully defeated usurpers in Africa. Theodosius the Great established the House of Theodosius, which ruled both the East and the West for over 50 years. He governed Moesia Prima or Superior in 373 or 374 where he defeated Rome's perennial problem, the Sarmatians, along the Danube. After his father, a successful general under Valentinian, was executed in 375, Theodosius retired to his family estates in Spain until 378. After the battle of Adrianople, Gratian recalled Theodosius, making him general and then emperor in the East after some initial successes against the Visigoths in January 379. Theodosius created a new prefecture, Illyricum, placing parts of the Balkans, notably Macedon and Moesia, in the hands of the East. This provided for numerous conflicts between East and West during the next few centuries.

Theodosius campaigned against the Visigoths for several years. After realizing that it was impossible to defeat the Visigoths, Theodosius decided to negotiate a treaty in 380, and celebrated a triumph at Constantinople. The treaty allowed the Visigoths to settle in the empire en masse and be under their own leaders. In the West, Magnus Maximus removed Gratian in Gaul and when Maximus invaded Italy in 382, Theodosius used barbarian units (probably Visigoths), headed west, and defeated him. Theodosius placed Valentinian II, Gratian's brother, under the control of the German Arbogast. Valentinian tried to exert more control and was found dead in 392. Arbogast promoted Eugenius as emperor until 394 when Theodosius defeated them, unifying the Roman world for the last time. This unity lasted only a few months, for in January 395 Theodosius died in Milan.

Theodosius expelled Arians from Constantinople and ordered their churches closed in the East. He likewise took actions against paganism, refusing to restore the Altar of Victory in the Roman senate, and he outlawed paganism in 392. During his reign Theodosius was known for his harshness. In 390 he massacred 7,000 citizens in Thessalonica for civil disorder. Later in 390, in visiting Italy, Ambrose ordered him to do penance under threat of excommunication. After this Ambrose exerted even more influence culminating in a decree in 391 outlawing paganism.

With Theodosius' death power passed to his sons Arcadius and Honorius. In the West, Arcadius was not able to stop the invasion and sack of Rome in 410. In the East, Honorius' son Theodosius II succeeded, ruling from 408 to 451.

Theodosius II (401–450)

Theodosius II, son of the Eastern emperor Arcadius and Aelia Eudoxia, was born in April 401, and crowned Augustus in January of 402. He received an excellent education centered on being a future ruler, and succeeded his father in 408. His elder sister Pulcheria instructed him in his moral education, on behaving as an emperor, and on being a Christian. Being so young when he took over, Theodosius' early reign was controlled by his generals, advisors, and his sister. In 409, after the Western general Stilicho was assassinated, relations between the West and East improved with Theodosius and his uncle Honorius, the Western emperor, holding the joint consulships. By 414 his sister Pulcheria had taken over the regency completely, even choosing Eudocia as his wife. These two women would continually fight for control of the emperor and the government. Although Pulcheria won the battle, having had Eudocia exiled for adultery, she lost the war when Theodosius became more independent in the 440s.

His foreign policy concerned Persia and the Huns; he even sent aid to the West to his uncle Honorius and cousin Valentinian III, and maintained Eastern influence in the Mediterranean. His military and diplomatic record was mixed; on the Eastern front he made a peace treaty with Persia in 422 which lasted nearly a century, but he failed to control the Goths and Huns in the West. The Huns successfully used the troubles Theodosius faced on both fronts (the Persians in the East and the Vandals in the West) to demand more money, which Theodosius refused, and which prompted war. After defeating a Roman army in 443, Attila and his Huns forced Theodosius to increase the annual tribute to 2,100 pounds of gold, with an immediate penalty of 6,000 pounds, and in 448 they raised it again. These exactions bankrupted the Eastern Empire.

Theodosius II opened a university in Constantinople and began the collection of laws from Constantine onward, culminating in the publication of the Theodosian Law Code in 438 (his greatest achievement), which became the basis for Justinian's reform in the East and the Visigothic Code in Spain in 507. On July 28, 450, Theodosius fell from his horse and died after naming the senator Marcian as his heir. Theodosius II ruled the longest of any Roman ruler, and with his death the House of Theodosius ended.

Valens (328–378)

Valens, like his brother Valentinian, grew up in southern Pannonia on the family estate, entering the army later in life, in the 360s. He was appointed co-emperor by his bother Valentinian I in March 364, with the task of strengthening the East. A year later, Valens had to contend with the usurper Procopius, a cousin of Julian, who seized Constantinople and capitalized on the Constantinian by name minting coins and demanding the loyalty of troops nearby. Valens had difficulty in maintaining control over his own troops' loyalty, but finally in the spring of 366 he defeated and executed Procopius. This rebellion's memory left Valens distrustful and shaken during the remainder of his reign.

Valens then began a campaign against the Visigoths who had supported Procopius. Pushing them across the Danube, Valens constructed forts along the Danube and finally made peace with the Visigoths. Unfortunately, one of the terms resulted in a loss of manpower for the Roman army. This hasty treaty was partly a result of new Persian problems in Armenia. Valens' army successfully defeated the Persians and a truce in 371 enhanced Rome's position in the East.

The peace with the Visigoths was damaged when corrupt officials refused to make good on promises of providing food for starving tribesmen. The Visigoths began to raid Roman territory and in 378, Valens marched against them near Adrianople. Distrusting intelligence and not waiting for support, Valens initiated battle. There, his infantry pushed the Visigothic infantry off the battle, but in their haste to attack the enemy's wagons the legions were caught off guard by the Visigothic cavalry and were shattered. Over two-thirds of the army, including Valens, was killed.

Valentinian I (321–375)

Valentinian I was recalled from retirement when the returning army from Julian's expedition promoted Jovian as emperor. After Jovian's death the army chose Valentinian as emperor in February 364. Born in 321 at Cibalis (modern Vinkovici) in southern Pannonia, Flavius Valentinianus (Valentinian) was the son of Gratianus the elder, who had been a famous general under Constantine. Valentinian traveled with his father to Africa, where he received a good education. He had risen through the ranks under Constantius II before being forced into retirement in Egypt by Julian in 362 for his Christianity. A month after being made emperor he elevated his brother Valens as emperor in the East while he retained the West. Valentinian and Valens traveled west, where they separated, with Valentinian moving into Gaul to fight the Alamanni. Valentinian did not move east to help his brother against the usurper Procopius; rather, he decided to make the West supreme. During his reign he fought the Alamanni on the Rhine and greatly strengthened the fortifications in the West. He fought across the Rhine into Germany proper and across the English Channel in 367 against the Picts and Saxons in Britain. Valentinian's generalship and command ability added vigor to the empire, extending Roman control for another 50 years. Valentinian in 369 began the construction of new defensive works and the rebuilding and strengthening of older fortresses on both sides of the Rhine. Valentinian had to deal with several revolts, most notably that of Macrinus (whom he never defeated), and Firmus in Africa put down by his general Theodosius, father of the future emperor Theodosius the Great. Valentinian continued to strengthen the army at the expense of other elements of society, but ensured Rome's survival. He did not become involved in the religious strife of the empire, but remained neutral. His death from a stroke in 375 (while berating a delegation of Alamanni) created a void from which the empire never recovered. His supervision of his cruel and corrupt officials was lax and his inability to control corruption continued to sap the empire.

The Valentinian household successfully reformed the empire but could not hold in check the Goths and other tribes being pushed to the west by the Huns. Their greatest achievements lay in reforming the economy and strengthening the defenses in the west.

Valentinian III (419–455)

Valentinian III, Western emperor from 425 to 455, was the last significant emperor in the West. The son of Constantius and Galla Placidia became emperor at the age of six when his uncle, the emperor Honorius died. Valentinian's cousin, the Eastern emperor Theodosius II, installed him at Rome. Theodosius undoubtedly planned to control him.

During the first 8 years his mother, Galla Placidia, controlled him. Aetius then supplanted her and became Valentinian's advisor. Throughout his reign Valentinian struggled to assert his position within the imperial household without much success. He had lost Africa to the Vandals in 442, and in 449 his sister Honoria invited Attila into the empire to help her against a planned marriage. Honoria had recently caused an imperial scandal by having relations with her steward Eugenius, who was executed when it was discovered. After the debacle with Attila she vanished from history.

During these intrigues Valentinian never ruled; rather, the palace bureaucrats and Aetius vied for power. With Aetius' failure to completely stop Attila, the palace bureaucrats convinced Valentinian to do away with the great general. Valentinian accused him of treason and on September 21, 454, stabbed Aetius himself. On March 16, 455, two of Aetius' bodyguards assassinated Valentinian on the Field of Mars, in revenge.

With the death of Valentinian the houses of Valentinian I and Theodosius I came to an end in the West. Although he never really ruled, and he lost great parts of the empire, the end of Valentinian created a distinct end of the continuity that had existed for nearly 80 years.

Valerian (?–260)

Publius Licinius Valerianus (Valerian) ruled as emperor from 253 to 260 with his son Gallienus. He rose through the ranks in the Roman government, possibly earning a consulship under Severus Alexander and helped in the rule under Decius. He commanded the legions along the Rhine in 253 and marched against Aemilian, whose troops rebelled and joined Valerian. Early in his reign Valerian persecuted the Christians. With the invasion of the Goths in the Balkans, Valerian marched east to meet them, and during the march he received news that Shapur I of Persia had attacked Armenia and Syria. Valerian moved against Shapur but his legions were weakened with disease and were defeated by the Persians. Valerian was captured, killed, and his body displayed in a Persian temple.

Zenobia (?–after 272)

Zenobia was the wife of Odaenath of Palmyra and queen; and after his murder, perhaps by Zenobia, she ruled Palmyra from 266 to 272 in the name of her son Vaballath. In 270, Zenobia, after the death of Claudius II Gothicus, invaded Syria, Asia Minor, and Egypt. Aurelian moved against her in 271 defeating the Palmyrene army at Antioch. After an initial peace, Zenobia rebelled again and Aurelian defeated her in 272, forcing her to march in Aurelian's triumph in Rome. Aurelian allowed her to live in Tibur and Rome, provided for by the state.

PRIMARY DOCUMENTS ILLUSTRATING LATE ROME

DOCUMENT 1
Biography

*These excerpts provide portraits of individuals: public and private fig-
ures. The first concerns the emperor Diocletian, the second Sabina, wife
of fifth-century poet and government official Ausonius, and the third
Ricimer, a fifth-century German general.*

*The first excerpt is from Eutropius, who wrote an abridgement of
Roman history for the emperor Valens. The selection presents the history
of the rule of the emperor Diocletian, providing not only important historical information, but also an idea of the era's literary style. Eutropius
served in the Eastern bureaucracy under Constantius II, Julian, and
Valens, and dedicated his work to Valens in gratitude for being promoted
to Secretary of State for General Petitions in the East, one of the most
important jobs in the imperial bureaucracy. He accompanied the emperor
in his campaigns along the Danube in 367–369. Eutropius later became
proconsul of Asia, and under Theodosius, prefect of Illyricum. In 387 he
was elected the Eastern consul, a great achievement for someone probably not born of the senatorial rank. The selection relates the career of Diocletian and the Tetrarchs, and is direct about their habits and mores.
Although Eutropius is critical of violence and bloodshed, he omits the persecutions. This extract is one of the few literary sources for the emperor
Diocletian and is generally a favorable portrait of him.*

*The second excerpt is from Ausonius' Parantalia, a collection of thirty
poems, mainly elegiacs, commemorating deceased relatives. This particu-*

lar poem is about Attusia Lucana Sabina, his wife, who had died young (at the age of twenty-eight), some 36 years before he wrote the poem.

The last selection concerns the German general Ricimer, who dominated the period after Valentinian III, making emperors at will. The selection refers to Avitus, father-in-law to Sidonius Apollinaris, who was on good relations with the Visigoth king Theodoric and had helped bring the Visigoths into the alliance with Aetius, against the Huns. When news of the death of the emperor Petronius (shortly after Valentinian's death arrived), Avitus was at the Visigoth court where they urged him to accept the crown. Avitus attempted to repel Gaiseric by sending Ricimer to Sicily where the German general successfully repelled an attack and won a naval victory; but Avitus' position in Rome worsened with a grain shortage, caused by Gaiseric, and the people hailed Ricimer on his return as the Deliverer of Italy. The following excerpt shows this struggle and how Ricimer worked behind the scene. For the next 16 years this German general would be the real power behind the throne.

1.A. Eutropius' Life of Diocletian

XIX. The victorious army, on returning from Persia, as they had lost their emperor Carus by lightning, and the Caesar Numerianus by a plot, conferred the imperial dignity on Diocletian, a native of Dalmatia, of such extremely obscure birth, that he is said by most writers to have been the son of a clerk, but by some to have been a freed man of a senator named Anulinus.

XX. Diocletian, in the first assembly of the army that was held, took an oath that Numerian was not killed by any treachery on his part; and while Aper, who had laid the plot for Numerian's life, was standing by, he was killed, in the sight of the army, with a sword by the hand of Diocletian. He soon after overthrew Carinus, who was living under the utmost hatred and detestation, in a great battle at Margum, Carinus being betrayed by his own troops, for though he had a greater number of men than the enemy, he was altogether abandoned by them between Viminacium and Mount Aureus. He thus became master of the Roman Empire; and when the peasants of Gaul made an insurrection, giving their faction the name Bagaudae, and having for leaders Amandus and Aelianus, he dispatched Maximian Herculius, with the authority of Caesar, to suppress them. Maximian, in a few battles of little importance, subdued the rustic multitude, and restored peace to Gaul.

XXI. During this period, Carausius, who, though of very mean birth, had gained extraordinary reputation by a course of active service in war, having received a commission in his post at Bononia, to clear the sea, which the Franks and Saxons infested, along the coast of Belgica and Armorica, and having captured numbers of the barbarians on several occasions, but having never given back the entire booty to the people of the province or sent it to the emperors, and there being a suspicion, in consequence, that the barbarians were intentionally allowed by him to congregate there, that he might seize them and their booty as they passed, and by that means enrich himself, assumed, on being sentenced by Maximian to be put to death, the imperial purple, and took on him the government of Britain.

XXII. While disorder thus prevailed throughout the world, while Carausius was taking arms in Britain and Achilleus in Egypt, while the Quinquegentiani were harassing Africa, and Narseus was making war upon the east, Diocletian promoted Maximian Herculius from the dignity of Caesar to that of emperor, and created Constantius and Maximian Galerius Caesars, of whom Constantius is said to have been the grandnephew of Claudius by a daughter, and Maximian Galerius to have been born in Dacia not far from Sardica. That he might also unite them by affinity, Constantius married Theodora the step-daughter of Herculius, by whom he had afterwards six children, brothers to Constantine; while Galerius married Valeria, the daughter of Diocletian; both being obliged to divorce the wives that they had before. With Carausius, however, as hostilities were found vain against a man eminently skilled in war, a peace was at last arranged. At the end of seven years, Allectus, one of his supporters, put him to death, and held Britain himself for three years subsequently, but was cut off by the efforts of Asclepiodotus, prefect of the Praetorian Guard.

XXIII. At the same period a battle was fought by Constantius Caesar in Gaul, at Lingonae, where he experienced both good and bad fortune in one day; for though he was driven into the city by a sudden onset of the barbarians, with such haste and precipitation that after the gates were shut he was drawn up the wall by ropes, yet, when his army came up, after the lapse of scarcely six hours, he cut to pieces about sixty thousand of the Alamanni. Maximian the emperor, too, brought the war to an end in Africa, by subduing the Quinquegentiani, and compelling them to make peace. Diocletian, meanwhile, besieging Achilleus in Alexandria, obliged him to surrender about eight months after, and put him to death. He used his victory, indeed, cruelly, and distressed all Egypt with severe proscriptions and massacres. Yet at the same time he made many judicious arrangements and regulations, which continue to our own days.

XXIV. Galerius Maximian, in acting against Narseus, fought, on the first occasion, a battle far from successful, meeting him between Callinicus and Carrae, and engaging in the combat rather with rashness than want of courage; for he contended with a small army against a very numerous enemy. Being in consequence defeated, and going to join Diocletian, he was received by him, when he met him on the road, with such extreme haughtiness, that he is said to have run by his chariot for several miles in his scarlet robes.

XXV. But having soon after collected forces in Illyricum and Moesia, he fought a second time with Narseus (the grand-father of Hormisdas and Sapor), in Greater Armenia, with extraordinary success, and with no less caution and spirit, for he undertook, with one or two of the cavalry, the office of a *speculator*. After putting Narseus to flight, he captured his wives, sisters, and children, with a vast number of the Persian nobility besides, and a great quantity of treasure; the king himself he forced to take refuge in the remotest deserts in his dominions. Returning therefore in triumph to Diocletian, who was then encamped with some troops in Mesopotamia, he was welcomed by him with great honor. Subsequently, they conducted several wars both in conjunction and separately, subduing the Carpi and Bastarnae, and defeating the Sarmatians, from which nations he settled a great number of captives in the Roman territories.

XXVI. Diocletian was of a crafty disposition, with much sagacity, and keen penetration. He was willing to gratify his own disposition to cruelty in such a way as to throw the odium upon others; he was however a very active and able prince. He was the first that introduced into the Roman Empire a ceremony suited rather to royal usages than to Roman liberty, giving orders that he should be adored, whereas all emperors before him were only saluted. He put ornaments of precious stones on his dress and shoes, when the imperial distinction had previously been only in the purple robe, the rest of the habit being the same as that of other men.

XXVII. But Herculius was undisguisedly cruel, and of a violent temper, and showed his severity of disposition in the sternness of his looks. Gratifying his own inclination, he joined with Diocletian in even the most cruel of his proceedings. But when Diocletian, as age bore heavily upon him, felt himself unable to sustain the government of the empire, he suggested to Herculius that they should both retire into private life, and commit the duty of upholding the state to more vigorous and youthful hands. With this suggestion his colleague reluctantly complied. Both of them, in the same day, exchanged the robe of empire for an ordinary dress, Diocletian at Nicomedia, Herculius at Milan, soon after a magnificent triumph which they celebrated at Rome over several nations, with a noble succession of pictures, and in which the wives, sisters, and children of Narseus were led before their chariots. The one then retired to Salonae, and the other into Lucania.

XXVIII. Diocletian lived to an old age in a private station, at a villa which is not far from Salonae, in honorable retirement, exercising extraordinary philosophy, inasmuch as he alone of all men, since the foundation of the Roman Empire, voluntarily returned from so high a dignity to the condition of private life, and to an equality with the other citizens. That happened to him, therefore, which had happened to no one since men were created, that, though he died in a private condition, he was enrolled among the gods.

Source: Eutropius, *Abridgment of Roman History*, from John Selby Watson, *Justin, Cornelius Nepos; and Eutropius*. London: George Bell and Sons, 1886, pp. 523–527.

1.B. Ausonius' Praise for His Wife Sabina

Thus far my dirge, fulfilling its sacred task, has sung in loving strains of those who, though dear, were mourned but in the course of nature. Now my grief and anguish and a wound that cannot bear a touch—the death of my wife snatched away untimely, must be told by me. High was her ancestry and noble in her birth from a line of senators, but yet Sabina was ennobled more by her good life. In youth I wept for you, robbed of my hopes in early years, and through these six and thirty years, unwedded, I have mourned, and mourn you still. Age has crept over me, but yet I cannot lull my pain; for ever it keeps raw and well-nigh new to me. Others receive of time a balm to soothe their grief: these wounds become but heavier with length of days. I tear my grey hairs mocked by my widowed life, and the more I live in loneliness, the more I live in heaviness. That my house is still and silent, and that my bed is cold, that I share not my ills with any, my good with any—these things feed my wound. I grieve if another has a worthy wife; and yet again I grieve if another has a bad: for pattern, you are ever present with me. However it be, you come to torture me: if one be bad, because you were like her. I mourn not for useless wealth or unsubstantial joys, but because in your youth you were torn from me, your youthful lord. Cheerful, modest, staid, famed for high birth as famed for beauty, you were the grief and glory of Ausonius your spouse. For before you could complete your eight and twentieth December, you deserted our two children, the pledges of our love. They by God's mercy, and as you ever prayed, flourish amid an abundance of such goods as you desired for them. And still I pray that they may prosper, and that at last my dust may bring the news to your ashes that they are living yet.

Source: Ausonius, *Parentalia*. Translated by Hugh G. Evelyn White. Cambridge, MA: Harvard University Press, 1919, pp. 71–72.

1.C. Avitus and Ricimer

When Avitus reigned at Rome there was famine in the city, and the people blaming Avitus compelled him to remove from the city of the Romans the allies from Gaul who had entered it along with him (that so there might be fewer mouths to feed). He also dismissed the Goths whom he had brought for the protection of Rome, having distributed among them money which he obtained by selling to merchants bronze stripped from public works, for there was no gold in the imperial treasury. This excited the Romans to revolt when they saw their city stripped of its adornments.

But Majorian and Ricimer, no longer held in fear of the Goths, openly rebelled, so that Avitus was constrained—terrified on the one hand by the prospect of internal troubles, on the other hand by the hostilities of the Vandals—to withdraw from Rome and set out for Gaul. But Majorian and Ricimer attacked him on the road and forced him to flee into a sanctuary, where he abdicated the throne and put off his imperial apparel. But Majorian's soldiers did not cease to blockade him, until he died of starvation, after a reign of eight months; others say that he was strangled.

Source: J. B. Bury, *A History of the Later Roman Empire*, vol. 1. London: Macmillian, 1889, p. 237.

DOCUMENT 2
The Circus

The following set of documents comes from the Roman Cassiodorus working in the Ostrogoths' Theodoric the Great (492–526) bureaucracy shortly after the collapse of Rome. In addition to showing that the institution of the Circus continued, the document shows a continual flourishing of Roman and Classical civilization past 476.

The first few letters (2.A–D) detail the ongoing problems of the unruly public in the Roman Circus, something attested in Byzantine sources for Constantinople. The Circus, with its large crowd, allowed public opinion to be voiced, often giving rise to potential violence. Theodoric attempted to prevent riots which had occurred in Constantinople.

The larger selection (2.E) is a letter describing the history and functions of the Circus. After giving rewards for Thomas the Charioteer, Theodoric relates the pleasures and problems associated with the games. This is one of the best descriptions of the games and its history (Figure 7). The third selection (2.F), an Egyptian papyrus, attests that gladiatorial games existed in the far reaches of the empire, and were probably common. The final selection (2.G), also an Egyptian papyrus, shows that victors in the games were entitled to certain benefits and privileges, namely, freedom from public duties. Athletic prowess and its ensuing economic gains are not recent phenomena.

2.A. Letter of King Theodoric to Albinus and Albienus, Viri Illustres and Patricians

Notwithstanding our greater cares for the Republic, we are willing to provide also for the amusement of our subjects. For it is the strongest possible proof of the age of the success of our labours that the multitude knows itself to be again at leisure.

The petition of the Green party in the circus informs us that they are oppressed, and that the factions of the circus are fatal to public tranquility. We therefore order you to assume the patronage of the Green party, which our father of glorious memory paid for. So let the spectators be assembled, and let them choose between Helladius and Theodorus which is fittest to be Pantomimist of the Greens, whose salary we will pay.

Source: Thomas Hodgkin, *The Letters of Cassiodorus*. London: Henry Frowde, 1886, pp. 155–156, Letter 20.

2.B. Letter of King Theodoric to Speciosus

If we are moderating under our laws the character of foreign nations, if the Roman law is supreme over all that is in alliance with Italy, how much more doth it become the Senate of the seat of civilization itself to have a surpassing reverence for law, that by the example of their moderation the beauty of their dignities may shine forth more eminently. For where shall we look for moderation, if violence stains Patricians? The Green party complain that they have been truculently assaulted by the Patrician Theodoric and the "Illustris and Consul Importunus," and that one life has been lost in the fray. We wish the matter to be at once brought before the Illustres Coelianus and Agapitus and examined into by them.

As to their counter-complaints of rudeness against the mob, you must distinguish between deliberate insolence and the license of the theatre. Who expects seriousness of character at the spectacles? It is not exactly a congregation of Catos that comes together at the circus. The place excuses some excesses. And besides, it is the beaten party which vents its rage in insulting cries. Do not let the Patricians complain of clamor that is really the result of a victory for their own side, which they greatly desired.

Source: Thomas Hodgkin, *The Letters of Cassiodorus*. London: Henry Frowde, 1886, pp. 159–160, Letter 27.

2.C. Letter of King Theodoric to the Roman People

The Circus, in which the King spends so much money, is meant to be for public delight, not for stirring up wrath. Instead of uttering howls and insults like other nations [the populace of Byzantium?], whom they have despised for doing so, let them tune their voices, so that their applause shall sound like the notes of some vast organ, and even the brute creation delight to hear it.

"Anyone uttering outrageous reproaches against any Senator will be dealt with by the Praefectus Urbis."

Source: Thomas Hodgkin, *The Letters of Cassiodorus*. London: Henry Frowde, 1886, pp. 161–162, Letter 31.

2.D. Letter of King Theodoric to Agapitus, Vir Illustris, Praefectus Urbis

The ruler of the city ought to keep the peace, and justify my choice of him. Your highest praise is a quiet people.

We have issued our "oracles" to the "amplissimus ordo" (i.e., the Senate) and to the people, that the custom of insulting persons in the Circus is to be put under some restraint; on the other hand, any Senator who shall be provoked to kill a free-born person shall pay a fine. The games alone meant to make people happy, not to stir them up to deadly rage. Helladius is to come forth into the midst and afford the people pleasure [as a pantomimist], and he is to receive his monthly allowance (menstruum) with the other actors of the Green Faction. His partisans are to be allowed to sit where they please.

Source: Thomas Hodgkin, *The Letters of Cassiodorus*. London: Henry Frowde, 1886, p. 162, Letter 32.

2.E. Letter of King Theodoric to Faustus, Praetorian Prefect

Constancy in actors is not a very common virtue, therefore with all the more pleasure do we record the faithful allegiance of Thomas the Charioteer, who came long ago from the East hither, and who, having become champion charioteer, has chosen to attach himself to "the seat of our Empire"; and we therefore decide that he shall be rewarded by a monthly allowance. He embraced what was then the losing side in the chariot races and carried it to victory—victory which he won so often that envious rivals declared that he conquered by means of witchcraft.

The sight of a chariot-race drives out morality and invites the most trifling contentions; it is the emptier of honorable conduct, the ever-flowing spring of squabbles: a thing which Antiquity commenced as a matter of religion, but which a quarrelsome posterity has turned into a sport.

For Aenomaus is said first to have exhibited this sport at Elis, a city of Asia, and afterwards Romulus, at the time of the rape of the Sabines, displayed it in rural fashion to Italy, no buildings for the purpose being yet founded. Long after, Augustus, the lord of the world, raising his works to the same high level as his power, built a fabric marvelous even to Romans, which stretched far into the Vallis Murcia. This immense mass, firmly girt round with hills, enclosed a space which was fitted to be the theatre of great events.

Twelve Ostia [gates] at the entrance represent the twelve signs of the Zodiac. These are suddenly and equally opened by ropes let down by the Hermulae [little pilasters]. The four colors worn by the four parties of charioteers denote the seasons: green for verdant spring, blue for cloudy winter, red for flaming summer, white for frosty autumn. Thus, throughout the spectacle we see a determination to represent the works of Nature. The Biga [two-horse chariot] is made in imitation of the moon, the Quadriga [four-horse chariot] of the sun. The circus horses, by means of which the servants of the Circus announce the heats that are to be run, imitate the herald-swiftness of the morning star. Thus it came to pass that while they deemed they were worshipping the stars, they profaned their religion by parodying it in their games.

A white line is drawn not far from the ostia to each Podium [balcony], that the contest may begin when the quadrigae pass it, lest they should interrupt the view of the spectators by their attempts to get each before the other. There are always seven circuits round the goals [Metae] to one heat, in analogy with the days of the week. The goals themselves have, like the decani of the Zodiac, each three pinnacles, round which the swift quadrigae circle like the sun. The wheels indicate the boundaries of East and West. The channel which surrounds the Circus presents us with an image of the glassy sea, whence come the dolphins which swim hither through the waters. The lofty obelisks lift their height towards heaven; but the upper one is dedicated to the sun, the lower one to the moon: and upon them the sacred rites of the ancients are indicated with Chaldee signs for letters.

The Spina [central wall or backbone] represents the lot of the unhappy captives, inasmuch as the generals of the Romans, marching over the backs of their enemies, reaped that joy which was the reward of their labors. The Mappa [napkin], which is still seen to give the signal at the games, came into fashion on this wise. Once when Nero was loitering over his dinner, and the populace, as usual, was impatient for the spectacle to begin, he ordered the napkin which he had used for wiping his fingers to be thrown out of window, as a signal that he gave the required permission. Hence it became a custom that the display of a napkin gave a certain promise of future circenses.

The Circus is so called from "circuitus:" circenses is, as it were, circuenses, because in the rude ages of antiquity, before an elaborate building had been prepared for the purpose, the races were exhibited on the green grass, and the multitude were protected by the river on one side and the swords [enses] of the soldiers on the other.

We observe, too, that the rule of this contest is that it be decided in twenty-four heats, an equal number to that of the hours of day and night. Nor let it be accounted meaningless that the number of circuits round the goals is expressed by the putting up of eggs, since that emblem, pregnant as it is with many superstitions, indicates that something is about to be born from thence. And in truth we may well understand that the most fickle and inconstant characters, well typified by the birds who have laid those eggs, will spring from attendance on these spectacles. It were long to describe in detail all the other points of the Roman Circus, since each appears to arise from some special cause. This only will we remark upon as preeminently strange, that in these beyond all other spectacles men's minds are hurried into excitement without any regard to a fitting sobriety of character. The Green charioteer flashes by: part of the people is in despair. The Blue gets a lead: a larger part of the City is in misery. They cheer frantically when they have gained nothing; they are cut to the heart when they have received no loss; and they plunge with as much eagerness into these empty contests as if the whole welfare of the imperiled fatherland were at stake.

No wonder that such a departure from all sensible dispositions should be attributed to a superstitious origin. We are compelled to support this institution by the necessity of humoring the majority of the people, who are passionately fond of it; for it is always the few who are led by reason, while the many crave excitement and oblivion of their cares. Therefore, as we too must sometimes share the folly of our people, we will freely provide for the expenses of the Circus, however little our judgment approves of this institution.

Source: Thomas Hodgkin, *The Letters of Cassiodorus*. London: Henry Frowde, 1886, pp. 226–229, Letter 51.

2.F. Relating to Gymnastic Sports in 323 C.E.

Dioscorides, logistes, of the Oxyrhyncite nome (subprovince). The assault at arms by the youths will occur tomorrow, the 24th. Tradition, no less than the distinguished character of the festival, requires that they do their uttermost in the gymnastic display. The spectators will be present at the two performances.

Source: William Stearns Davis, *Readings in Ancient History: Illustrative Extracts from the Sources II. Rome and the West*. Boston: Allyn and Bacon, 1913, p. 244.

2.G. Announcing Privileges to a Victor in the Games

At a meeting of our body a dispatch was read from Theodorus, recently chosen in place of Areion, the scribe, to proceed to his highness, the Prefect [of Egypt] and attend his "immaculate" court. In this dispatch he explained that he is victor in the games and exempted from inquiries. We have, therefore, nominated Aurelianus to serve [as deputy to the Governor at Alexandria] and we send you word accordingly that this fact may be brought to his knowledge, and no time be lost in his departure and attendance upon the court.

Source: William Stearns Davis, *Readings in Ancient History: Illustrative Extracts from the Sources II. Rome and the West*. Boston: Allyn and Bacon, 1913, p. 245.

DOCUMENT 3
Country Life

The following two excerpts display the importance of the country life.
Egyptian papyri contain a wealth of information attesting to private
lives, and in the following papyri invitations are sent from one owner to

another pointing to continual traditions of hosts and guest. Also included is a request for dancing girls for a private party, probably for the upper class.

The second selection is a letter from Sidonius Apollinaris who wrote in the fifth century. The theme is hospitality and Sidonius describes the opulence that existed in some upper-class homes. The letter is meant to describe his time as a guest at two wealthy friends' homes or villas with a considerable amount of leisure time and eager to keep their friend Sidonius occupied. Although one should not assume that the description was a regular day in the life of the wealthy, the letter does show how rich magnates had considerable amounts of free time. The reference to tennis players is interesting, but it is unclear what game is actually being played. The image presented is one of extensive parties and entertainment including hunting, carousing, and gaming. The ability to engage in these pastimes rested on the burden of unmentioned laborers. One wonders what the laborers would have written concerning Sidonius' visit, if he would be seen as the oppressive "gentleman" coming into their region (see below for oppression).

3.A. Invitations to Parties

Chaereman requests your company at dinner, at the table of the lord Serapis at the Serapaeum, to-morrow the 15th, at 9 o'clock.

Greeting, my dear Serenia, from Petosiris. Be sure, dear, to come upon the 20th for the birthday festival of the god, and let me know whether you are coming by boat or by donkey, in order that we may send for you accordingly. Take care not to forget. I pray for your continued health.

To Aureleus Theon, keeper of the training school, from Aurelius Asclepiades, son of Philadelphus, president of the council of the village of Bacchias. I desire to hire from you Tisais, the dancing girl, and another, to dance for us at the above village for (fifteen?) days from the 13th Phaophi by the old [Egyptian] calendar. You shall receive as pay 36 drachmae a day, and for the whole period 3 artabai of wheat, and 15 couples of loaves; also three donkeys to fetch them and take them back.

Source: William Stearns Davis, *Readings in Ancient History: Illustrative Extracts from the Sources II. Rome and the West.* Boston: Allyn and Bacon, 1913, pp. 245–246.

3.B. Sidonius' Description of Wealthy Villas and Entertainment

Sidonius wishes health to his friend Donidius.

You ask me why, though I set out for Nismes some time ago, I have not yet returned home. I will tell you the agreeable cause of my delay, since I know that the things which please me please you too.

The fact is that I have been spending some days in a very pleasant country with two most delightful men, my hereditary friend Tonantius Ferreolus, and my cousin Apollinaris. Their estates adjoin one another and their houses are not far apart, a long walk but a short ride. The hills which rise behind are covered with vineyards and olive yards. The view from each house is equally charming; the one looks upon woods, and the other over a wide expanse of plain. So much for the dwellings; now for the hospitality shown to us there.

As soon as they found out that I was on my return journey, they stationed skilful scouts to watch not only the high-road but every little track and sheep-walk into which I could possibly turn aside, that I might not by any chance escape from their friendly snares. When I had fallen into their hands, not very reluctantly I must confess, they at once administered to me a solemn oath not to entertain one thought of continuing my journey till seven days were over. Then, every morning a friendly strife arose between my hosts whose kitchen should first have the honor of preparing my repast, a strife which I could not adjust by a precisely equal alternation of my visits, although I was bound to one house by friendship and to the other by relationship, because Ferreolus, as a man who had held the office of Prefect, derived from his age and dignity a claim beyond that of mere friendship to take precedence in entertaining me. So we were hurried from pleasure to pleasure. Scarce had we entered the vestibule of either house when lo! on one side the pairs of tennis-players stood up to oppose one another in the ring; on the other, amid the shouts of the dicers, was heard the frequent rattle of the boxes and the boards. Here too were books in plenty; you might fancy you were looking at the breast-high book-shelves of the grammarians, or the wedge-shaped cases of the Athenaeum, or the well-filled cupboards of the book-sellers. I observed however that if one found a manuscript beside the chair of one of the ladies of the house, it was sure to be on a religious subject, while those which lay by the seats of the fathers of the family were full of the loftiest strains of Latin eloquence. In making this distinction, I do not forget that there are some writings of equal literary excellence in both branches, that Augustine may be paired off against Varro, and Prudentius against Horace. Among these books Origen, "the Adamantine," translated into Latin by Turranius Rufinus, was frequently perused by readers holding our faith. I cannot understand why some of our Arch-divines should stigmatize him as a dangerous and heterodox author.

While we were engaged, according to our various inclinations, in studies of this nature, punctually as the water-clock marked 5 [11 A.M.], there would come into the room a messenger from the chief cook to warn us that the time for refreshment had arrived. At dinner we made a full and rapid meal, after the manner of senators, whose custom it is to set forth a large banquet with few dishes, though variety is produced by sometimes cooking the meat dry and sometimes with gravy. While we were drinking we had merry stories told, which at once amused and instructed us. To be brief, the style of the repast was decorous, handsome, and abundant.

Then rising from table, if we were at Voroangus (the estate of Apollinaris) we walked back to the inn where was our baggage, and there took our siesta; if at Prusianum (the name of the other property) we had to turn Tonantius and his brothers—nobles as they were, and our equals in age—out of their couches, as we could not easily carry our sleeping-apparatus about with us.

When we had shaken off our noontide torpor, we rode on horseback for a little while to sharpen our appetites for supper. Both of my hosts had baths in their houses, but neither of them happened to be in working order. However, when my attendants and the crowd of their fellow-revelers, whose brains were too often under the influence of the hospitable wine-cup, had made a short pause in their potations, they would hurriedly dig a trench near to the fountain or the river. Into this they tossed a heap of burnt stones, and over it they would weave a hemisphere of hazel-twigs. Upon this framework were stretched sheets of coarse Cilician canvas, which at once shut out the light, and beat back the steam rising from the hot flints sprinkled with water. Here we often passed hours in pleasant and witty talk, while our limbs, wrapped in the fizzing steam, gave forth a wholesome sweat. When we had spent as long as we chose in this rude sudatorium [sweating room], we plunged into the heated waters to wash away the perspiration; and, having so worked off all tendency to indigestion, we then braced our bodies with the cold waters of the well, the fountain, or the river. For I should have mentioned that midway between the two houses flows the river Vuardo,[1] red with its tawny gravel, except when the melting snow makes pale its waters, gliding tranquilly over its pebbly bed, and well-stocked with delicate fish.

I would also describe the luxurious suppers which we used to sit down to, if my talkative vein, which knows no check from modesty, were not summarily stopped by the end of my paper. And yet it would be pleasant to tell over again their delights if I did not blush to carry my scrawl over to the back of the sheet. But now, as we are really in act to depart, and as you, with Christ's help, are going to be good enough to pay us an immediate visit, it will be easier to talk over our friends suppers when you and I are taking our own; only let the end of this week of feasting restore to me as soon as possible my vanished appetite, since no refinements of cookery can so effectually soothe an overcharged stomach as the remedy of abstinence. Farewell.

Source: Thomas Hodgkin, *Italy and Her Invaders*, vol. II, 2nd ed. Oxford: Clarendon Press, 1892, pp. 325–328, The Country-house Epistle, ii.9.

DOCUMENT 4
Roman Persecutions

The history of the persecutions has usually been written by Christians, the group that suffered and ultimately prevailed. The first set of documents describe the edicts issued by Diocletian including the fourth edict calling for universal sacrifice where the individual would offer incense, libations, and a prayer or oath to the gods of Rome. A corollary to this edict is the receipt of universal sacrifice (4.C) during the Decian persecutions. The meticulous record keeping of the Romans is evident. This record keeping is seen in the excerpt from officials demanding the surrender of sacred books. In this extract (4.D), the Roman officials clearly know who are Christians and wish them to give some works so that they may record that the Christians had complied with imperial orders.

The final document is an inscription from Asia Minor by pagan villagers requesting that Christians not be allowed to continue. This inscription shows that anti-Christian sentiment was not confined to the imperial family or governors, but had its roots in the local population, who saw Christians as enemies and dangerous individuals.

4.A. The First Edict of Diocletian

. . . Diocletian and Maximian, that the assemblies of the Christians should be abolished. . . .

Source: C. F. Cruse, *The Ecclesiastical History of Eusebius Pamphilus, Bishop of Caesarea, In Palestine.* London: Henry G. Bohn, 1851, p. 330.

4.B. The Edicts of Diocletian

It was the nineteenth year of the reign of Diocletian, and the month of Dystrus, called by the Romans March, in which the festival of our Savior's passion was at hand, when the imperial edicts were every where published, to tear down the churches to the foundation, and to destroy the sacred Scriptures by fire; and which commanded, also, that those who were in honorable stations should be degraded, but those who were freedmen should be deprived of their liberty, if they persevered in their adherence to Christianity. The first edict against us was of this nature; but it was not long before other edicts were also issued, in which it was ordered that all the prelates in every place should first be committed to prison, and then by every artifice constrained to offer sacrifice to the gods.

Source: C. F. Cruse, *The Ecclesiastical History of Eusebius Pamphilus, Bishop of Caesarea, In Palestine.* London: Henry G. Bohn, 1851, p. 303.

4.C. Certificate Attesting to Sacrificing

To the Commissioners of Sacrifice of the Village of Alexander's Island: from Aurelius Diogenes, the son of Satabus, of the Village of Alexander's Island, aged 72 years; scar on his right eyebrow.

I have always sacrificed regularly to the gods, and now, in your presence, in accordance with the edict, I have done sacrifice, and poured the drink offering, and tasted of the sacrifices, and I request you to certify the same, Farewell.

Handed in by me, Aurelius Diogenes.

I certify that I saw him sacrificing . . . nonus (magistrate's signature partly obliterated.)

In the first year of the Emperor, Caesar Gaius Messius Quintus Trajanus Decius, Pius, Felix, Augustus the second of the month Epith.

Source: Herbert B. Workman, *Persecution in the Early Church*, 2nd ed. Cincinnati: Jennings and Graham, 1906, p. 341.

4.D. Roman Official Report of Seizing Christian Sacred Books

When [the magistrates and a policeman, guided by the apostatizing secretaries of the Bishop] came to the house of Felix the tailor, he brought out five books, and when they came to the house of Projectus he brought out five big and two little books. Victor the schoolmaster brought out two books, and four books of five volumes each. Felix the "Perpetual Flamen" said to him, "Bring your Scriptures out: you have more." Victor the schoolmaster said, "If I had had more I should have brought them out." When they came to the house of Eutychius who was a "Caesarian" [i.e., in the government civil service], the flamen said, "Bring out your books that you may obey the law." "I have none," he replied. "Your answer" said Felix "is taken down." At the house of Coddeo, Coddeo's wife brought out six books. Felix said, "Look and see if you have not got some more." The woman said, "I have no more." Felix said to Bos, the policeman, "Go in and see if she has any more." The policeman reported, "I have looked and found none."

Source: William Stearns Davis, *Readings in Ancient History: Illustrative Extracts from the Sources II. Rome and the West.* Boston: Allyn and Bacon, 1913, pp. 289–290.

4.E. Pagan Petition to the Emperor Maximin to Punish Christians

To the saviors of the whole human race, to the divinities, the Augusti, the Caesars, Galerius Valerius Maximinus [Flavius Valerius] Constantinus, and Valerius Licinianus Licinius, the petition and supplication of the people of Lycia and Pamphylia.

The gods, your kinsmen, most illustrious emperors, having always shown manifest favor to all who have their religion earnestly at heart and pray to them for the perpetual health of you, our invincible Lords, we have thought it well to have recourse to your immortal sovereignty, and to request that the Christians, who long ago were disloyal, and still persist in the same mischievous intent, should at last be put down and not be suffered, by any absurd novelty, to offend against the honor due to the gods. This end will best be attained, if by your divine and perpetual decree, commandment be laid upon all that the malpractices of the detestable devotion of the atheists be forbidden and prevented; and all be required to attend constantly upon the cult of the gods your kinsmen, invoking them on behalf of your eternal and incorruptible sovereignty, as is most patently to the advantage of all your subjects.

Source: B. J. Kidd, *Documents Illustrative of the History of the Church*, vol. I to A.D. 313. New York: Macmillan Company, 1920, pp. 227–228. No. 176, A Petition to Maximin.

DOCUMENT 5
Christianity

Lactantius, in his The Death of the Persecutors *(Chapter 25), recounts Christianity's triumph in Galerius' Edict of Toleration. Although still attacking the Christians for their stubbornness, Galerius decides that Rome cannot eradicate the Christians, and to forestall destruction, orders toleration. Galerius, however, clearly wants to control the Christians, ordering that they must pray for the state and its well-being. This selection provides an example of a hostile source against the pagan rulers of the Tetrarchy.*

With the triumph of Christianity, Constantine and his successors issued numerous laws giving benefits to Christians and favoring the religion, further promoting and enhancing its position in the Roman Empire. Constantine (5.B) orders North African officials that Christian clergy are exempt from public duties. These exemptions would be expanded to other, nonclergy members. The problem was that an increasing number of clergy exempt from taxes invariably led to abuses. In the final section Constantine orders that those who try to escape taxation by claiming to be clergy will be punished.

5.A. Galerius' Edict of Toleration

Amongst our other measures for the advantage of the Empire, we have hitherto endeavored to bring all things into conformity with the ancient laws and public order of the Romans. We have been especially anxious that even the Christians, who have abandoned the religion of their ancestors, should return to reason. For they have fallen, we know not how, into such perversity and folly that, instead of adhering to those ancient institutions which possibly their own forefathers established, they have arbitrarily made laws of their own and collected together various peoples from various quarters.

After the publication, on our part, or an order commanding the Christians to return to the observance of the ancient customs, many of them, it is true, submitted in view of the danger, while many others suffered death. Nevertheless, since many of them have continued to persist in their opinions and we see that in the present situation they neither duly adore and venerate the gods nor yet worship the god of the Christians, we, with wonted clemency, have judged it wise to extend a pardon even to these men and permit them once more to become Christians and reestablish their places of meeting; in such manner, however, that they shall in no way offend against good order. We propose to notify the magistrates in another mandate in regard to the course that they should pursue.

Wherefore it should be the duty of the Christians, in view of our clemency, to pray to their god for our welfare, for that of the Empire, and for their own, so that the Empire may remain intact in all its parts, and that they themselves may live safely in their habitations.

Source: James Harvey Robinson, *Readings in European History*, vol. I. Boston: Ginn and Company, 1904, pp. 22–23.

5.B. Constantine's Order Exempting Christian Clergy from Taxes

[§ 1] Greeting to thee, our most esteemed Anulinus. Since it appears from many circumstances that when that religion is despised, in which is preserved the chief reverence for the most holy celestial Power, great dangers are brought upon public affairs; but that, when legally adopted and observed, it affords the most signal prosperity to the Roman name and remarkable felicity to all the affairs of men, through the divine beneficence—it has seemed good to me, most esteemed Anulinus, that those men who give their services with due sanctity and with constant observance of this law, to the worship of the divine religion, should receive recompense for their labors.

[§ 2] Wherefore it is my will that those within the province entrusted to thee, in the Catholic Church, over which Caecilianus presides, who give their services to this holy religion, and who are commonly called clergymen, be entirely exempted from all public duties, that they may not by any error or sacrilegious negligence be drawn away from the service due to the Deity, but may devote themselves without any hindrance to their own law. For it seems that, when they show greatest reverence to the Deity, the greatest benefits accrue to the State. Farewell, our most esteemed and beloved Anulinus.

Source: B. J. Kidd, *Documents Illustrative of the History of the Church*, vol. I to A.D. 313. New York: Macmillan Company, 1920, p. 243. No. 193, Constantine to Anulinus.

5.C. Constantine's 319 C.E. Law Exempting Clerics

Those who exercise the functions of divine worship, that to be is to say those who are called clerics [clerici], shall be exempt from all public burdens, lest otherwise they might be called away from their sacred duties through some one's malicious interference.

Source: James Harvey Robinson, *Readings in European History*, vol. I. Boston: Ginn and Company, 1904, p. 24. Codex Theodosius tit. ii, 2 (319).

5.D. Constantine's 326 C.E. Law Controlling Privileges of Clerics

Immunity from public burdens is to be granted neither by custom nor upon anyone's plea that he is a clergyman; nor may persons join the order of the clergy easily or in too great numbers. But when a cleric dies another shall be chosen in his stead. He shall not be of decurion rank by descent, nor possess sufficient means easily to bear the public burdens. Should doubt arise between a city and the clergy in regard to any candidate, if justice indicates that he should bear the public burdens and he should appear, either by descent or owing to his patrimony, to be suitable for the rank of decurion, he shall leave the clergy and be turned over to the city. For it is proper that the rich should bear the burdens of the world and that the poor should be supported by the wealth of the Church.

Source: James Harvey Robinson, *Readings in European History*, vol. I. Boston: Ginn and Company, 1904, p. 24. Codex Theodosius tit. ii, 6 (326).

5.E. Constantius' 361 C.E. Law Favoring Christianity

In every city, in every town, hamlet, and burg, whoever, according to the spirit of the Christian law, shall have sincerely striven to bring home to all its supreme and peculiar merits shall enjoy permanent protection. We should rejoice and be exceeding glad in the faith, knowing that our empire is maintained more by religion than by officials or by the labor and sweat of the body.

Source: James Harvey Robinson, *Readings in European History*, vol. I. Boston: Ginn and Company, 1904, p. 25. Codex Theodosius tit. ii, 16 (361).

DOCUMENT 6
The Church's Supremacy

The victory of Christianity over paganism led to increased powers by the church. This became apparent in a series of events that occurred during the fourth century. The first excerpt points to the church using the imperial government to enforce its ideas of orthodoxy over heretics. The power of the imperial government was now used to enforce religious ideology and doctrine. This began the process of direct government involvement in Christianity. The second selection describes the conflict between Bishop of Milan Ambrose, and the emperor Theodosius over the emperor's massacre in Thessalonica. The incident and its subsequent history put the civil government under the authority of the church, profoundly influencing political history for the next 1,000 years as both church and state constantly fought for control of policies and governments. Ambrose's arguments and actions articulated the church's position that civil authority was under the authority of the church, which could interpret God's wishes in political actions.

6.A. Supremacy of Catholic Religion over Heresies and Non-Christians

Lest the Donatists and other deluded heretics and those who, like the Jews and the Gentiles (commonly called "pagans"), cannot be brought into the communion of the Catholic religion, should conclude that the force of the laws formerly directed against them had declined, let all the magistrates take note that those provisions of the law are to be faithfully observed, and that they should not hesitate to enforce all that we have decreed against the heretics.

Source: James Harvey Robinson, *Readings in European History*, vol. I. Boston: Ginn and Company, 1904, p. 27. Codex Theodosius tit. v, 46 (409).

6.B. How St. Ambrose Humiliated Theodosius the Great

Thessalonica is a large and populous city: it is situated in the province of Macedonia, and is the metropolis of Thessaly, Achaia, and of several other provinces which are under the administration of the governor of Illyria. A sedition arose in this city, and some of the magistrates were stoned and dragged through the streets. When the emperor was informed of this occurrence, his anger rose to the highest pitch: and, instead of curbing it by the suggestions of reason, he gratified his vindictive desire for vengeance by unsheathing the sword most unjustly and tyrannically against all; slaying alike the innocent and guilty. It is said that seven thousand persons were put to death without any of the forms of law, and without even having judicial sentence passed upon them; but that, like ears of corn in the time of harvest, they were alike cut down.

Ambrose, of whom we have so often spoken, when apprized of this deplorable catastrophe, went out to meet the emperor, who, on his return to Milan, desired to enter as usual the holy church; but Ambrose prohibited his entrance, saying, "You do not reflect it seems, O emperor, on the guilt you have incurred by the great massacre which has taken place; but now that your fury is appeased, do you not perceive the enormity of the crime? It may be that the greatness of your empire prevents your discerning the sins which you have committed, and that absolute power obscures the light of reason. It is, however, necessary to reflect on our nature which is subject to death and to decay; for we are made of dust, and unto dust we must return. You must not be dazzled by the splendor of the purple in which you are clothed, and be led to forget the weakness of the body which it enrobes. Your subjects, O emperor, are of the same nature as yourself, and not only so, but they are likewise your fellow-servants. For there is one Lord and Ruler of all, and He is the Maker of all creatures, whether princes or people. How would you look upon the temple of the one Lord of all? How would you walk upon such holy ground? How could you lift up in prayer hands steeped in the blood of unjust massacre? How could you with such hands presume to receive the most sacred body of our Lord? How could you carry his precious blood to a mouth, whence the word of fury issued, commanding the wanton effusion of innocent blood? Depart, then, and do not by a second crime augment the guilt of the first. Submit to the wholesome bonds which God the Lord of all has ordained; for such bonds possess healing virtue and power to restore you to health."

The emperor, who had been brought up in the knowledge of the sacred Scriptures, and who well knew the distinction between the ecclesiastical and the temporal power, submitted to this rebuke; and with many groans and tears returned to his palace. More than eight months after, the festival of our Savior's birth occurred. The emperor shut himself up in his palace, mourned bitterly, and shed floods of tears. This was observed by Rufin, the controller of the palace, and he took the liberty of inquiring the cause of his tears. The emperor, sighing yet more piteously, and weeping still more bitterly, replied, "You, O Rufin, may be at ease, and may be able to divert yourself, for you do not feel the evils under which I groan. I weep and sigh when I reflect on the calamity in which I am involved; the church of God is open to servants and to mendicants, and they can freely enter and pray to the Lord. But to me the church is closed, and so are the doors of heaven. The following words of our Lord dwell upon my memory: 'Whatsoever you shall bind on earth shall be bound in heaven.'" "If you will permit me," said Rufin, "I will run to the bishop and beseech him to unloose your bonds." "You will not be able to persuade him," said the emperor. "I see the justice of the sentence which he has pronounced against me, and I know that respect for imperial power will never lead him to transgress the divine law."

Rufin, however, persisted in declaring that he could obtain some promise from Ambrose. The emperor, therefore, commanded him to go immediately, while he himself, animated by the hope that Rufin would obtain some concession, followed very shortly after.

As soon as St. Ambrose saw Rufin, he thus addressed him: "You imitate, O Rufin, the impudence of dogs. You were the adviser of this cruel massacre, and now you have divested yourself of every feeling of shame, and neither blush nor tremble at having given vent to your fury against the image of God." Rufin addressed him in a supplicatory tone, and told him that the emperor was coming to him. Ambrose, inspired by Divine zeal, replied, "I declare to you, O Rufin, that I forbid him from entering the gates of the holy church. If he change his empire into tyranny, I will gladly receive death."

On hearing this determination, Rufin sent to the emperor to inform him of what the bishop had said, and to advise him to remain within the palace. But the emperor, having received this message when he had reached the middle of the market-place, exclaimed, "I will go and receive the rebukes which I so justly deserve." When he arrived at the entrance of the church, he did not go into the sacred edifice, but went to the bishop who was sitting in his stranger's house, and besought him to unloose his bonds. Ambrose accused him of having acted in a tyrannical manner, of having risen in opposition against God, and of having trampled upon his laws. Theodosius replied, "I do not oppose the laws which have been laid down, neither do I intend to enter within the sacred doors contrary to your injunctions; but I beseech you, in consideration of the mercy of our common Lord, to unloose me from these bonds, and not to shut against me the door which is opened by the Lord to all who truly repent." "What repentance," asked the bishop, "have you then manifested for so great a crime? What remedy have you applied to so severe a wound?" The emperor replied, "It is your office to point out the remedy, and mine to receive and to comply with it." "As you acted by the impulse of passion," said the holy Ambrose, "and enacted the sentence according to the dictates of resentment rather than of reason, let a law be drawn up to cancel henceforth all decrees passed in haste and fury; and to decree that when sentence of death or of proscription has been signed against anyone, thirty days are to elapse before the sentence is carried into execution, and that on the expiration of this period the case is to be brought before you; for your resentment will then be calmed, and will leave your reason and judgment at liberty to examine the facts, and to decide whether the sentence be just or unjust. If it be proved to be unjust it ought to be revoked, but if just it ought to be confirmed. The delay of this number of days will not injure the cause of justice."

The emperor listened to this advice; and, deeming it to be excellent, he immediately ordered the law to be committed to writing, and he signed the document with his own hand. St. Ambrose then unloosed his bonds. The emperor, who was full of faith, took courage to enter the holy church; he prayed neither in a standing nor a kneeling posture, but throwing himself on the ground, he said, with David, "My soul cleaved unto the dust, quicken thou me according to thy word" (Psal. cxix. 25). He tore his hair, struck his forehead, and shed torrents of tears as he implored forgiveness of God. When the time came to present offerings on the communion table, he went up weeping no less than before, to present his gift; and, as usual, remained afterwards within the enclosed space. The great Ambrose, however, did not suffer this in silence, but acquainted him with the distinction between different places in the church. He first asked him what he wanted; and, on his replying that he remained for the purpose of partaking of the holy mysteries, he directed his deacon to address him in the following words: "The priests alone, O emperor, are permitted to enter within the palisades of the altar, all others must not approach it. Retire, then, and remain with the rest of the laity. A purple robe makes emperors, but not priests."

The faithful emperor gladly listened to this representation, and sent word back to Ambrose, that it was not from arrogance that he had remained within the palisades of the altar, but because such was the custom at Constantinople, and that he owed him thanks for his advice on the occasion. Such were the virtues which adorned the emperor and the bishop. I greatly admire the boldness and fervent zeal of the one, and the submission and pure faith of the other. When Theodosius returned to Constantinople, he observed the pious regulation which had been explained to him by the great bishop. When a festival occurred he repaired to the church, and after having presented his gift at the altar, immediately retired. Nectarius, the bishop of the church, asked him why he did not remain within the precincts of the altar: he sighed and said, "I have learnt, after great difficulty, the difference between an emperor and a priest. It is not easy to find a man capable of teaching me the truth. Ambrose alone deserves the title of bishop." Such were the valuable results of the rebukes of a man of eminent virtue.

Source: Edward Walford, *Ecclesiastical History of Theodoret*. London: Henry G. Bohn, 1854, pp. 219–223.

DOCUMENT 7
Roman Bureaucracy

The following extract is from the late-fourth-century document the
Notitia Dignitatum *or Register of Dignitaries, illustrating the imperial
bureaucracy for both the East and the West, including the disposition of
provinces, military units, departments, officials, and minor offices. This
document is the only extensive document listing the imperial offices and is
an example of the Roman Empire's record keeping and thoroughness. The
example below describes the offices for the markets, store houses, mints,
and materials used by the imperial household, and those involved in taxes
and overseeing the imperial estates. The second document is an oath by
the egg-sellers affirming their intention not to participate in the black market. The officials in the Sacred Bounties would oversee such markets, ensuring the food supply and stability of the markets.*

7.A. *Notitia Dignitatum or Register of Dignitaries*

XIII.
THE COUNT OF THE SACRED BOUNTIES.

Under the control of the illustrious count of the sacred bounties:

The counts of the bounties in all the dioceses,
The counts of the markets:
in the East and Egypt,
in Moesia, Scythia and Pontus,
in Illyricum.
The provosts of the store-houses,
The counts of the metals in Illyricum,
The count and the accountant of the general tribute of Egypt,
The accountants of the general tribute,
The masters of the linen vesture,
The masters of the private vesture,
The procurators of the weaving-houses,

The procurators of the dye-houses,
The procurators of the mints,
The provosts of the goods despatch,
The procurators of the linen-weavers.

The staff of the aforesaid count of the sacred bounties includes:

The chief clerk of the whole staff,
The chief clerk of the bureau of fixed taxes,
The chief clerk of the bureau of records,
The chief clerk of the bureau of accounts,
The chief clerk of the bureau of gold bullion,
The chief clerk of the bureau of gold for shipment,
The chief clerk of the bureau of the sacred wardrobe,
The chief clerk of the bureau of silver,
The chief clerk of the bureau of *miliarensia*,
The chief clerk of the bureau of coinage and other clerks of the
    above-mentioned bureaus,
A deputy chief clerk of the staff, who is chief clerk of the secretaries,
A sub-deputy chief clerk, who deals with the goods despatch,
A fourth clerk who deals with requests, and other palatine [officials]
    of the aforesaid staff.

The count of the bounties is entitled to as many post-warrants in the
year as his occasions may require.

XIV.
THE COUNT OF THE PRIVATE DOMAIN.

Under the control of the illustrious count of the private domain:

The imperial estates,
The accountants of the private domain,
The private baggage train,
The provosts of the herds and stables,
The procurators of the pastures.

The staff of the aforesaid illustrious count of the private domain:

A chief clerk of the whole staff,

A chief clerk of remitted taxes,

A chief clerk of the fixed taxes,

A chief clerk of receipts,

A chief clerk of the bureau of private bounties, and other clerks of the aforesaid bureaus,

A deputy chief clerk of the whole staff, who has charge of the documents of that staff, and other palatine [officials].

The count of the private domain is entitled to as many post-warrants in the year as his occasions may require.

Source: William Fairley, *Notitia Dignitatum or Register of Dignitaries*. Translations and Reprints from the Original Sources of European History, vol. vi, no. 4. Philadelphia: Department of History of the University of Pennsylvania, 1899, pp. 12–13.

7.B. Declaration to a Local Magistrate by an Egg Seller, Showing the Close Watch Kept by City Authorities over the Trades

To Flavius Thennyras, logistes of the Oxyrhynchite district, from Aurelius Nilus, son of Didymus, of the illustrious and most illustrious city of Oxyrhynchos, an egg seller by trade. I hereby agree on the august, divine oath by our lord the Emperor and the Caesars to offer my eggs in the market place publicly for sale, and to supply to the said city, every day without intermission; and I acknowledge that it shall be unlawful for me in the future to sell secretly or in my house. If I am detected in so doing, I shall be liable to penalty.

Source: William Stearns Davis, *Readings in Ancient History: Illustrative Extracts from the Sources II. Rome and the West*. Boston: Allyn and Bacon, 1913, p. 246.

DOCUMENT 8
Roman Oppression

The following two documents detail Roman oppression and corruption in Gaul, typical through out the empire. In the first source, Sidonius presents a vivid description of the governor Seronatus who abuses everyone. Sidonius clearly condemns Seronatus, who, however, continued in his po-

sition. The letter illustrates the effects of Roman oppression with flight from the towns and farms. This in turn gave more power to the large estates' owners. In the second piece Salvian details the oppression of the Romans compared to the invading Germans. Salvian lived during the fifth century and his work, De gubernatione Dei *or* On the Government of God, *attempts to explain the theme of divine providence. Writing for many Catholics who had just been overrun by Arian Germans, Salvian attempted to explain the events by examining the Roman Christians and their less-than-sterling behavior. For Salvian the Roman oppression, especially heavy taxes, led the population to welcome the German invaders. The two samples indicate a theme consistently expressed by others, that the Romans drove their own people into the hands of the German invaders. This view, however, was no different than any other time in Roman history.*

8.A. Sidonius' Letter about an Oppressive Gallic Governor

Sidonius wishes health to his friend Pannychius.

If you have not already heard that Seronatus is returning from Toulouse, let this letter inform you of the fact. Already Evanthius is on his way to Clausetia, and is forcing people to clear away the rubbish from the works that have been let out on contract, and to remove the fallen leaves from his path. Poor man! if there is an uneven surface anywhere, he himself, with trembling hand, brings earth to fill up the trenches, going before the beast whom he is escorting from the valley of Tarmis, like the little mussels who pioneer the mighty body of the whale through the shallow places and rocky channels of the sea.

Seronatus, however, as quick to wrath as he is unwieldy in bulk, like a dragon just rolled forth from his cave, comes towards us from the district of Gabala, whose inhabitants he leaves half dead with fright. This population, scattered into the country from their towns, he is now exhausting with unheard-of imposts; now entangling them in the winding meshes of false accusations, and scarcely permitting the laborers at length to return home, when they have paid him a year's tribute in advance. The sure and certain sign of his approaching advent is the gangs of unhappy prisoners who are dragged in chains to meet him. Their anguish is his joy, their hunger is his food, and he seems to think it an especially fine thing to degrade before he punishes them, making the men grow

their hair long, and the women cut theirs. If any here and there meet
with a chance pardon, it will be due to a bribe, or to his flattered van-
ity, but never to compassion.

But to set forth all the proceedings of such a beast would exhaust the
rhetoric of a Cicero and the poetry of a Virgil. Therefore, since it is said
that this pest is approaching us (whose ravages may God guard us from!),
do you forestall the disease by the counsels of prudence; compromise your
lawsuits if you have any; get security for your arrears of tribute; do not
let the wicked man have any opportunity of hurting the good, or of lay-
ing them under an obligation. In fine, do you wish to hear what I think
of Seronatus? Others fear his fines and his punishments: to me the so-
called benefits of the robber seem even more to be dreaded.

Source: Thomas Hodgkin, *Italy and Her Invaders*, vol. II, 2nd ed. Oxford: Clarendon Press, 1892, pp. 338–340. The Oppressive Governor Epistle, V. 13.

8.B. Salvian's Account of Roman Oppression

In what respects can our customs be preferred to those of the Goths
and Vandals, or even compared with them? And first, to speak of affec-
tion and mutual charity (which, our Lord teaches, is the chief virtue, saying, "By this shall all men know that ye are my disciples, if ye have love
one to another "), almost all barbarians, at least those who are of one
race and kin, love each other, while the Romans persecute each other.
For what citizen does not envy his fellow-citizen? What citizen shows to
his neighbor full charity?

[The Romans oppress each other with exactions] nay, not each other:
it would be quite tolerable, if each suffered what he inflicted. It is worse
than that; for the many are oppressed by the few, who regard public exactions as their own peculiar right, who carry on private traffic under the
guise of collecting the taxes. And this is done not only by nobles, but by
men of lowest rank; not by judges only, but by judges' subordinates. For
where is the city—even the town or village—which has not as many
tyrants as it has curials? . . . What place is there, therefore, as I have said,
where the substance of widows and orphans, nay even of the saints, is
not devoured by the chief citizens? . . . None but the great is secure from
the devastations of these plundering brigands, except those who are
themselves robbers.

[Nay, the state has fallen upon such evil days that a man cannot be safe unless he is wicked.] Even those in a position to protest against the iniquity which they see about them dare not speak lest they make matters worse than before. So the poor are despoiled, the widows sigh, the orphans are oppressed, until many of them, born of families not obscure, and liberally educated, flee to our enemies that they may no longer suffer the oppression of public persecution. They doubtless seek Roman humanity among the barbarians, because they cannot bear barbarian inhumanity among the Romans. And although they differ from the people to whom they flee in manner and in language; although they are unlike as regards the fetid odor of the barbarians' bodies and garments, yet they would rather endure a foreign civilization among the barbarians than cruel injustice among the Romans.

So they migrate to the Goths, or to the Bagaudes, or to some other tribe of the barbarians who are ruling everywhere, and do not regret their exile. For they would rather live free under an appearance of slavery than live as captives under an appearance of liberty. The name of Roman citizen, once so highly esteemed and so dearly bought, is now a thing that men repudiate and flee from. . . .

It is urged that if we Romans are wicked and corrupt, that the barbarians commit the same sins, and are not so miserable as we. There is, however, this difference, that if the barbarians commit the same crimes as we, yet we sin more grievously. . . . All the barbarians, as we have already said, are pagans or heretics. The Saxon race is cruel, the Franks are faithless, the Gepidae are inhuman, the Huns are unchaste,—in short, there is vice in the life of all the barbarian peoples. But are their offenses as serious as ours? Is the unchastity of the Hun so criminal as ours? Is the faithlessness of the Frank so blameworthy as ours? Is the intemperance of the Alemanni so base as the intemperance of the Christians? Does the greed of the Alani so merit condemnation as the greed of the Christians? If the Hun or the Gepid cheat, what is there to wonder at, since he does not know that cheating is a crime? If a Frank perjures himself, does he do anything strange, he who regards perjury as a way of speaking, not as a crime?

Source: James Harvey Robinson, *Readings in European History*, vol. I. Boston: Ginn and Company, 1904, pp. 28–30. Salvian De gubernatione Dei v. cc. 4ff; iv, c. 14.

DOCUMENT 9
Constantinople: The New Rome

The foundation of Constantinople changed the perception of Roman power. The city of Rome was no longer premier or the capital; instead a new Christian city, Constantinople, would take its place. The excerpt clearly indicates that Constantine desired this new city to be Christian, but modeled on Rome. Sozomen gives the mystical account of Constantine's decision caused by Divine intervention. Constantine planned to place his city at Troy, Rome's ancestral city, for Aeneas fled Troy to Italy. Constantine instead received God's order to establish the capital at the ancient city of Byzantium. A more plausible reason lay in Byzantium's strategic position as a bridge between the Greek East and the Latin West. The city flourished and ultimately replaced Rome as the center of the Mediterranean world for nearly a millennium, becoming the intellectual center for law, history, architecture, and Classical scholarship. With its strategic location and defenses, the city successfully withstood the continual onslaughts from all sides until 1204 and the Fourth Crusades. With its two natural harbors, Constantinople became the commercial center for the Mediterranean, controlling trade with the Far East, Medieval Europe, and the Islamic world.

9.A. How Constantine Founded Constantinople

The emperor [Constantine] always intent on the advancement of religion, erected magnificent [Christian] temples to God in every place, particularly in metropolises, such as Nicomedia in Bithynia, Antioch on the Orontes, and Byzantium. He greatly improved this latter city, and made it equal to Rome in power and influence; for, when he had settled the affairs of the empire according to his own mind, and had freed himself from foreign foes, he resolved upon founding a city which should be called by his own name, and should be equal in celebrity to Rome. With this intention he repaired to a plain at the foot of Troy, near the Hellespont, above the tomb of Ajax, where, it is said, the Achaians intrenched themselves when besieging Troy; and here he laid the plan of a large and beautiful city, and built the gates on an elevated spot of ground, whence they are still visible from the sea to sailors. But when he had advanced thus far, God appeared to him by night, and commanded him seek another site for his city. Led by the hand of God, he arrived at Byzantium in Thrace, beyond Chalcedon in Bithynia, and here he was desired to build his city, and to render it worthy of the name of Constantine. In obedience to the command of God, he therefore enlarged the city formerly called Byzantium, and surrounded it with high walls; he also erected magnificent dwelling-houses, and being aware that the former population was insufficient for so great a city, he peopled it with men of rank and their households, whom he summoned thither from Rome and from other countries. He imposed taxes to cover the expenses of building and adorning the city, and of supplying its inhabitants with food. He erected all the requisite edifices, a hippodrome, fountains, porticoes and other beautiful embellishments. He named it Constantinople and New Rome, and constituted it the Roman capital for all the inhabitants of the North, the South, the East, and the shores of the Mediterranean, from the cities on the Danube, and from Epidamnus and the Ionian Gulf, to Cyrene and that part of Libya called Bonium. He created another senate, which he endowed with the same honors and privileges as that of Rome, and he sought to render the city which bore his name equal in every respect to Rome in Italy: nor were his wishes thwarted, for, by the assistance of God, it became the most populous and wealthy of cities. I know of no cause to account for this extraordinary aggrandizement, unless it be the piety of the builder and of the inhabitants, and their compassion and liberality towards the poor. The zeal they manifested for Christianity was so great that many of the Jewish inhabitants, and most of the Greeks, were converted. As this city became the capital of the empire during the period of religious prosperity, it was not polluted by altars, Grecian temples, nor sacrifices; and although Julian authorized the introduction of idolatry for a short pace of time, it soon afterwards became extinct. Constantine further honored this new city of Christ by adorning it with numerous and magnificent houses of prayer, in which the Deity vouchsafed to bless the efforts of the emperor by giving sensible manifestations of his presence.

Source: Edward Walford, _The Ecclesiastical History of Sozomen._ London: Henry G. Bohn, 1854, pp. 53–54.

DOCUMENT 10
Battle of Adrianople and Its Aftermath

The battle of Adrianople became the first great disaster leading to the collapse of the Western Empire. Ammianus presents the events leading up to the battle showing Valens' impending defeat as a forgone conclusion, not because of Visigoth superiority, but because of Valens' behavior, his rashness, obstinacy, and fear of giving up glory to his nephew Gratian.

The selection from Jordanes, written from a pro-Gothic point, addresses the conditions after the defeat, showing it was divine judgment. The final selection is from Jerome where he describes the virtual onslaught of the barbarians coming into the Roman Empire. It is a poignant picture of the troubles facing the West, especially Gaul and Spain. Although a Christian, Jerome still feels connected to the past glories of pagan Rome.

10.A. Valens' Impetuous Behavior

3. Three days afterwards, when the barbarians, who were advancing slowly, because they feared an attack in the unfavorable ground which they were traversing, arrived within fifteen miles from the station of Nice, which was the aim of their march, the emperor, with wanton impetuosity, resolved on attacking them instantly, because those who had been sent forward to reconnoiter (what led to such a mistake is unknown) affirmed that their entire body did not exceed ten thousand men.

4. Marching on with his army in battle array, he came near the suburb of Hadrianople, where he pitched his camp, strengthening it with a rampart of palisades, and then impatiently waited for Gratian. While here, Richomeres, Count of the Domestici, arrived, who had been sent on by that emperor with letters announcing his immediate approach.

5. And imploring Valens to wait a little while for him that he might share his danger, and not rashly face the danger before him single handed, he took counsel with his officers as to what was best to be done.

6. Some, following the advice of Sebastian, recommended with urgency that he should at once go forth to battle; while Victor, master-general of the cavalry, a Sarmatian by birth, but a man of slow and cautious temper, recommended him to wait for his imperial colleague,

and this advice was supported by several other officers, who suggested that the reinforcement of the Gallic army would be likely to awe the fiery arrogance of the barbarians.

7. However, the fatal obstinacy of the emperor prevailed, fortified by the flattery of some of the princes, who advised him to hasten with all speed, so that Gratian might have no share in a victory which, as they fancied, was already almost gained.

Source: C. D. Yonge, *The Roman History of Ammianus Marcellinus*. London: Henry G. Bohn, 1862, pp. 608–609.

10.B. Gothic View of the Battle of Adrianople

When the Emperor Valens heard of this at Antioch, he made ready an army at once and set out for the country of Thrace. Here a grievous battle took place and the Goths prevailed. The Emperor himself was wounded and fled to a farm near Hadrianople. The Goths, not knowing that an emperor lay hidden in so poor a hut, set fire to it (as is customary in dealing with a cruel foe), and thus he was cremated in royal splendor. Plainly it was a direct judgment of God that he should be burned with fire by the very men whom he had perfidiously led astray when they sought the true faith, turning them aside from the flame of love into the fire of hell.

Source: Jordanes, *The Origin and Deeds of the Goths*. Translated by Charles C. Mierow. Princeton, NJ: Princeton University Press, 1908, pp. 43–44.

10.C. Jerome's Lament over the Invasion of the West

Nations innumerable and most savage have invaded all Gaul. The whole region between the Alps and the Pyrenees, the ocean and the Rhine, has been devastated by the Quadi, the Vandals, the Saimati, the Alani, the Gepidae, the hostile Heruli, the Saxons, the Burgundians, the Alemanni and the Pannonians. O wretched Empire! Mayence, formerly so noble a city, has been taken and ruined, and in the church many thousands of men have been massacred. Worms has been destroyed after a long siege. Rheims, that, powerful city, Amiens, Arras, Speyer, Strasburg,—all have seen their citizens led away captive into Germany. Aquitaine and the provinces of Lyons and Narbonne, all save a few towns, have been depopulated; and these the sword threatens without, while hunger ravages within. I cannot speak without tears of Toulouse, which the merits of the holy Bishop Exuperius have prevailed so far to save from destruction. Spain, even, is in daily terror lest it perish, remembering the invasion of the Cimbri; and whatsoever the other provinces have suffered once, they continue to suffer in their fear.

I will keep silence concerning the rest, lest I seem to despair of the mercy of God. For a long time, from the Black Sea to the Julian Alps, those things which are ours, have not been ours; and for thirty years, since the Danube boundary was broken, war has been waged in the very midst of the Roman Empire. Our tears are dried by old age. Except a few old men, all were born in captivity and siege, and do not desire the liberty they never knew. Who could believe this? How could the whole tale be worthily told? How Rome has fought within her own bosom not for glory, but for preservation—nay, how she has not even fought, but with gold and all her precious things has ransomed her life. . . .

Source: James Harvey Robinson, *Readings in European History*, vol. I. Boston: Ginn and Company, 1904, pp. 44–45. St. Jerome, Ep. ad Ageruchiam.

DOCUMENT 11
Sack of Rome in 410

Alaric's sack of Rome in 410 sent shockwaves throughout the Roman Empire, as seen in the first selection from Jerome (writing in Bethlehem), who clearly viewed it as the end of an era. He is in disbelief when describing the ravages of the invasion. He views the invaders as impure, not worthy to control the empire. Jordanes, writing for the Goths, views the sacking of Rome differently, as an event which could have been far worse, for Alaric was not a savage. The Gothic king ordered it to be sacked but not destroyed. The chronicles present it as a matter of fact, although they too express their outrage. The chronicles for 410 connect the two, where one states that because of the sacking, only an Eastern consul existed. Finally, a century later the Byzantine writer Procopius (11.F) writes the fullest version of what happened, although he also gave way to popular

*gossip. His account is important since it provides a vivid description of
how Alaric successfully seized the capital.*

11.A. Jerome's Shock of Rome's Sack

Who could believe that Rome, built upon the conquest of the whole
world, would fall to the ground? that the mother herself would become
the tomb of her peoples? that all the regions of the East, of Africa and
Egypt, once ruled by the queenly city, would be filled with troops of slaves
and handmaidens? that to-day holy Bethlehem should shelter men and
women of noble birth, who once abounded in wealth and are now beg-
gars?

Source: James Harvey Robinson, *Readings in European History*, vol. I. Boston:
Ginn and Company, 1904, p. 45. St. Jerome, *Commentaria in Ezechielem preface
bk. 3.*

11.B. A Pro-Gothic View of the Sack of Rome

When they had plundered and spoiled it, they also laid waste Aemilia,
and then hastened toward the city of Rome along the Flaminian Way,
which runs between Picenum and Tuscia, taking as booty whatever they
found on either hand. When they finally entered Rome, by Alaric's express command they merely sacked it and did not set the city on fire, as
wild peoples usually do, nor did they permit serious damage to be done
to the holy places. Thence they departed to bring like ruin upon Cam-
pania and Lucania, and then came to Bruttii.

Source: Jordanes, *The Origin and Deeds of the Goths*. Translated by Charles C.
Mierow. Princeton, NJ: Princeton University Press, 1908, p. 48.

11.C. Prosper of Aquitaine, Entry for the Year 410

Senator Varanes.

Rome was captured by the Goths under the command of Alaric, and
for this reason there was only a consul for the east, a practice followed
the next year as well.

11.D. Gallic Chronicle of 452

Finally, the capital of the world, Rome herself, was most foully exposed to sack at the hands of the Goths.[65]

11.E. Chronicle of Hydatius

Alaric, king of the Goths, entered Rome. Although killing took place inside and outside the city, all who sought sanctuary in the holy places were spared.

[Galla] Placidia, the daughter of Theodosius, the sister of the emperor Honorius, was captured in the city.

11.F. The Byzantine Historian Procopius' Account of Alaric's Capture of Rome

But I shall now tell how Alaric captured Rome.

After much time had been spent by him in the siege, and he had not been able either by force or by any other device to capture the place, he formed the following plan. Among the youths in the army whose beards had not yet grown, but who had just come of age, he chose out three hundred whom he knew to be of good birth and possessed of valor be-yond their years, and told them secretly that he was about to make a present of them to certain of the patricians in Rome, pretending that they were slaves. And he instructed them that, as soon as they got inside the houses of those men, they should display much gentleness and moderation and serve them eagerly in whatever tasks should be laid upon them by their owners; and he further directed them that not long afterwards, on an appointed day at about midday, when all those who were to be their masters would most likely be already asleep after their meal, they should all come to the gate called Salarian and with a sudden rush kill the guards, who would have no previous knowledge of the plot, and open the gates as quickly as possible. After giving these orders to the youths, Alaric straightway sent ambassadors to the members of the senate, stating that he admired them for their loyalty toward their emperor, and that he would trouble them no longer, because of their valor and faithfulness, with which it was plain that they were endowed to a remarkable degree, and in order that tokens of himself might be preserved among men both noble and brave, he wished to present each one of them with some domestics. After making this declaration and sending the youths not long afterwards, he commanded the barbarians to make preparations for the departure, and he let this be known to the Romans. And they heard his words gladly, and receiving the gifts began to be exceedingly happy, since they were completely ignorant of the plot of the barbarian. For the youths, by being unusually obedient to their owners, averted suspicion, and in the camp some were already seen moving from their positions and raising the siege, while it seemed that the others were just on the point of doing the very same thing. But when the appointed day had come, Alaric armed his whole force for the attack and was holding them in readiness close by the Salarian Gate; for it happened that he had encamped there at the beginning of the siege. And all the youths at the time of the day agreed upon came to this gate, and, assailing the guards suddenly, put them to death; then they opened the gates and received Alaric and the army into the city at their leisure. And they set fire to the houses which were next to the gate, among which was also the house of Sallust, who in ancient times wrote the history of the Romans, and the greater part of this house has stood half-burned up to my time; and after plundering the whole city and destroying the most of the Romans, they moved on. At that time they say that the Emperor Honorius in Ravenna received the message from one of the eunuchs, evidently a keeper of the poultry, that Rome had perished. And he cried out and said, "And yet it has just eaten from my hands!" For he had a very large cock, Rome by name; and the eunuch comprehending his words said that it was the city of Rome which had perished at the hands of Alaric, and the emperor with a sigh of relief answered quickly: "But I, my good fellow, thought that my fowl Rome had perished." So great, they say, was the folly with which this emperor was possessed.

Source: Procopius, *History of the Wars*. Translated by H. B. Dewing. Cambridge, MA: Harvard University Press, 1916, pp. 13–19.

DOCUMENT 12
Death of Valentinian and Gaiseric's Sack of Rome

Valentinian III's assassination of Aetius removed Rome's last chance for survival. In the first selection Procopius (12.A) relates how Valentinian raped the wife of Maximus, a nobleman, who then uses Aetius' murder to seek revenge and advance. The historian John of Antioch (12.B) shows how Maximus used Aetius' murder to provoke two of Aetius' retainers who then slew Valentinian. Procopius (12.C) then shows how Maximus revealed his true nature after becoming emperor, by seizing Valentinian's widow and not punishing the murderers of Valentinian. The Chronicles (12.D–E) show that Maximus could not prevent the invasion by Gaiseric, who had been asked by Valentinian's widow to intervene. Procopius (12.F) finally relates that Maximus is then killed by the mob, and Gaiseric plunders the city. The pillaging of Rome is complete and a century later Procopius describes some of the plunder recovered. The two events are clearly intertwined, resulting in a Roman emperor's daughter married to a Vandal king's son.

12.A. Assassination of Aetius by Valentinian

And I shall now relate in what manner Valentinian died.

There was a certain Maximus, a Roman senator, of the house of that Maximus who, while usurping the imperial power, was overthrown by the elder Theodosius and put to death, and on whose account also the Romans celebrate the annual festival named from the defeat of Maximus. This younger Maximus was married to a woman discreet in her ways and exceedingly famous for her beauty. For this reason a desire came over Valentinian to have her to wife. And since it was impossible, much as he wished it, to meet her, he plotted an unholy deed and carried it to fulfillment. For he summoned Maximus to the palace and sat down with him to a game of draughts, and a certain sum was set as a penalty for the loser; and the emperor won in this game, and receiving Maximus' ring as a pledge for the agreed amount, he sent it to his house, instructing the messenger to tell the wife of Maximus that her husband bade her come as quickly as possible to the palace to salute the queen Eudoxia. And she, judging by the ring that the message was from Maximus, entered her litter and was conveyed to the emperor's court. And she was received by those who had been assigned this service by the emperor, and led into a certain room far removed from the women's apartments, where Valentinian met her and forced her, much against her will. And she, after the outrage, went to her husband's house weeping and feeling the deepest possible grief because of her misfortune, and she cast many curses upon Maximus as having provided the cause for what had been done. Maximus, accordingly, became exceedingly aggrieved, at that which had come to pass, and straightway entered into a conspiracy against the emperor; but when he saw that Aetius was exceedingly powerful, for he had recently conquered Attila, who had invaded the Roman domain with a great army of Massagetae and the other Scythians, the thought occurred to him that Aetius would be in the way of his undertaking. And upon considering this matter, it seemed to him that it was the better course to put Aetius out of the way first, paying no heed to the fact that the whole hope of the Romans centered in him. And since the eunuchs who were in attendance upon the emperor were well-disposed toward him, he persuaded the emperor by their devices that Aetius was setting on foot a revolution. And Valentinian, judging by nothing else than the power and valor of Aetius that the report was true, put the man to death. Whereupon a certain Roman made himself famous by a saying which he uttered. For when the emperor enquired of him whether he had done well in putting Aetius to death, he replied saying that, as to this matter, he was not able to know whether he had done well or perhaps otherwise, but one thing he understood exceedingly well, that he had cut off his own right hand with the other.

Source: Procopius, *History of the Wars*. Translated by H. B. Dewing. Cambridge, MA: Harvard University Press, 1916, pp. 39–43.

12.B. Assassination of Valentinian

And after the murder of Aetius, Valentinian slew also Boethius, the prefect, who was a very dear friend of Aetius. And having exposed their bodies unburied in the forum, he immediately summoned the senate, and brought many charges against the men: this was a precaution against a revolt on account of the fate of Aetius. And Maximus, after the death of Aetius, went to Valentinian, seeking to be promoted to the consulship; and failing it he desired to obtain the rank of patrician, but in this too was foiled by Heraclius, who countervailed the aims of Maximus and persuaded Valentinian that being well rid of the oppressive influence of Aetius he ought not to transfer his power to Maximus. Thwarted in both his wishes, Maximus was wroth, and he sent for two Scythians (Huns), brave in war, named Optila and Thraustila, who had fought campaigns with Aetius, and were intimate with Valentinian. When he met them pledges were exchanged, and he accused the Emperor of the murder of Aetius and advised them to take vengeance on him, suggesting that they would win very great advantages by justly avenging the victim.

"A few days later, it seemed good to Valentinian to ride in the Campus Martius with a few guards, accompanied by Optila and Thraustila and their attendants. And when he dismounted and proceeded to practice archery, Optila and those with him attacked him. Optila struck Valentinian on the temple, and when the prince turned to see who struck him, dealt him a second blow on the face and felled him. And Thraustila slew Heraclius. And the two assassins taking the imperial diadem and the horse hastened to Maximus. . . . They escaped all punishment for their deed. But a strange marvel happened to the corpse of Valentinian. A swarm of bees lit upon it, and drained and wiped away all the blood that flowed from it to the ground. Thus died Valentinian, having lived thirty-seven years."

Source: J. B. Bury, *A History of the Later Roman Empire*, vol. 1. London: Macmillian, 1889, p. 182.

12.C. Procopius' Account of Maximus and Eudoxia's Plea to Gaiseric to Avenge Valentinian

So after the death of Aetius, . . .

Later on Maximus slew the emperor with no trouble and secured the tyranny, and he married Eudoxia by force. For the wife to whom he had been wedded had died not long before. And on one occasion in private he made the statement to Eudoxia that it was all for the sake of her love that he had carried out all that he had done. And since she felt a repulsion for Maximus even before that time, and had been desirous of exacting vengeance from him for the wrong done Valentinian, his words made her swell with rage still more against him, and led her on to carry out her plot, since she had heard Maximus say that on account of her the misfortune had befallen her husband. And as soon as day came, she sent to Carthage entreating Gaiseric to avenge Valentinian, who had been destroyed by an unholy man, in a manner unworthy both of himself and of his imperial station, and to deliver her, since she was suffering unholy treatment at the hand of the tyrant. And she impressed it upon Gaiseric that, since he was a friend and ally and so great a calamity had befallen the imperial house, it was not a holy thing to fail to become an avenger. For from Byzantium she thought no vengeance would come, since Theodosius had already departed from the world and Marcian had taken over the empire.

Source: Procopius, *History of the Wars*. Translated by H. B. Dewing. Cambridge, MA: Harvard University Press, 1916, pp. 45–47.

12.D. Prosper of Aquitaine's Account of Maximus and Gaiseric's Sack of Rome

Valentinian for the eighth time and Anthemius.

As this murder was carried out, moreover, Maximus, twice possessor of the consulship and holder of the patrician dignity, took up the imperial power. Although people believed he would be in every way beneficial to the endangered state, it did not take long for him to show by example the kind of mind he had. Not only did he not punish the killers of Valentinian, but he received them as friends; and he forbade the Augusta, Valentinian's wife, to mourn the loss of her husband and within a few days forced her to marry him. But he was not to indulge this lack of restraint for long. After another month he got news of the arrival of Gaiseric from Africa, and many nobles and commoners fled the city. When he gave permission for everyone to leave and wished himself to get away in haste, on the seventy-seventh day after his seizure of power, he was torn to pieces by the royal slaves; thrown in pieces into the Tiber, he was even deprived of burial. After this end to Maximus, a Roman captivity, deserving of many tears, immediately followed, and Gaiseric obtained the city devoid of all protection. Holy Bishop Leo met him outside the gates and his supplication mollified him through the power of God to such an extent that, when everything was given into his hands, he was held back nevertheless from burning, killing, and torture. Then for fourteen days, through an untrammeled and open search, Rome was emptied of all its wealth, and many thousands of captives, all that were satisfactory as to age or occupation, along with the queen and her children, were taken away to Carthage.

Source: From Roman to Merovingian Gaul: A Reader. Edited and translated by Alexander Callander Murray. Peterborough, ON: Broadview Press, 2000, p. 75, entry for the year 455. Copyright © 2000 by Alexander Callander Murray. Reprinted by permission of Broadview Press.

12.E. Chronicle of Hydatius' Account of Gaiseric

Before Avitus was made Augustus, Gaiseric entered Rome—at the invitation of Valentinian's widow, according to a lying rumor that was spread about. He plundered the wealth of the Romans and returned to Carthage, taking with him Valentinian's widow, his two daughters, and Gaudentius, the son of Aetius.

Source: From Roman to Merovingian Gaul: A Reader. Edited and translated by Alexander Callander Murray. Peterborough, ON: Broadview Press, 2000, p. 43. Copyright © 2000 by Alexander Callander Murray. Reprinted by permission of Broadview Press.

12.F. Procopius' Account of Gaiseric Plundering Rome

And Gaiseric, for no other reason than that he suspected that much money would come to him, set sail for Italy with a great fleet. And going up to Rome, since no one stood in his way, he took possession of the palace. Now while Maximus was trying to flee, the Romans threw stones at him and killed him, and they cut off his head and each of his other members and divided them among themselves. But Gaiseric took Eudoxia captive, together with Eudocia and Placidia, the children of herself and Valentinian, and placing an exceedingly great amount of gold and other imperial treasure in his ships sailed to Carthage, having spared neither bronze nor anything else whatsoever in the palace. He plundered also the temple of Jupiter Capitolinus, and tore off half of the roof. Now this roof was of bronze of the finest quality, and since gold was laid over it exceedingly thick, it shone as a magnificent and wonderful spectacle. But of the ships with Gaiseric, one, which was bearing the statues, was lost, they say, but with all the others the Vandals reached port in the harbor of Carthage. Gaiseric then married Eudocia to Honoric, the elder of his sons; but the other of the two women, being the wife of Olybrius, a most distinguished man in the Roman senate, he sent to Byzantium together with her mother, Eudoxia, at the request of the emperor. Now the power of the East had by now fallen to Leon, who had been set in this position by Aspar, since Marcian had already passed from the world. . . . And there was also silver weighing many thousands of talents and all the royal treasure amounting to an exceedingly great sum (for Gaiseric had despoiled the Palatium in Rome, as has been said in the preceding narrative), and among these were the treasures of the Jews, which Titus, the son of Vespasian, together with certain others, had brought to Rome after the capture of Jerusalem. And one of the Jews, seeing these things, approached one of those known to the emperor and said: "These treasures I think it inexpedient to carry into the palace in Byzantium. Indeed, it is not possible for them to be elsewhere than in the place where Solomon, the king of the Jews, formerly placed them. For it is because of these that Gaiseric captured the palace of the Romans, and that now the Roman army has captured that the Vandals." When this had been brought to the ears of the Emperor, he became afraid and quickly sent everything to the sanctuaries of the Christians in Jerusalem.

Source: Procopius, *History of the Wars.* Translated by H. B. Dewing. Cambridge, MA: Harvard University Press, 1916, pp. 47–49, 281.

DOCUMENT 13
The Empire

The following two excerpts indicate the position of the empire in general and Gaul in particular, from an emperor's and a poet's perspectives. The first is the preamble to Diocletian's price edict in 301, a panegyric by Diocletian on the empire and how unscrupulous individuals have taken advantage of the people, especially the military, through greed or avarice. The preamble is more than a justification of the emperor's decision to impose a limit on prices; it is a glorification of his rule and how he and his fellow emperors have defeated external foes, and are now attempting to solve the rise in inflation. The second excerpt is by the poet Ausonius, writing in the fourth century about the Moselle River. The poem not only catalogued the expanse of the river, its fishes, vineyards growing on its banks, its rich shore; it also praised the calmness and serenity of the region as it flowed past Trier in Germany, the seat of power in the West. The Moselle is therefore a poem praising not only the region but the serenity and peace of the emperor and the empire.

13.A. Diocletian's Price Edict

THE EDICT OF DIOCLETIAN FIXING MAXIMUM PRICES

1. The national honor and the dignity and majesty of Rome demand that the fortune of our State—to which, next to the immortal gods, we may, in memory of the wars which we have successfully waged, return thanks for the tranquil and profoundly quiet condition of the world—be also faithfully administered and duly endowed with the blessings of that peace for which we have laboriously striven; to the end that we, who under the gracious favor of the gods have repressed the furious depredations, in the past, of barbarous tribes by the destructions of those nations themselves, may for all time gird with the bulwarks due to justice the peace which has been established.

2. To be sure, if any spirit of self-restraint were holding in check those practices by which the raging and boundless avarice is inflamed, an avarice which, without regard for the human race, not yearly or monthly or daily only, but almost every hour and even every moment, hastens to-

ward its own development and increase; or if the common fortunes could with calmness bear this orgy of license, by which, under their unhappy star, they are from day to day ripped to pieces—peradventure there would seem to be room left for shutting our eyes and holding our peace, since the united endurance of men's minds would ameliorate this detestable enormity and pitiable condition.

3. But since it is the sole desire of untamed fury to feel no love for the ties of our common humanity; and since among the wicked and lawless it is held to be, so to speak, the religious duty of an avarice that swells and grows with fierce flames, that, in harrying the fortunes of all, it should desist of necessity rather than voluntarily; and since those whom extreme poverty has brought to a perception of their most wretched condition cannot further keep their eyes shut; it suits us, who are the watchful parents of the whole human race, that justice step in as an arbiter in the case, in order that the long-hoped-for result, which humanity could not achieve by itself, may, by the remedies which our forethought suggests, be contributed toward the general alleviation of all.

4. And of this matter, it is true, as the common knowledge of all recognizes and indisputable facts proclaim, the consideration is almost too late, since we form plans or delay discovered remedies in the hope that, as was to be expected from natural justice, humanity, detected in most odious crimes, might work out its own reformation; for we thought it far better that the censure of intolerable robbery should be removed from the court of public opinion by the feeling and decision of those men themselves, who rush daily from bad to worse and in a sort of blindness of mind tend toward outrages upon society, and whom their grave misdoing has branded as enemies alike to individuals and to the community, and guilty of the most atrocious inhumanity.

5. Therefore we proceed promptly to apply the remedies long demanded by the necessity of the case, and that too, feeling no concern about complaints that our corrective interference may, as coming unseasonably or unnecessarily, be considered cheaper or less valuable even in the eyes of the wicked, who, though seeing in our silence of so many years a lesson in self-restraint, nevertheless refused to follow it.

6. For who has so dull a breast, or is so alien to the feeling of humanity, that he can be ignorant, nay rather has not actually observed that in commodities which are bought and sold in markets or handled in the daily trade of cities, the wantonness in prices had progressed to such

a point that the unbridled greed for plundering might be moderated neither by abundant supplies nor by fruitful seasons?

7. So that there is clearly no doubt that men of this sort, whom these occupations have engaged, are always mentally calculating and even seeking, from the motions of the stars, to take advantage of the very winds and seasons, and by reason of their wickedness cannot bear that the fields be watered and made productive by the rains of heaven, so as to give hope of future crops, since they consider it a personal loss for abundance to come to the world by the favorable moods of the sky itself.

8. And to the avarice of those who are always eager to turn to their own profit even the blessings of the gods, and to check the tide of general prosperity, and again in an unproductive year to haggle about the sowing of the seed and the business of retail dealers; who, individually possessed of immense fortunes which might have enriched whole peoples to their heart's content, seek private gain and are bent upon ruinous percentages of profit—to their avarice, ye men of our provinces, regard for common humanity impels us to set a limit.

9. But now, further, we must set forth the reasons themselves, whose urgency has at last compelled us to discard our too long protracted patience, in order that—although an avarice which runs riot through the whole world can with difficulty be laid bare by a specific proof, or rather fact—none the less the nature of our remedy may be known to be more just, when utterly lawless men shall be forced to recognize, under a definite name and description, the unbridled lusts of their minds.

10. Who therefore can be ignorant that an audacity that plots against the good of society is presenting itself with a spirit of profiteering, wherever the general welfare requires our armies to be directed, not only in villages and towns, but along every highway? That it forces up the prices of commodities not fourfold or eightfold, but to such a degree that human language cannot find words to set a proper evaluation upon their action? Finally, that sometimes by the outlay upon a single article the soldier is robbed both of his bounty and of his pay, and that the entire contributions of the whole world for maintaining the armies accrue to the detestable gains of plunderers, so that our soldiers seem to yield the entire fruit of their military career, and the labors of their entire term of service, to these profiteers in everything, in order that the pillagers of the commonwealth may from day to day carry off all that they resolve to have?

11. Being justly and duly moved by all these considerations above included, since already humanity itself seemed to be praying for release, we resolved, not that the prices of commodities should be fixed—for it is not thought just that this be done, since sometimes very many provinces exult in the good fortune of the low prices which they desire, and as it were in a certain privileged state of abundance—but that a maximum be fixed; in order that, when any stress of high prices made its appearance—which omen we prayed the gods might avert—avarice, which could not be checked on the so-to-speak endlessly extending plains, might be confined by the bounds of our statute and the limits set in the law promulgated to control them.

12. It is our pleasure, therefore, that those prices, which the concise items of the following list indicate, be held in attention throughout our whole domain, in such a way that all men understand that freedom to exceed them is removed; while at the same time, in those places where goods manifestly abound, the happy condition of cheap prices shall not thereby be hampered—and ample provision is made for cheapness, if avarice is limited and curbed.

13. Between sellers, moreover, and buyers whose custom it is to enter trading-ports and visit provinces overseas, this restraint will have to be a mutual action, that, while they already of themselves know that in the need imposed by high prices the price-limits cannot be exceeded at the time of retailing such a reckoning of places and bargainings and of the whole transaction be figured out, that under it there is manifestly a fair agreement that those who transport the goods shall nowhere sell at an unduly high price.

14. Because, therefore, it is an established fact that among our ancestors also the methods employed in new enactments was that boldness be curbed by a prescribed penalty—since very rarely is a status found for men which will benefit them with their free consent, but it is always fear, justest teacher of duties, which will restrain and guide them in the right path—it is our pleasure that if anyone have acted with boldness against the letter of this statute, he shall be subjected to capital punishment.

15. And let none think that a hard penalty is set, though when the time comes the observance of moderation will be a refuge for averting the peril.

16. He also shall be subject to the same peril, who in eagerness to purchase has come to an agreement with an avarice which retails in violation of the statutes.

17. From such guilt also he too shall not be considered free, who, having goods necessary for food or usage, shall after this regulation have thought that they might be withdrawn from the market; since the penalty ought to be even heavier for him who causes need than for him who makes use of it contrary to the statutes.

18. We therefore appeal to the devotion of all, that the decision made for the public welfare be observed with generous obedience and due scrupulousness, especially since by such a statute provision is manifestly made not only for the individual states and peoples and provinces, but for the whole world, for whose ruin a few, we learn, have raged exceedingly, whose greed neither length of time nor the riches which they are seen to have desired, have been able to moderate or satisfy.

Source: Roland G. Kent, "The Edict of Diocletian Fixing Maximum Prices." *The University of Pennsylvania Law Review* 69 (1920): 35–47.

13.B. Ausonius' Poem *Moselle*

Horned Moselle, worthy to be renowned throughout foreign lands, and not to be renowned in those parts alone where at thy farthest source thou dost reveal the gilded glory of a bull-like brow; or where amid embaying fields thou dost wind thy peaceful course; or where below German harbors thou dost clear thy outfall;—if any praise shall choose to breathe upon this feeble strain, if anyone shall deign to waste his leisure on my verse, thou shall pass upon the lips of men, and be cherished with joyful song. Of thee springs and living lakes shall learn, of thee azure rivers, of thee ancient groves, the glory of our villages; to thee Druna, to thee Druentia [The Drome and the Durance], wandering uncertainly between her shifting banks, shall do reverence with all the Alpine streams, and Rhodanus who, flowing through that twofold city, gives a name to the Right Bank [Arles]; thee will I praise to the dark meres and deep-voiced tributaries, thee will I praise to sea-like Garonne.

Source: Ausonius, *Moselle*. Translated by Hugh G. Evelyn White. Cambridge, MA: Harvard University Press, 1919, p. 263.

GLOSSARY OF
SELECTED TERMS

Adlocutio: An address or speech.

Adventus: A ceremony relating to the arrival of an important person, usually an emperor. Typically the surrounding area was required to furnish supplies for the entourage.

Anchorite: Refers to an individual who lives a life of seclusion, usually religious. In the early church a form of monasticism in the East where individuals lived alone.

Annona: Originally meant grain supply, but in general meant a tax on land.

Archaeology: A study of past people's life through artifacts.

Arianism: A follower of Arius who preached against the traditional Christian church.

Augustus: Originally the proper name for Rome's first emperor; afterwards was used as part of the imperial title. During the late empire denoted the senior emperor(s).

Aureus: Roman gold coin originally worth 25 *denarii* or silver coins. Under Diocletian, 60 *aurei* were in a pound of gold. Constantine modified the coin, creating the *Solidus*.

Boule: Greek name for a town council.

Cenobite: A member of a religious group living and working together in a monastic community.

Christianity: Monotheistic religion believing that Jesus was the Jewish Messiah.

Church: A term used in early Christianity to refer to the official organization of Christianity. During the second century C.E. became synonymous with Catholic and by the fourth century referred to the Western church led by the pope.

Clarissime: A term to designate an individual of the upper class.

Coloni: A peasant who was forced to live in a region and work for a powerful landowner and who could not leave the region.

Cursus publicus: The government postal or courier service; later meant the public roads.

Damnatio: An official act by the Roman senate in which someone was condemned and their memory erased, usually with their names, statues, or busts on official monuments destroyed.

Debasement: The process of adding lower-quality metal, usually bronze, to higher-quality metal, usually silver, to increase the number of coins in circulation without increasing substantially the cost of production.

Decurion: A member of the town council that appointed and oversaw magistrates and other appointed officials.

Dekaprotoi: A member of a city's board of ten which collected taxes.

Denarius: Originally a Roman silver coin, but by the late empire a unit of account.

Dominate: The term describing the Roman Empire after Diocletian, indicating absolute control by the emperor.

Donatist: A follower to a group in North Africa which argued for harsh penalties for Christians who handed over (traditors) sacred books.

Equestrian: The business class in republican Rome, during the Roman Empire also became part of the imperial bureaucracy.

Gaul: The region of modern-day France, Low Countries, western Germany, and northwest Switzerland.

Gnosticism: A sect which claimed to posses "special knowledge" of salvation.

Holy Roman Empire: The title of Charlemagne's empire created in 800 C.E.

Honestores: Persons of higher birth.

Humiliores: Persons of lower birth.

Insula: An apartment house or a large house subdivided into apartments.

Judaism: Monotheistic religion established in ancient Palestine by the Hebrew people.

Liturgies: Forced public service without pay.

Magister Militum: Master of the soldiers, in charge of the military, especially under weak emperors.

Manichaeanism: A Gnostic religion preached by Mani of Babylon.

Mansiones: Stopping points on the cursus publicus for official couriers.

Manus: Complete disciplinary control over the wife by the husband at the time of marriage. During the late empire manus had virtually disappeared.

Monotheism: The belief in one God; it originally began with Judaism and was then preached by the Christians, exclusive of other cults.

Mystery religions: A group of nonexclusive cults professing individual salvation and happiness through the worship of their god or goddess.

Napoleonic codes: Law codes developed by Napoleon of France in the early 1800s based on the law codes of Justinian.

Navicularii: Ship owners who carried Rome's food supply from Egypt and North Africa. Originally independent merchants, under Constantine they became hereditary.

Neo-Platonism: An attempt by Plotinus and his followers to explain the universe through Platonic philosophy; it later espoused the use of magic and cosmology.

Orthodox: Originally meant conforming to the established teachings of the Christian religion. During Constantine's age referred to the Catholics in the dispute with Donatists and Arians. In the late empire became associated with the Patriarch of Constantinople.

Paganism: Belief in non-Judaic or Christian god(s). Originally meant the worship of gods by rural inhabitants, and then more generally polytheism.

Palestine: The region of modern-day Israel, Lebanon, Jordan, and Syria.

Patrician: A Roman aristocrat, a member of a privileged class.

Plebeian: The common people.

Polytheism: The belief in more than one god.

Praetorian Prefect: Originally military commanders of the imperial guard, they became adjutants of the emperor and under Constantine became responsible for judicial and financial matters.

Principate: The term used to describe the Roman Empire from Augustus to Diocletian.

Rescript: An official or authoritative order or decree.

See: The authority or jurisdiction of a bishop.

Senator: The ruling elite during the republic and empire.

***Solidus*:** The gold coin issued by Constantine and struck at 72 to the pound. It became the universal coin of trade in the late empire.

Tetrarchy: The rule of four instituted by Diocletian in 293 with Maximian, Constantius, and Galerius as his colleagues.

Theurgy: The intervention of the divine or supernatural in the lives of humans which Neo-Platonists believed was usually achieved through beneficent magic.

Traditor: An individual who handed over to the Roman officials sacred Christian books.

Villa: A living complex comprising more than just a home. The villa rusticus (rustic) developed from a simple farmstead to a more elaborate living environment which could include a house, often palatial, baths, store houses, stables, and other outbuildings, often in an enclosed environment.

NOTES

INTRODUCTION

1. *Gladiator*, directed by Ridley Scott, Universal Studios, 2000.
2. See the volume *The Rise of the Roman Empire* in this series.
3. See the volume *The Emergence of Christianity* in this series.

CHAPTER 1

1. The term *pagan* here means polytheism. Although many Christians view the term *pagan* as a pejorative term, it originally came from the Latin word *pagus*, meaning from the country. The term *pagan* is concerned with original rural rites which evolved into a polytheistic state religion.
2. See the volume *The Emperor Justinian and the Byzantine Empire* in this series.

CHAPTER 3

1. See the volumes *The Emergence of Judaism*, *The Emergence of Christianity*, and *The Reign of Cleopatra* in this series for a discussion of the multicultural composition of Alexandria.
2. Pliny, *The Letters of the Younger Pliny* (London: Penguin, 1963), 10.33–10.34.

CHAPTER 6

1. Donald Kagan. *Decline and Fall of the Roman Empire: Why Did It Collapse?* (Boston: Heath, 1962).
2. C. iv. St. 145 Chile Harld's Pilgrimage.

PRIMARY DOCUMENTS ILLUSTRATING LATE ROME

1. The Gard of the celebrated Pont du Gard.

ANNOTATED BIBLIOGRAPHY

Ancient Works

Abinnaeus, Flavius. *The Abinnaeus Archive: Papers of a Roman Officer in the Reign of Constantius II*. Edited by Sir Harold Idris Bell. Oxford: Clarendon Press, 1962. One of the numerous archives recovered from Egyptian papyri deals with a low-level military administrator and his dealings with officials and local individuals.

The Acts of the Christian Martyrs. Translated by Herbert Musurillo. Oxford: Clarendon Press, 1972. A collection of authentic acts translated, an important source for early hagiography and Diocletian's persecutions.

Ammianus Marcellinus. *The Later Roman Empire*. Translated by Walter Hamilton. New York: Penguin Books, 1986. The last great Latin historian details the careers of Constantius II, Julian, and Valens. Although incomplete, his work is important for understanding the military disasters of Julian and Valens. This translation is abridged.

Ammianus Marcellinus. Translated by John Carew Rolfe. 3 vols. Cambridge, MA: Harvard University Press; London: Loeb Classical Library, 1935–1939. The entire surviving work is translated.

Ante-Nicene Christian Library: Translations of the Writings of the Fathers down to A.D. 325. Edited by Alexander Roberts and James Donaldson. Edinburgh: T. and T. Clark, 1867–1872. Many of the earliest Christian texts are translated, including some of the more obscure ones.

Arnobius of Sicca. *The Case Against the Pagans*. Translated by George Englert McCracken. Westminster, MD: Newman Press, 1949. Arnobius was a fourth-century convert and apologist; his work provides a good example of the arguments used by learned converts who were not trained as theologians.

Augustine, Bishop of Hippo. *The City of God*. New York: Modern Library, 1950. The Christian theologian refutes the pagan view that Christianity caused Rome's fall.

————. *Confessions*. Translated by Henry Chadwick. Oxford: Oxford University Press, 1991. A classic work, detailing his journey to Christianity.

Cassiodorus. *The Letters of Cassiodorus, being a Condensed Translation of the Variae epistolae of Magnus Aurelius Cassiodorus Senator*. Translated by Thomas Hodgkin. London: H. Frowde, 1886. A collection of letters from a bureaucrat describing life in Roman Italy after 476; they are important for showing that the institutions and concepts of Roman life continued even after the last emperor had been deposed.

————. *The Variae of Magnus Aurelius Cassiodorus Senator being Documents of the Kingdom of the Ostrogoths in Italy Cassiodorus, Senator; Theodoric, King of the Ostrogoths*. Translated by S.J.B. Barnish. Liverpool: Liverpool University Press, 1992. The various works are concerned with the new post-Roman government of Theodoric.

The Chronicle of John, Bishop of Nikiu. Translated from Zotenberg's Ethiopic Text by R. H. Charles. London: Willams and Norgate, 1916. A vivid Christian account drawn mainly from the Egyptian point of view, but often unreliable.

The Chronicle of Joshua the Stylite. Translated by W. Wright. Cambridge: Cambridge University Press, 1882. Work describing the city of Edessa and the East during the Late Roman period by one of its own citizens.

Chronicon Paschale 284–628 AD. Translated with notes and introduction by Michael Whitby and Mary Whitby. Liverpool: Liverpool University Press, 1989. Work detailing the history of Western Christianity during the fourth and fifth centuries. Although not always reliable, it does provide useful information on popularly held ideas.

The Civil Law, Including the Twelve Tables, the Institutes of Gaius, the Rules of Ulpian, the Opinions of Paulus, the Enactments of Justinian, and the Constitutions of Leo. Translated by S. P. Scott. New York: AMS Press, 1973 [1932]. Translation of civil laws from Justinian's code, this is important for showing the evolution of legal ideas during the late empire; the translation is flawed, however. Is also available online at: http://www.constitution.org/sps/sps.htm.

Eusebius. *The History of the Church from Christ to Constantine*. Translated by G. A. Williamson; revised and edited with a new introduction by Andrew

Louth. New York: Penguin Books, 1989. An official account of Christianity written after its acceptance during the reign of Constantine, this ancient history provides the most detailed story of Christianity.

————. *In Praise of Constantine: A Historical Study and New Translation of Eusebius' Tricennial Orations.* Translated by H. A. Drake. Berkeley: University of California Press, 1976. A Panegyric written near the end of Constantine's life, provides a good source for the official view of Constantine's accomplishments.

————. *Life of Constantine, Introduction, Translation and Commentary.* Translated by Averil Cameron and Stuart G. Hall. Oxford: Oxford University Press, 1999. Eusebius' account is often flawed since he views Constantine as the Christian protector.

Eutropius. *The Breviarium ab Urbe Condita of Eutropius: The Right Honourable Secretary of State for General Petitions: Dedicated to Lord Valens, Gothicus Maximus & Perpetual Emperor.* Translated by H. W. Bird. Liverpool: Liverpool University Press, 1993. General history down to Valens provides information often ignored by Christian historians or missing from Ammianus.

Jerome, Saint. *The Letters of St. Jerome.* Translated by Thomas Comerford Lawler. New York: Newman Press, 1963. Important letters from a Church Father deals with all aspects of life and religion during the fourth and fifth centuries.

Johnson, Allan Chester, Paul Robinson Coleman-Norton, [and] Frank Card Bourne. *Ancient Roman Statutes: a Translation, with Introduction, Commentary, Glossary, and Index.* Clark, NJ: Lawbook Exchange, 2003. A collection of ancient laws from Greece and Rome provides a representative sampling dealing with economic, political, social, and military aspects.

Jordanes. *The Gothic History of Jordanes in English Version.* Translated by Charles Christopher Mierow. Cambridge: Speculum Historiale; New York: Barnes & Noble, 1960. Pro-Gothic account by a Romanized Goth presents information differing from Roman accounts.

Lactantius. *Minor Works.* Translated by Sister Mary Francis McDonald. Washington, DC: Catholic University of America Press, 1965. Includes the works: *The Wrath of God, The Death of the Persecutors,* and *The Phoenix,* arguing against paganism.

————. *The Works of Lactantius.* Translated by William Fletcher. Edinburgh: T. & T. Clark, 1871. Works from the Latin rhetorician and court instructor that justify, defend, and articulate the case for Christianity.

Lieu, Samuel N. C. *The Emperor Julian: Panegyric and Polemic: Mamertinus Claudius; John Chrysostom, Saint; Ephraem, Syrus Saint.* Liverpool: Liverpool University Press, 1986. Collection of important sources shows various views in favor of and opposed to Julian.

Maas, Michael. *Readings in Late Antiquity: A Sourcebook.* London: Routledge, 2000. Good collection of various sources on all aspects of ancient life.

Nixon, C.E.V., and Rodgers, Barbara Saylor. *In Praise of Later Roman Emperors: The Panegyrici Latini: Introduction, Translation, and Historical Commentary, with the Latin Text of R.A.B. Mynors.* Berkeley: University of California Press, 1994. Important collection of Latin Gallic panegyrics details the history and official imperial view of emperors, especially for the First and Second Tetrarchy.

Orosius, Paulus. *The Seven Books of History Against the Pagans.* Translated by Roy Joseph Deferrari. Washington, DC: Catholic University of America Press, 1964. Late Roman history account from a Christian defends Christianity from the pagan charge that the new religion destroyed Rome.

Salvian, of Marseilles. *On the Government of God; A Treatise Where in Are Shown by Argument and by Examples Drawn from the Abandoned Society of the Times the Ways of God Toward His Creatures. Indited by Salvian as a Warning and Counsel.* Translated by Eva Matthews Sanford. New York: Octagon Books, 1966 [1931]. Late Roman account from a Christian arguing that the end of Rome came from the corrupt government.

Sidonius, Apollinaris. *Poems and Letters.* 2 vols. Translated by William Blair Anderson. Cambridge, MA: Harvard University Press, 1936–1965, Loeb Classical Library. Work detailing the life of the late fourth century Gaul, provides examples of all aspects of life and politics.

Themistius. *Politics, Philosophy, and Empire in the Fourth Century: Select Orations of Themistius.* Translated by P. J. Heather and David Moncur. Liverpool: Liverpool University Press, 2001. Works addressed to Eastern Emperors of fourth century comparing them to Plato's idea of the just king.

The Theodosian Code and Novels, and the Sirmondian Constitutions. Edited by Clyde Pharr. [Princeton, NJ:] Princeton University Press, 1952. Excellent translation of Rome's other great legal code dealing with the enactments after Diocletian to Theodosius II.

Victor, Sextus Aurelius *Liber de Caesaribus.* Translated by H. W. Bird. Liverpool: Liverpool University Press, 1994. A collection of imperial biographies beginning with Augustus down to the end of the fourth century; he is important for the later period before Constantine where literary sources are lacking.

Zosimus. *New History*. Translated with Commentary by Ronald T. Ridley. Canberra: Australian Association for Byzantine Studies, 1982. Byzantine pagan author writing down to the fifth century, blamed Christianity, especially Constantine, for Rome's fall.

Modern Works

Ackerman, James S. *The Villa: Form and Ideology of Country Houses*. Princeton, NJ: Princeton University Press, 1990. A general work discusses the villa from antiquity to the twentieth century.

Adam, Jean Pierre. *Roman Building: Materials and Techniques*. Bloomington: Indiana University Press, 1994. This thorough technical work discusses all aspects of building, and is an excellent starting point in any research on Late Roman architecture and construction.

Alföldi, Andreas. *A Conflict of Ideas in the Late Roman Empire: The Clash between the Senate and Valentinian I*. Oxford: Clarendon Press, 1952. An important work, discusses post-Constantinian politics between a Christian emperor and pagan senate.

Andreau, Jean. *Banking and Business in the Roman World*. Cambridge: Cambridge University Press, 1999. A description of the history of finances focused mainly during the late republic and early empire.

Auguet, Roland. *Cruelty and Civilization: The Roman Games*. New York: Routledge, 1994. The work presents a complete examination and history of the Roman games: gladiators, hunts, and races; is a good introductory work.

Baker, George Philip. *Constantine the Great and the Christian Revolution*. New York: Barnes & Noble, 1967 [1930]. A standard work on the life of Constantine portrays him in a balanced light.

Barnes, Timothy David. *Ammianus Marcellinus and the Representation of Historical Reality*. Ithaca, NY: Cornell University Press, 1998. Barnes provides a thorough reexamination and evaluation of Ammianus, challenging many of the traditional views of scholarship. This should be the starting point for any analysis of Ammianus.

———. *Athanasius and Constantius: Theology and Politics in the Constantinian Empire*. Cambridge, MA: Harvard University Press, 1993. The author attempts to place Athanasius in the broader context of the Roman Empire under Constantius II. The work is as much a history/biography of Athanasius as Constantius.

————. *Constantine and Eusebius.* Cambridge, MA: Harvard University Press, 1981. Scholarly work covers the reign of Constantine and the influence of Eusebius on Constantine's image.

————. *The New Empire of Diocletian and Constantine.* Cambridge, MA: Harvard University Press, 1982. Excellent source work examining various components of the imperial court, individuals, military actions, and imperial journeys.

Barton, I. M. *Roman Domestic Buildings.* Exeter: University of Exeter Press, 1996. Describes the different types of private buildings.

Blockley, R. C. *East Roman Foreign Policy: Formation and Conduct from Diocletian to Anastasius.* Leeds: Francis Cairns, 1992. Work describes the relationship between Rome and the Sassanids focusing on the military and diplomatic acts.

Bowder, Diana. *The Age of Constantine and Julian.* New York: Barnes & Noble Books, 1978. Provides a general history of the fourth century focusing on Constantine's new Christian empire and Julian's reaction; presents Constantine as a sincere Christian.

Bowersock, G. W. *Julian the Apostate.* Cambridge, MA: Harvard University Press, 1978. Standard scholarly work on Julian focuses on his career and his impact.

Brown, Peter Robert Lamont. *Augustine of Hippo: A Biography.* Berkeley: University of California Press, 1967. Excellent biography of the great Christian writer describes not only his life but his environment.

————. *The Making of Late Antiquity.* Cambridge, MA: Harvard University Press, 1978. Good general account of the political, social, and cultural world of the Mediterranean from 400–700 C.E.

————. *Society and the Holy in Late Antiquity.* Berkeley: University of California Press, 1982. Discusses the interaction between the new state religion Christianity and society.

Burckhardt, Jacob. *The Age of Constantine the Great.* Garden City, NY: Doubleday, 1956. Classic account of Constantine describes how he created the new Christian empire.

Burns, Thomas S. *Barbarians within the Gates of Rome: A Study of Roman Military Policy and the Barbarians, ca. 375–425* A.D. Bloomington: Indiana University Press, 1994. Attempt to place the military picture of the late Roman Empire in perspective.

Bury, J. B. *History of the Later Roman Empire from the Death of Theodosius I to the Death of Justinian.* New York: Dover Publications, 1958. Standard reference work on the fifth century provides a useful historical description of the Germanic invaders.

Cameron, Alan. *Circus Factions: Blues and Greens at Rome and Byzantium.* Oxford: Clarendon Press, 1976. Scholarly work examines the social, political, military, religious, and imperial history of the games.

Cameron, Averil. *The Later Roman Empire,* A.D. *284–430.* Cambridge, MA: Harvard University Press, 1993. General work on the fourth century provides an excellent overview of the Constantinian emperors.

Casey, P. J. *Carausius and Allectus: The British Usurpers.* New Haven, CT: Yale University Press, 1995 [1994]. Author presents a thorough examination of the British separatist movement during Diocletian's reign, especially useful for the numismatic evidence.

Chambers, Mortimer. *The Fall of Rome; Can It Be Explained?* New York: Holt, Rinehart and Winston, 1963. The volume gives a collection of extracts from modern scholars examining the various reasons for Rome's fall. The work provides a good introduction to the various modern theories.

Cherry, David. *Frontier and Society in Roman North Africa.* Oxford: Clarendon Press; New York: Oxford University Press, 1998. The work provides an examination of Roman influence before the fourth century. The work is a good starting place in attempting to understand the world of the Donatist movement.

Clark, Gillian. *Women in Late Antiquity: Pagan and Christian Lifestyles.* Oxford: Clarendon Press, 1993. Presents an overview of women's personal lives and how law, morality, and religious concerns affected their lives.

Coello, Terence. *Unit Sizes in the Late Roman Army.* Oxford: Tempus Reparatum, 1996. An examination of the Late Roman army as it pertains to the *Notitia Dignitatum.*

Connolly, Peter, and Hazel Dodge. *The Ancient City: Life in Classical Athens and Rome.* New York: Oxford University Press, 1998. Popular book on the city of Rome provides animated illustrations on ancient buildings and daily life.

Corcoran, Simon. *The Empire of the Tetrarchs: Imperial Pronouncements and Government, A.D. 284–324.* Oxford: Clarendon Press; New York: Oxford University Press, 1996. Scholarly work on the legal documents of Diocletian, which provide a justification for the Tetrarch's rule.

Digeser, Elizabeth DePalma. *The Making of a Christian Empire: Lactantius and Rome.* Ithaca, NY: Cornell University Press, 2000. Examines Lactantius' influence on Constantine and his government.

Downey, Glanville. *Antioch in the Age of Theodosius the Great.* Norman: University of Oklahoma Press, 1962. Excellent work on the topography, social setting, and history of Antioch, one of Rome's most important cities in the East.

———. *Constantinople in the Age of Justinian.* Norman: University of Oklahoma Press, 1960. Presents the city of Constantinople as it appeared at the end of the fifth century.

Dudden, F. Homes. *The Life and Times of St. Ambrose.* Oxford: Clarendon Press, 1935. Describes Roman society during the late fourth century and Ambrose's impact on Roman history.

Duncan-Jones, Richard. *The Economy of the Roman Empire: Quantitative Studies.* Cambridge: Cambridge University Press, 1974. The author provides evidence and rationale for the use of statistics to understand imperial Roman society.

Elsner, Jas. *Imperial Rome and Christian Triumph: the Art of the Roman Empire A.D. 100–450.* New York: Oxford University Press, 1998. Excellent work detailing the fusion of Roman and Christian ideologies seen in art.

Fagan, Garrett G. *Bathing in Public in the Roman World.* Ann Arbor: University of Michigan Press, 1999. Modern work detailing the importance of the bath complex in Roman society.

Fox, Robin Lane. *Pagans and Christians.* New York: Knopf, 1987. Describes the social and cultural world of Christian and pagan struggles, easily readable.

Fraschetti, Augusto, ed. *Roman Women.* Translated by Linda Lappin. Chicago: University of Chicago Press, 1994. The work has chapters on individual Roman women from the late republic to the end of the empire.

Frend, W.H.C. *The Rise of Christianity.* Philadelphia: Fortress Press, 1984. Standard work describes the growth of Christianity and its position in the

Roman world. The author describes the various problems facing Christianity during its early period.

Garnsey, Peter, and Richard P. Saller. *The Roman Empire: Economy, Society, and Culture*. Berkeley: University of California Press, 1987. Describes their interaction, especially by using archaeological material to provide new models and directions.

Gibbon, Edward. *The Decline and Fall of the Roman Empire*. Edited by D. M. Low. New York: Harcourt, Brace, 1960. This classic work provides a starting point for all further work on the Late Roman period.

Gordon, Colin Douglas. *The Age of Attila; Fifth-century Byzantium and the Barbarians*. Ann Arbor: University of Michigan Press, 1960. Places Attila in the context of fifth-century Rome and his importance in Eastern relations.

Grant, Michael. *The Army of the Caesars*. New York: Scribner's, 1974. A general introductory discussion of the early imperial army provides some useful background information on the struggle between the army and the emperors.

———. *The Collapse and Recovery of the Roman Empire*. New York: Routledge, 1999. The work is a good introduction and popular account of the third century and its crisis.

———. *Constantine the Great: The Man and His Times*. New York: Scribner's; Maxwell Macmillan International, 1994. A general biography of Constantine and his career, geared for the general reader.

———. *From Rome to Byzantium: The Fifth Century* A.D. New York: Routledge, 1998. A general description of the collapse of the Roman West and the predominance of the East.

Greene, Kevin. *The Archaeology of the Roman Economy*. Berkeley: University of California Press, 1986. Author presents a series of examples of various archaeological sites and ideas as they relate to the Roman economy, a good starting place to understand their interaction.

Hanfmann, George. *From Croesus to Constantine: The Cities of Western Asia Minor and Their Arts in Greek and Roman Times*. Ann Arbor: University of Michigan Press, 1975. This work provides an overview of the development of the cities of modern-day Turkey with their archaeological and monumental materials.

Hans Campenhausen, Freiherr von. *The Fathers of the Latin Church*. Stanford, CA: Stanford University Press, 1969 [1964]. Gives the careers and discusses the works of the Latin Fathers Tertullian, Cyprian, Lactantius, Ambrose, Jerome, Augustine, and Boethius.

Harl, Kenneth W. *Coinage in the Roman Economy, 300 B.C. to A.D. 700.* Baltimore, MD: Johns Hopkins University Press, 1996. An attempt to place coinage in the wider political system of the Roman world; shows the interaction of coinage, the government, and society.

Harries, Jill. *Sidonius Apollinaris and the Fall of Rome, A.D. 407–485.* Oxford: Clarendon Press; New York: Oxford University Press, 1994. An excellent scholarly work on Sidonius and fifth-century Gaul, this volume provides the biographical and historical background for his voluminous letters.

Harries, Jill, and I. N. Wood. *The Theodosian Code.* Ithaca, NY: Cornell University Press, 1993. A collection of articles by experts focusing on different aspects of the code, such as its background, sources, Licinius' laws, Christianity in the code, and the code's later history.

Haywood, Richard Mansfield. *The Myth of Rome's Fall.* New York: Crowell, 1958. A popular work that introduces students and the public to the end of Rome. The author argues against Spengler and Toynbee, who believed in a philosophical ideology of history. The author argues for a gradual transformation that was inevitable.

Heather, P. J. *Goths and Romans, 332–489.* Oxford: Clarendon Press; New York: Oxford University Press, 1991. Good examination of the interaction between the Goths and Rome and their entry into the Roman Empire.

Hodgkin, Thomas. *Theodoric the Goth, the Barbarian Champion of Civilization.* London: G. P. Putnam's Sons, 1891. Standard work on post-476 Rome describes the new kingdom of the Goths.

Humphrey, John H. *Roman Circuses: Arenas for Chariot Racing.* Berkeley: University of California Press, 1986. The work provides a thorough review of the archaeological sites and the remains of the circuses in the Roman world, and includes copious pictures illustrating the sites.

Isaac, Benjamin H. *The Limits of Empire: The Roman Army in the East.* Oxford: Clarendon Press; New York: Oxford University Press, 1990. Author provides a detailed survey of the Eastern provinces of the empire, and the problems along the imperial frontier.

James, Edward. *The Franks.* Oxford: Basil Blackwell, 1988. A good introduction to the history of the Franks before and after the fall of the West, concentrates mainly on Clovis and his creation of the Frankish monarchy.

Jones, A.H.M. *The Decline of the Ancient World*. New York: Holt, Rinehart and Winston, 1966. Jones gives a popular version of his *Later Roman Empire*.

————. *The Later Roman Empire, 284–602: A Social Economic and Administrative Survey*. 2 vols. Norman: University of Oklahoma Press, 1964. Excellent standard scholarly work from which all modern studies stem.

————. *The Roman Economy: Studies in Ancient Economic and Administrative History*. Totowa, NJ: Rowman and Littlefield, 1974. A collection of his important articles collected and reprinted, allowing for detailed analysis of different aspects of Late Roman society.

Kagan, Donald. *Decline and Fall of the Roman Empire: Why Did It Collapse?* Boston: Heath, 1962. Gives short excerpts of various modern scholars' theories for Rome's fall.

King, Noel Quinton. *The Emperor Theodosius and the Establishment of Christianity*. Philadelphia: Westminster Press, 1960. General work on the rule of Theodosius and his role in making Christianity the official state religion.

Krautheimer, Richard. *Rome, Profile of a City, 312–1308*. Princeton, NJ: Princeton University Press, 1980. Work provides an excellent physical overview of the Christian city of Rome.

Lançon, Bertrand. *Rome in Late Antiquity: Everyday Life and Urban Change*, A.D. *312–609*. New York: Routledge, 2000. Author gives an excellent introduction and description of the various components of the city of Rome; this is a good starting place for examining the city.

Lasko, Peter. *The Kingdom of the Franks: North-west Europe before Charlemagne*. New York: McGraw-Hill, 1971. General introduction to the art, history, and archaeology of the Franks, geared to the general audience.

Lenski, Noel. *Failure of Empire: Valens and the Roman State in the Fourth Century* A.D. Berkeley: University of California Press, 2002. Scholarly work on the rule of Valens leading to the disaster at Adrianople.

Liebeschuetz, J.H.W.G. *From Diocletian to the Arab Conquest: Change in the Late Roman Empire*. Northampton, England: Variorum, 1990. A series of articles addressing various subjects relating to the Late Roman world.

L'Orange, Hans Peter. *Art Forms and Civic Life in the Late Roman Empire*. Princeton, NJ: Princeton University Press, 1965. Traces the changes in art during the Late Roman period; argues for a fundamental shift away from Rome toward the provinces.

Luttwak, Edward. *The Grand Strategy of the Roman Empire from the First Century A.D. to the Third*. Baltimore, MD: Johns Hopkins University Press, 1976. Describes the changes in imperial military strategy and how it changed during the crises of the third century, arguing for an imperial planning of the defense in depth.

MacCormack, Sabine. *Art and Ceremony in Late Antiquity*. Berkeley: University of California Press, 1981. Discusses the various imperial ceremonies as seen in art and how they relate to creation of a more formal court ceremony.

MacMullen, Ramsay. *Christianity and Paganism in the Fourth to Eighth Centuries*. New Haven, CT: Yale University Press, 1997. Shows that Christianity did not become universal with the Constantinian age, but rather the struggle between the two continued.

———. *Constantine*. New York: Dial Press, 1969. The author gives a good general biography of the emperor; geared for introductory study.

———. *Corruption and the Decline of Rome*. New Haven, CT: Yale University Press, 1988. Author argues that late Rome became more oppressive and regimented.

———. *Soldier and Civilian in the Later Roman Empire*. Cambridge, MA: Harvard University Press, 1963. Work describes the interaction and struggle between the military and civilians during the post-Diocletianic period.

Mänchen-Helfen, Otto. *The World of the Huns: Studies in Their History and Culture*. Berkeley, University of California Press, 1973. Work provides a thorough examination of the Huns, exploring all aspects of their society, history, religion, art, and economy.

Markus, R. A. *The End of Ancient Christianity*. New York: Cambridge University Press, 1990. Examines the forces that changed the Christian world from the fourth through the sixth centuries.

Matthews, John. *The Roman Empire of Ammianus*. Baltimore, MD: Johns Hopkins University Press, 1989. Exhaustive, seminal, and scholarly work on all aspects of Ammianus; describes the Roman Empire during his time.

———. *Western Aristocracies and Imperial Court, A.D. 364–425*. Oxford: Clarendon Press, 1975. Scholarly work detailing the history and personalities of the Valentianian and Theodosian regimes. The work is an excellent starting point in understanding the position of pagan and Christian senators and their interaction with the emperors and each other.

Mattingly, Harold. *Christianity in the Roman Empire*. New York: W.W. Norton, 1967. Author provides a good introduction to the rise of Christianity in the Roman Empire for the general reader.

McKay, Alexander Gordon. *Houses, Villas, and Palaces in the Roman World*. Ithaca, NY: Cornell University Press, 1975. An excellent examination of the various forms of Roman structures in the different regions of the empire.

Millar, Fergus. *The Roman Near East, 31* B.C.–A.D. *337*. Cambridge, MA: Harvard University Press, 1993. Provides a comprehensive discussion of the East during the early empire; is especially useful in assembling the various source materials for the military reorganization by Diocletian and Constantine.

Moorhead, John. *Theodoric in Italy*. Oxford: Clarendon Press; New York: Oxford University Press, 1992. Scholarly work gives the career of Theodoric in fifth–sixth-century Italy.

Nicasie, Martinus Johannes. *Twilight of Empire: The Roman Army from the Reign of Diocletian until the Battle of Adrianople*. Amsterdam: J. C. Gieben, 1998. A description of the Late Roman army focuses on the reforms made by Constantine toward the creation of the mobile armies.

O'Donnell, James Joseph. *Cassiodorus*. Berkeley: University of California Press, 1979. A thorough scholarly study of the life and works of Cassiodorus; discusses not only his background but his interactions with Theodoric and his writings.

Ogilvie, R. M. *The Library of Lactantius*. Oxford: Clarendon Press, 1978. A standard work describes the life, influence, and writing of Lactantius.

Oost, Stewart Irvin. *Galla Placidia Augusta*. Chicago: University of Chicago Press, 1988. Author presents a balanced biography of the imperial woman who attempted to bring about a union between Rome and the Visigoths.

Paoli, Ugo Enrico. *Rome: Its People, Life and Customs*. New York: D. McKay Company, 1963. A good popular discussion of everyday life in Rome during the empire, this volume is geared to the general audience.

Parker, Henry Michael Denne. *The Roman Legions*. New York: Barnes & Noble, 1958 [reprinted, with corrections]. The starting point for further studies on the imperial army; although mainly concerned with the pre-Diocletianic army, provides useful information on the makeup of the legions.

Pelikán, Jaroslav Jan. *The Excellent Empire: The Fall of Rome and the Triumph of the Church.* San Francisco: Harper & Row, 1987. The author discusses the work of Gibbon and the impact Christian writers had on Gibbon's view of history.

Percival, John. *The Roman Villa: An Historical Introduction.* Berkeley: University of California Press, 1976. Classic work on the Roman villa describing its evolution and function in Rome; indispensable in understanding the position of the villa in Roman society.

Rees, Roger. *Layers of Loyalty in Latin Panegyric,* A.D. *289–307.* New York: Oxford University Press, 2002. A scholarly discussion of the Latin speeches made during Diocletian's and Constantine's reign, placing them in the historical context of imperial patronage.

Ricciotti, Giuseppe. *The Age of Martyrs.* Milwaukee: Bruce Publishing Company, 1959. The author does a good job of describing and placing the final persecutions in a historical setting; easily readable.

————. *Julian the Apostate.* Milwaukee: Bruce Publishing Company, 1960. Popular biography of Julian attempts to place him within his struggles with Christianity.

Rivet, A.L.F. *The Roman Villa in Britain.* New York: Praeger, 1969. Standard work on the rise and development of villas in England provides a good introduction to the various stages in British development.

Rowlandson, Jane. *Landowners and Tenants in Roman Egypt: The Social Relations of Agriculture in the Oxyrhynchite Nome.* Oxford: Oxford University Press, 1996. A systematic study of landed estates describes their interaction with the countryside using papyri.

Shiel, Norman. *The Episode of Carausius and Allectus: The Literary and Numismatic Evidence.* Oxford: British Archaeological Reports, 1977. A detailed description of the primary sources, literary, archaeological, and numismatic, surrounding Carausius and Allectus.

Simmons, Michael Bland. *Arnobius of Sicca: Religious Conflict and Competition in the Age of Diocletian.* Oxford: Clarendon Press; New York: Oxford University Press, 1995. Scholarly work describes Arnobius' position in Christian apologists and Diocletian's response to Christianity.

Southern, Pat. *The Roman Empire from Severus to Constantine.* New York: Routledge, 2001. General history of third century, focuses mainly on the early period and its collapse.

Southern, Pat, and Karen R. Dixon. *The Late Roman Army*. New Haven, CT: Yale University Press, 1996. An excellent overview of the Late Roman army, especially its units and their functions, the work is useful in showing the changes that occurred due to the Germanic invasions.

Strong, Donald Emrys, and J.M.C. Toynbee. *Roman Art*. New York: Penguin, 1976. Standard introduction gives a good overview to the various forms of art.

Talbert, Richard J. A. *Barrington Atlas of the Greek and Roman World, and Map-by-Map Directory*. Princeton, NJ: Princeton University Press, 2000. An excellent, up-to-date atlas; a must for locating the various sites.

Thompson, E. A. *The Huns*. Oxford: Blackwell Publishers, 1996. A thorough examination of the Huns, their history and society, this work focuses mainly on the political and military exploits of Attila.

————. *Romans and Barbarians: The Decline of the Western Empire*. Madison: University of Wisconsin Press, 1982. A reprint of a series of scholarly articles, together with added sections, discusses the fifth-century Germanic settlements and their aftermath. The chapters deal with Gaul, Italy, Noricum, and Spain, providing detailed information and analysis of the end of Roman rule and the rise of Germanic power in each area.

Vanderspoel, John. *Themistius and the Imperial Court: Oratory, Civic Duty, and Paideia from Constantius to Theodosius*. Ann Arbor: University of Michigan Press, 1995. Provides a reassessment of Themistius' life and works within the framework of the fourth-century oratory at Constantinople. The author argues for a new interpretation showing that Themistius is not a flatterer out for personal gain, but rather a leader and orator of Constantinople.

Vogt, Joseph. *The Decline of Rome*. Translated by Janet Sondheimer. New York: New American Library, 1968. The author describes the collapse of Rome, presenting the cultural and social changes which occurred during the fourth century.

Wand, J.W.C. *Doctors and Councils*. London: The Faith Press, 1962. A series of lectures covers the lives of Greek and Latin Fathers along with the four main councils in the East against Arius.

Warmington, B. H. *The North African Provinces from Diocletian to the Vandal Conquest*. Cambridge: Cambridge University Press, 1954. Excellent work describes the African provinces and their organizations during the fourth and fifth centuries.

Williams, Stephen. *Diocletian and the Roman Recovery*. New York: Methuen, 1985. A general popular account of Diocletian and his reign.

Williams, Stephen, and J.G.P. Friell. *Theodosius: The Empire at Bay*. New Haven, CT: Yale University Press, 1995 [©1994]. A detailed and comprehensive summary of the emperor's life and his policies, especially on Theodosius' treatment of Christianity.

Wilson, Roger John Anthony. *Piazza Armerina*. Austin: University of Texas Press, 1983. Discusses and describes the great villa in Sicily; attempts to answer the question of whom it was built for or by.

Internet Sources

www.julen.net/ancient/ The ancient world Web site provides a good introduction to the variety of sources available.

www.art.man.ac.uk/cla/home.htm The Centre for Late Antiquity provides information concerning Late Antiquity and Early Medieval history.

www.ccel.org/p/pearse/morefathers/home.html and www.ccel.org/fathers2/ Early Church Fathers sites provides English translations on the Web.

iam.classics.unc.edu/ The Interactive Ancient Mediterranean site provides excellent material for maps.

classics.mit.edu/ The Internet Classics Archive has many ancient texts in translations available on the Web.

www.fordham.edu/halsall/ancient/asbook10.html The Internet Source Book for Late Antiquity provides sources covering a wide spectrum.

www.constitution.org/sps/sps.htm Justinian's law code. The translation is flawed, however.

www.perseus.tufts.edu/ The Perseus Digital Library is a valuable resource tool for any aspect of Ancient History.

www.sc.edu/ltantsoc/#sour The Society for Late Antiquity has numerous links to all aspects of Late Antiquity.

INDEX

About the Author

JAMES W. ERMATINGER is Professor and Chair of the Department of History at Southeast Missouri State University in Cape Girardeau, Missouri. He received his B.S. and M.A. from San Diego State University and his Ph.D. from Indiana University. He is the author of *The Economic Reforms of Diocletian* (1996), as well as articles on Late Roman history.